KNOW HOW

THE COMPLETE GUIDE TO
VEGETABLE GARDENING

Create, Cultivate, and Care for Your Perfect Edible Garden

From the Editors of
GARDENING KNOW HOW

COOL
SPRINGS
PRESS

CONTENTS

PART ONE
THE VEGETABLE GARDEN'S FOUNDATIONS

PART TWO
PLANT PROFILES

THE COMPLETE GUIDE TO

VEGETABLE GARDENING

Quarto.com

© 2024, Moseley Road Inc.

First Published in 2024 by Cool Springs Press, an imprint of The Quarto Group, 100 Cummings Center, Suite 265-D, Beverly, MA 01915, USA.
T (978) 282-9590 F (978) 283-2742

Cool Springs Press titles are also available at discount for retail, wholesale, promotional, and bulk purchase. For details, contact the Special Sales Manager by email at specialsales@quarto.com or by mail at The Quarto Group, Attn: Special Sales Manager, 100 Cummings Center, Suite 265-D, Beverly, MA 01915, USA.

28 27 26 25 24   1 2 3 4 5

ISBN: 978-0-7603-8626-2

Digital edition published in 2024
eISBN: 978-0-7603-8627-9

Library of Congress Cataloging-in-Publication Data available.

Produced by Moseley Road Inc.
Cover Design and Page Layout: Lisa Purcell/Moseley Road Inc.
Cover Image: Matthew Taylor/Alamy Stock Photo

Printed in China

FOOD FOR THOUGHT

Welcome to our second book, *Gardening Know How: The Complete Guide to Vegetable Gardening*. I am so excited to introduce this book to everyone who has ever thought of growing edible plants in the garden, whether in pots, plots, or acres. Thanks to our savvy staff of gardening gurus, our online presence has blossomed into a virtual almanac for gardening enthusiasts and a leading source of online gardening guidance for more than 100 million visitors per year. For us, this book is a natural extension of our intention to bring you the best gardening help, wherever you happen to be.

All my life, I've had a passion for gardening. Growing vegetables in the garden is particularly rewarding at so many levels. Observing the magical way that seeds turn into food and the clearly superior quality of fresh vegetables in our meals has me hooked on vegetable gardening for life. And, it's not just the process of growing food, but it's also the crunch of a freshly picked cucumber or the earthy flavor of a crimson garden beet, steamed to perfection, that make healthy eating a memorable experience. The vegetables that are commercially grown and transported to our grocery stores can't compare with rings from sweet garden onions and corn kernels that pop with flavor.

As the head of GARDENING KNOW HOW, I am delighted to see this book come to fruition. It is a rich compilation of facts and information that explores the joys, the work, and the occasional setbacks involved in vegetable gardening. Solutions, easy to understand instructions, and enlightening ideas are the hallmarks of our savvy crew of gardening gurus, who spend their days working toward making your gardening experience the very best it can be.

If you'd like to explore a topic in more depth, you can access additional info using the links and QR codes contained in this book. They'll connect you directly to our website, where you can also attend courses, watch enjoyable videos, and get to know our unique digest of helpful articles. GARDENING KNOW HOW's primary intention is to provide our visitors with whatever they need to be successful at gardening.

I am thrilled to be part of a team of gardening wizards and support staff who appreciate the extraordinary rewards that vegetable gardening offers. Sit back, and enjoy the wide range of reliable tips, ideas, and cutting-edge guidance that we've compiled for this book, and plan to grow your best vegetables ever. Our collective hope at GARDENING KNOW HOW is that everyone might experience the countless wonders of nature in their own homes and yards.

As always, from myself and my team of vegetable-growing experts, we at GARDENING KNOW HOW wish you Happy Gardening!

Peggy Doyle
Brand Director
GARDENING KNOW HOW

Gardening
KNOW HOW
LEARNING CHANNEL

Create a
Butterfly Garden

Garden to Table

Regenerative
Gardening

Video How-To

The Perfect Match: Herb Garden Guide
A Guide to Companion Planting Your Herb Garden

Backyard Stories

INTRODUCTION

THE JOY OF GROWING YOUR OWN FOOD

A vegetable, or kitchen, garden can help save money and provide your family with fresh, healthy foods. It can contain any combination of veggies, fruits, and herbs.

Grocery prices are going up. It's a fact of life we can't escape, and it's probably an ongoing trend. But you can substantially reduce those food bills if you have a flourishing vegetable garden. It is one of the better ways to ensure access to fresh produce, as well as knowing what chemicals, if any, are going into your food. It also allows you to enjoy the great outdoors as you tend your vegetable plot.

WHAT IS A KITCHEN GARDEN?
During the Middle Ages—possibly even going back to Greek and Roman times—families grew the vegetables or fruits they regularly ate—beans, tubers, or berries, say—in small garden plots near their homes. They also cultivated the herbs that flourished in their region, along with the flowering plants that kept insect or animal pests away. These early kitchen gardens later transitioned into English cottage gardens and French potagers.

Because these gardens were located so near the home, they often acquired attractive trappings. Many featured charming elements like rail or picket fences, pebbled paths, ornamental sundials, or stone benches. They became places of refuge on occasion, where the cook/gardener could steal a moment of peaceful repose among nature's bounty.

That tradition has been carried on in the modern kitchen garden, which is a space focused on growing edible produce, but also one that offers a certain aesthetic appeal.

CREATING A KITCHEN GARDEN
Your garden design and plant choices will rely heavily upon what your family enjoys eating. If they love salads or vegetable dishes, your goal will be simple—sow and harvest fresh green produce. But some gardeners use a kitchen garden to fulfill most of their fruit and vegetable needs. Dwarf fruit trees, fruiting vines and canes, greens and root vegetables, and summer crops, such as corn and tomatoes, all feature prominently in such a garden. Still, even limited spaces can provide plenty of food if you sow successive crops, use vertical supports, and plant small amounts of diverse foods. The kitchen garden can be as basic as a raised bed or as ambitious as a large plot with room to expand.

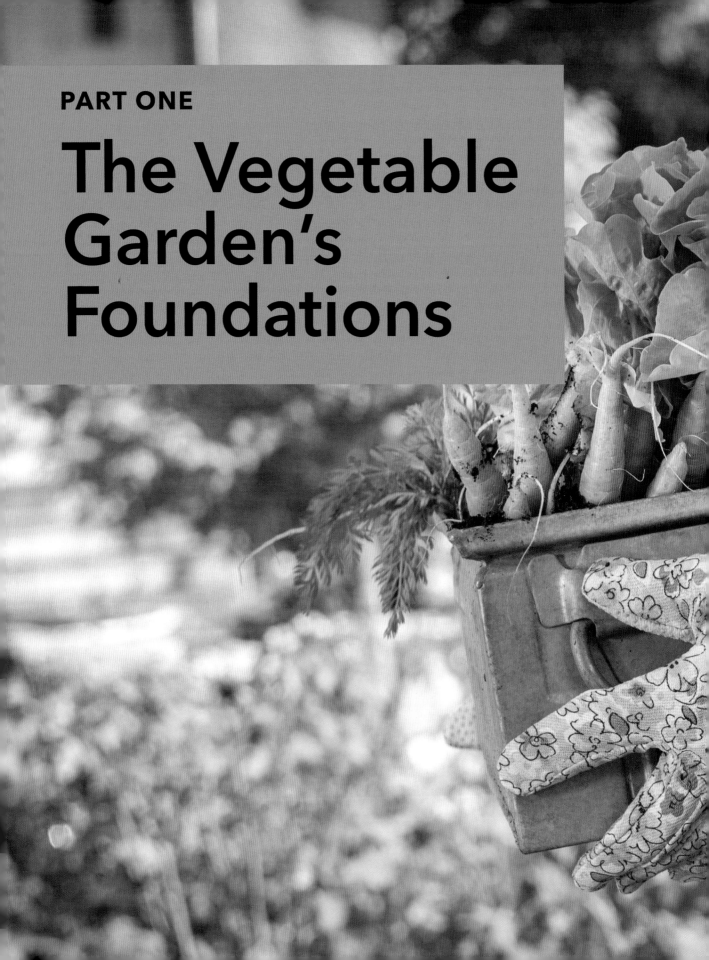

PART ONE

The Vegetable Garden's Foundations

CHAPTER ONE
EDIBLE GARDEN BASICS

From understanding your climate to assessing your soil to gathering and storing your tools and equipment, there are many important factors to consider when undertaking the work of creating an edible garden. In this chapter, all the big issues will be discussed, including how to plan your garden—whether outdoors, indoors, or in containers. You will learn how to work with your site, improve your soil, and fertilize your plants, as well as how to use mulch and compost. Discover the best practices for planting and maintaining a healthy garden, including weed and pest control, succession and companion planting, and organic gardening. And, finally, learn how to store and preserve the bountiful harvest of your hard work.

UNDERSTAND YOUR CLIMATE

Your regional climate is a critical factor that you need to take into consideration when determining which plants you can successfully grow in your vegetable garden.

Climate and weather are the most important factors that influence the growth of plants. Climate is determined by geographical location, whereas weather is the result of how nature decides to affect that climate on a daily basis.

For outdoor gardens, climate influences key planting factors. How long or short is your growing season? How warm does it get at night during summers in your area? How much rainfall do you get on average each year? When is your area's first frost date, and when is its last?

CLIMATE FACTORS

A region's temperature ranges, rainfall levels, and amount of sunshine will determine which plants can thrive there. Other factors, such as the terrain, can also influence the climate.

TEMPERATURE

Both soil and air temperatures must be taken into account when planting vegetables. The ideal soil temperature for planting and growing most vegetables is 65°F to 75°F (18°C to 24°C). Cool-weather vegetables, such as those of the cabbage family, leafy greens, and many root vegetables, require a minimum average soil temperature of 40°F to 50°F (4°C to 10°C) for planting. The average air temps should range between 60°F and 85°F (15°C to 29°C) for sustained growth, with 70°F (21°C) the optimal number. For cool-weather crops, the maximum is 86°F (30°C); above that, these crops will bolt—meaning they will flower and set seed—in other words, they will stop growing. Warm-weather vegetables, such as tomatoes, peppers, and summer squashes, require a minimum average soil temperature of 50°F (10°C) for planting and an average minimum air temps of 75°F (24°C) for sustained growth. The maximum for these plants is 110°F (43°C); above that, they wither and die. They are also likely to die if air temps dip to 32°F (0°C).

Is it a frost or a freeze?

Winter's chill brings extreme weather changes to your edible garden plants. Watching the evening news you will find words like *frost* and *freeze* frequently interspersed. But what's the difference between the two? The subtle distinction means all the difference in plant protection.

Various factors affect the severity of cold weather. The dew point, wind chill, and other variations can send temperatures plummeting more than indicated on a thermometer. Many of our garden denizens are sensitive, and special steps need to be taken to protect plants from a freeze. Frost protection for plants might also be necessary if a plant is not hardy to expected temperatures. Often our first cold spurt is in the form of a freeze. The difference between frost and freeze is not necessarily temperature, but where the cold attacks.

Frosting is when a plant is exposed to temperatures of 32°F (0°C). It is usually observed on the exterior of the plant. The plant radiates heat at night, which releases water vapor that freezes on its surfaces. The early-autumn frosts often cause the plants to die. A freeze is generally a longer event and occurs when the interior

A light rain falls on mustard sprouts. A region's rainfall level is just one factor of climate that determines whether certain plants will thrive or not in your garden.

temperature of the plant gets to 32°F (0°C). The frozen interior tissue warms during the day, and the cells release water and break down. The indicators are dark brown to black spots and water-soaked areas that become mushy, resulting in the death of annual and sensitive plants.

RAINFALL AND HUMIDITY

Most vegetables will thrive with about 1 to 2 inches (2.5 to 5 cm) of moisture each week during the growing season. Excessive soaking after showers and storms can ruin a plant's roots, which in turn affects how it will grow. Too much rain can mean water pools in the soil, flooding your plants and washing seeds away. The result can be stunted or poorly producing plants.

Humidity, which is the presence and percentage of water vapor in the air, is yet another factor that affects your garden and can influence the success or failure of your plantings. Plants require moisture, which would make it seem like humidity is good for gardens. But when it's really sunny and hot out—let's call that tomato weather—and humidity increases significantly, it can bring along with it a number of unpleasant companions, like gray mold, powdery mildew, downy mildew, and late blight fungus. Fortunately, the return of hot, dry weather will often halt the incursion.

LIGHT AND SHADE

A sunny climate can host a productive vegetable garden. Vegetables, like all plants, rely on the sun to kick-start photosynthesis. The optimal number of sunlight hours can vary from plant to plant, but the fastest-growing vegetables usually need six to eight hours of full sun each day, without shade supplied by trees, shrubs, or fences.

TERRAIN

The terrain that surrounds your home will also affect your garden's

MORE INFO
Microclimates

Sometimes your particular surroundings can end up creating a microclimate. This is a local set of atmospheric conditions, especially ones that differ from the surrounding area. The difference may be slight or significant, and it might affect an area of only a few square yards or meters—as with a cave or a garden bed—or an area of many square miles or kilometers. Microclimates can be found in most places but are most pronounced in topographically dynamic zones, such as mountainous areas, islands, and coastal areas. Heavy urban areas, where brick, concrete, and asphalt all heat up in the sun then re-radiate that heat into the ambient air, can create what is referred to as an "urban heat island," or UHI. This microclimate is also driven by a lack of cooling vegetation.

Being aware of your regional climate, any microclimates, and your hardiness zone makes it easier to factor in the growing season, timing and amount of rainfall, and temperature ranges in order to ensure the plants you've chosen are right for your location.

climate. Nearby woodlands or mountains might protect your plants from wind and rain. If you live in an open grassland or a desert area, wind might become something you need to prepare for with stakes and burlap wraps. Gardens located above lakes or rivers might benefit from the sunlight reflected off the water. Proximity to forests and large masses of water, like lakes or oceans, can affect the climate through transpiration and evaporation.

HARDINESS ZONES

The term *hardiness zone* denotes a geographic area defined as having a certain average annual minimum temperature and refers to how well a plant will survive cold. In some systems, other statistics are included in the calculations. The original and most widely used system is the USDA Plant Hardiness Zone Map, developed by the United States Department of Agriculture as a rough guide that divides North America into 11 zones by long-term average annual extreme minimum temperatures. The lower the number is, the lower the temperatures in that zone. Each zone represents 10 degrees of temperature difference. These same

ranges have also been applied to much of the rest of the planet. For example, Europe can be divided into 11 zones, with temperatures ranging from -60°F to 50°F (-51°C to 10°C). In the UK, however, the USDA zones do not work particularly well because they are designed for continental climates and subtropical climates. Other countries (such as Canada) have adapted the USDA zones in various forms. Most of the larger countries and regions of the world have their own version of a hardiness map. Australia, New Zealand, Africa, Canada, China, Japan, Europe, Russia, South America, and many more have a similar system.

Where the USDA zones fall short, however, is that they don't account for other factors, such as freeze dates, freeze-thaw cycles, the effects of snow cover, precipitation, and elevation. The limitations of the USDA zones are most felt in the western United States. If you live in this area, check the Sunset climate zones. This system uses the minimum temperatures to determine which plants will grow best where, along with the length of the growing season, summer temperatures, wind, humidity, and rainfall.

WORK WITH YOUR SITE

The key factors of a location's available light, topography, aspect, and drainage will determine what kinds of vegetables, fruits, and herbs will grow and thrive there.

Before selecting a garden plot, consider the factors that will affect your plants—things like sunlight, wind, drainage, access to water, foot traffic patterns, and, for an edible garden, ease of access to the plants when its time to harvest.

Location-wise, your choices of where to plant your garden are limited by the extent of your property. If tall trees shade the entire yard, that is your lot, literally. On the other hand, if the sun beats down upon the lawn without a lick of shade, at least you can plant several saplings and begin to add some cover. Likewise, there are other solutions to problem locations: hilly terrain can be terraced, lackluster flat terrain can be built up into berms or raised beds. Dry terrain can be irrigated or turned into a drought-resistant xeriscape that supports the numerous types of herbs and vegetables that can be successfully incorporated into these water-thrifty landscapes. For every challenge your yard may present, there is some way for a clever and resourceful vegetable gardener to ameliorate it.

You must also deal with the question of size, of determining how large your garden should be. Maybe it's better to have one small garden in a sunny location in which you grow sun-lovers like corn, summer squashes, and melons, and a larger shade garden situated under a row of trees that can support shade-tolerant vegetables, such as many members of the cabbage family. That way you've created two productive plots.

For an edible garden, placement near the kitchen is ideal, but sunlight trumps proximity to the house when it comes to the needs of most vegetables, herbs, and fruits. If the sunniest spot is out near the garage or in a far corner of the property, that's where the produce garden must go.

AVAILABLE LIGHT

The level of sunlight varies from season to season, sometimes even hour to hour. As the sun moves across the sky, the quality of the light changes, often softening, even in a sunny garden. Similarly, a shady garden will get dappled sunlight peeking through the tree canopy at some point in the day.

The sunny yard

You are to be envied if your yard enjoys more than six hours of sunshine—most edible species require full sun. Particularly sun-loving produce includes tomatoes, corn, green beans, cucumbers, okra, melons, sweet potatoes, pumpkins, zucchini, eggplant, and jalapeño peppers. Herbs that like to bask in full sun include basil, tarragon, dill, lavender, chives, thyme, and stevia.

Even homeowners with limited space can dedicate a corner of their outdoor space to an edible garden plot. Planted in spring, this suburban raised garden bed is loaded with a variety of herbs and vegetables ready to be harvested in summer.

The topography of your property will determine how you organize your produce plots. If your property is sloped, the best solution for hillsides is to plant your vegetables across the slope using contour rows, terraces, or raised beds.

Dig Deeper

LEARN MORE AT GARDENING KNOW HOW

Scan the QR code or follow the link below to learn more about how to work with sloping garden terrain.

"Growing a Vegetable Garden on a Hillside"
LINK: gkh.us.294

ASPECT

The aspect of a garden refers to which direction the plants face in terms of sunlight, exposure to rain or snow, and the like. In the Northern Hemisphere, south-facing gardens (north-facing beds in the Southern Hemisphere) receive more hours of sunshine and are therefore the best locations to plant in cooler regions. In hotter regions, north-facing gardens make more sense, reducing potentially damaging exposure to the tropic sun.

The shady yard

Do not despair if much of your yard is overhung with trees or shadowed by buildings. Many produce plants require full sun, but there are a good number that can survive a shady garden. Leafy greens such as spinach, lettuce, and kale all tolerate shade and cool temperatures. Pea plants, pears, plums, rhubarb, and many herbs can also tolerate or even thrive in shady conditions.

TOPOGRAPHY

The literal ups and downs of your landscape can make gardening . . . interesting. But a wise gardener soon learns to make the most of a rocky hillside or parched plateau. Your topography also affects the type of sunlight you receive. In temperate regions the sun does not position itself directly overhead, even at noon, so its rays tend to

fall more or less perpendicular to a slope, and with some intensity. On flat ground, however, the sun's rays are dissipated across a wider area, so their strength is diluted.

Uphill battles

Some of the world's most productive gardens have been planted on uneven hillsides. Landscaping aids such as railroad ties, concrete retaining stones, even bricks, can create a terraced garden that invites the eye to travel upward from layer to layer. Tiered plantings of produce and grasses also prevent soil erosion and, when mulched, can help retain moisture. Plants with fibrous root systems like grasses, wheat, and rosemary can help preserve soil in hilly conditions. Coir netting or windbreaks can also be used to keep soil in place on especially windy terraces.

DRAINAGE

Few things are worse for plants than a waterlogged garden. If the lawn remains squishy after a rainfall in the area where you plan to excavate for an edible garden, you need to either pick a new location or choose one of these solutions.

- Aerate the soil to facilitate drainage.
- Dig in large amounts of compost or other organic matter that will aid drainage.
- Create slopes that direct water to a surface drain or into garden beds with moisture-loving plants.
- Install land drains—underground perforated pipes that channel water away from flooding zones.
- Use absorbent mulch to remove water from the garden.
- Add more plants to the area, which will quickly drink up the excess water.

A Gallery of
VEGETABLE GARDEN STYLES

A vegetable garden can be as simple as a few pots of tomatoes on an apartment balcony to a row of herbs on a windowsill to extravagant veggie plots shaded with fruit trees that fill a backyard. Just about anyone can find space to plant a few vegetables, herbs, and fruits to fill the table with healthy, fresh produce.

TRADITIONAL PLOTS
For those with outdoor space, traditional plots of in-ground rows have long been the standard. You can mix this type with raised beds

RAISED BED OR TIERED GARDEN
Attractive raised beds allow you to control the soil for each kind of plant. They can be low to the ground or tiered to save space.

TABLETOP BED
Taking the raised bed format and bringing it up to waist height can save a gardener's back as they care for the plants within it.

CHILDREN'S PLOT
Kids love to get down in the dirt. Make this fun time productive with a garden filled with easy growers like carrots, lettuce, beans, and squash.

KEYHOLE GARDENING
Organic materials layered in a circular raised bed with a center composting well funnels nutrients from food waste into the soil.

ROOF GARDEN
Turning rooftop space into a garden is increasingly popular in many cities. Plots can be small individual ones or a community garden.

WINDOWSILL GARDEN
From herbs to small vegetables like cherry tomatoes, many species will thrive in a sunny spot on an interior windowsill.

BALCONY OR DECK GARDEN
Apartment dwellers with a sunny balcony or deck can cultivate a variety of vegetables, such as tomatoes, squash, herbs, and lettuce.

GREEN WALL
A smart way to cultivate vegetables when space is limited is by going vertical, creating a green wall of plants either indoors or out.

CONTAINER GARDENING
Containers using any available space provide a mobile garden for those with limited room to grow their own food.

COMMUNITY GARDEN
For those who lack outdoor space, community gardens are great ways to cultivate a plot or two and meet like-minded friends.

KNOW YOUR SOIL

The success or failure of a garden depends on many factors, but arguably the most critical of these is soil quality. It truly is the foundation of your vegetable garden.

Soil furnishes growing plants with nutrients, water, and air. It allows for healthy root systems and multiplication of bulbs, tubers, or corms. Put simply, poor soil produces poor plants, and high-quality soil produces high-quality plants. Rich, dark loam may be every gardener's wish, but few are ever blessed with it from the start. Instead, the typical plot of ground has its own blend of minerals and organic and inorganic matter that largely determines which vegetable crops or fruit trees can be successfully grown there. Enrichment is the solution for creating a more forgiving plot. Although conditioning soil is a continuous process that takes patience and hard work, this labor will pay off in healthy foliage, beautiful blooms, and bountiful harvests. But first, you need to determine what type of soil you are dealing with and what its pH level is.

SOIL TYPES

There are six soil types: clay, sand, silt, peat, chalk, and loam. Each is based on the dominating size of the particles within it. The first three are those most commonly found by gardeners. The following provides descriptions of each type.

Clay soil
Clay soil feels lumpy and sticky when wet and rock hard when dry. It lacks drainage, but is full of nutrients. When enhanced, it will support development and growth of high-yielding, vigorous summer crop vegetables. Early vegetables are difficult to grow in clay soil because of its cool, compact nature. Brussels sprouts and cabbage often grow better in clay soil than looser loams because their roots benefit from the firm anchorage it gives.

Silty soil
Silty soil is soft and feels somewhat "soapy." It retains moisture well and is frequently rich in nutrients. Easily cultivated, silty soil can be compacted with little effort. Adding composted organic matter will improve its draining abilities, and it will also improve its structure while adding vital nutrients. The result will support most vegetable and fruit crops, especially shallow-rooted lettuces, onions, beans, and members of the brassica family.

Sandy soil
Sandy soil feels gritty; it drains easily, dries out quickly, and is easy to cultivate. It warms up fast in spring but holds fewer nutrients; these can wash away during wet spells. For best

---

MORE INFO
Aspects of Garden Soil

In addition to general soil types, there are other aspects you should consider when the quality of your garden soil needs improvement.

1. Tilth. This is the soil's physical condition and larger-scale structure. It includes whether or not the soil has aggregates (clumps) and what size they are, whether it has channels where water can enter and drain, and its level of aeration. Soil with good tilth provides a structure that supports healthy root growth.

2. Water-holding capacity. This is partially a function of the soil type, but other things can alter it. Ideally, soil should be well drained but hold enough water to support healthy plant growth.

3. Nutrient-holding capacity. This is the soil's ability to hold onto mineral nutrients. Clay soils, with a greater nutrient-holding capacity, can be very fertile, yet they may need work to overcome their tendency to become compacted or too clumpy.

4. Percentage of organic matter. This is very important in promoting biological activity in the soil; it affects the water and nutrient-holding capacity and the tilth.

results, add organic amendments, such as glacial rock dust, kelp meal, or greensand, and be sure to mulch. Sandy soil supports lettuce, strawberries, peppers, corn, squash, tomatoes, and root crops like beets, carrots, and potatoes.

Peaty soil
Peaty soil is dark, damp, and spongy due to its higher levels of peat (partially decayed vegetation). This acidic soil slows down decomposition, which leads to fewer nutrients. It heats up quickly in spring and can retain water, which requires drainage. Blend peaty soil with organic matter and compost, as well as lime to reduce acidity. Brassicas, legumes, root crops, and salad crops thrive in well-drained peaty soils.

Chalky soil
Large-grained and often stony, chalky soil drains freely and usually overlays chalk or limestone bedrock. Because this soil is alkaline, it can cause stunted growth and yellowish leaves. Using appropriate fertilizers and balancing the pH will help improve its ability to support vegetables. Adding humus improves water retention and workability. Chalky soil supports vegetables like spinach, Brussels sprouts, beets, beans, sweet corn, kale, cauliflower, and cabbage.

Loamy soil
A mix of sand, silt, and clay, loamy soil is fine textured, slightly damp, and tends to be acidic. Its desirable qualities include great structure, adequate drainage, moisture retention, plenty of nutrients, and easy cultivation. It warms up quickly in spring, yet resists drying out in summer. Adding organic nutrients is essential to soil vitality. It is ideal for many vegetable crops, such as tomatoes, green beans, peppers, cucumbers, onions, and lettuce, as well as many berries.

DETERMINING SOIL TYPE
There are a number of simple tests you can perform at home that will help determine your soil type. The results will guide you when it comes time to add amendments.

Water test
Simply pour some water onto a bare spot of soil. If it drains quickly, that indicates a sandy or gravelly soil. With clay soils, the water will take its time sinking in.

Squeeze test
Scoop up a handful of soil and softly compress it in your fist. If the soil is sticky and slick to the touch and remains in the same shape when you release the pressure, it is clay soil. If the soil feels spongy, it's peaty soil. Sandy soil feels gritty and easily crumbles apart. Loamy and silty soils feel smooth textured and hold their shape for a short period of time.

Squeezing a handful of soil is a simple method of determining a soil's type.

Settle test
Add a handful of soil to a transparent container, add water, and shake it well. Leave the soil to settle for at least 12 hours before you evaluate it.

- Clay and silty soils will produce cloudy water with a layer of particles at the bottom.
- Sandy soils will leave the water mostly clear, and the particles will form a layer at the bottom of the container.
- Peaty soils show many particles floating on the surface; the water will be slightly cloudy with only a thin layer at the bottom.
- Chalky soils will leave a layer of whitish, gritty fragments on the bottom, and the water will be a pale gray.
- Loamy soil will leave the water quite clear, with layered particles at the bottom.

TESTING SOIL
Two important factors of soil are its nutrient content and its pH level. A soil test kit (available at garden centers and online) allows you to assess its primary nutrients (nitrogen, phosphorus, and potassium), as well as pH levels. Determining your soil's condition allows you to fertilize effectively and economically. Test periodically throughout the growing season.

Most vegetables prefer slightly acidic soils with a pH level of between 6.0 and 7.0, the levels at which nutrients and minerals tend to be most available to plants. Generally speaking, regions with soft water will have acid soil; hard-water areas will likely have alkaline.

LEARN MORE AT GARDENING KNOW HOW

Scan the QR code or follow the link below to learn how working in garden soil is good for your mental well-being.

"Anti-depressant Microbes: How Dirt Makes You Happy"
LINK: gkh.us/60021

IMPROVE YOUR SOIL

Most of us are not so lucky as to have land with the perfect soil in which to grow our vegetables, but there are many ways of amending it so that it can support healthy crops.

Your garden soil might have originally had a healthy structure and contained all the nutrients plants require, but over time the ground compacted and the nutrients were used up. If the soil has had organic amendments added continuously, however, it may be rich enough without additions. This is when you need a soil test (see page 21). Various soil-testing meters can be purchased at nurseries and other plant centers. You can also send a soil sample to your local Agricultural Extension office for analysis.

It is important to know your soil's pH, as well. For most plants, a healthy pH is between 6.0 and 7.0. Lower numbers indicate acidic soil, which reduces a plant's ability to access nutrients. Acidic soil will benefit from an application of lime prior to fertilizing, which will help neutralize the pH.

TYPES OF AMENDMENTS

Beds that utilize ground soil often need amendments to create the optimal growing conditions. There are two types of amendments: organic and inorganic. Organic or natural amendments include a number of materials, such as straw, leaves, and biosolids.

Compost and peat are also used to fertilize the soil and prevent pest infestation. Beneficial fungi and bacteria gain energy from the organic matter in the soil and will soon break down these amendments. Vermicompost, or biohumus, is a water-soluble, nutrient-rich organic substance produced by worms that makes an excellent, nutrient-rich organic fertilizer and soil conditioner.

Amendments like manure and grass clippings decompose rapidly and will quickly improve soil. Compost and peat decompose more slowly; they are used when the goal is to achieve long-lasting soil improvement.

Inorganic amendments include tire pieces, pea gravel, and sand. Over time, these can deplete the soil's naturally occurring nutrients.

IMPROVING SOIL

Sandy, clay, and silty are the soil types most often seen in home gardens (see pages 20 to 21). Their qualities will determine what specific kinds of amendments you require.

Sandy soil

Water quickly runs out of sandy soil, so it can be hard for it to retain the nutrients that plants need to thrive. Sandy soil is filled with sand—small pieces of eroded rock—so it has a gritty texture and few pockets to hold water or nutrients. Look for amendments that increase its ability to retain water and nutrients. Well-rotted manure or compost (including grass clippings, humus, and leaf mold) will provide a fast solution. You can also add vermiculite or peat, but they only increase soil's ability to hold onto water and will add little nutrient value. When amending sandy soil,

To amend soil for growing vegetables, a gardener begins the process of preparing a soil mixture from vermicompost, vermiculite, and perlite.

watch the salt levels. Compost and manure contain high levels that can damage growing plants. If your sandy soil is already high in salt, such as in a seaside garden, use plant-based compost or sphagnum peat, two amendments with the lowest salt levels.

Clay soil

Sticky, damp clay soil does hold nutrients and, when amended, it has good fertility. But clay soils have very fine particles, and their tiny pore spaces leave little room for roots to find needed air or water. The best way to improve clay is to work in a large amount of organic materials, such as manure, leaf mold, compost, and peat moss to a depth of 1 to 2 feet (30 to 60 cm). Break up any clods or clumps to allow the formation of those necessary air pockets. Perlite and crushed pumice will also keep the soil loose.

Silty soil

This type of soil has real possibilities—it holds moisture and is often rich in nutrients. Its main drawback is that it can lack drainage and structure. By working in some composted organic matter, you will be adding nutrients, as well as improving drainage and structure.

COMPACTED SOIL SOLUTIONS

Compacted soil occurs when something collapses the air pockets in between its components. It has a variety of causes: pressure from foot traffic or heavy machinery, like cars; if the ground is worked in less-than-ideal conditions—say, the soil is too wet when you till; if the soil doesn't have enough organic material to fluff it up; working the soil when it is too dry; and working it too often.

Roots in compacted soil must work harder to grow, which means that there will be fewer roots, and the plant will take up fewer nutrients and less water. There are a number of amendments that specifically loosen compacted soil.

Gypsum

Gypsum is calcium sulfate, a mineral that excels at breaking up compacted soil, especially clay.

Adding lime to garden soil

Lime

Lime, ground limestone, raises soil pH but also helps to loosen soil.

Vermiculite

Vermiculite, a hydrous phyllosilicate mineral, takes the form of glossy flakes in shades from dark gray to sandy brown. In garden beds or pots, it increases water and nutrient retention and aerates the soil.

Perlite

Perlite is an amorphous volcanic glass that improves aeration and modifies soil substructure, keeping it loose and well-draining.

MORE INFO
Lasagna Gardening

Lasagna gardening is a simple way to improve garden soil that uses fully biodegradable waste materials you are likely to have around the house. The method, also known as sheet mulching or sheet composting, promises "no digging, no tilling, no weeding." It was formulated to create the conditions for a productive plot.

Start in autumn by layering the grass of the designated garden plot with 5 inches (12.5 cm) of brown matter (for carbon)—shredded leaves, cardboard, newspaper, peat, or pine needles—then 3 inches (7.5 cm) of green matter (for nitrogen)—grass clippings, garden trimmings, or vegetable scraps. Repeat these layers for 20 inches (50 cm), and then cover

with 5 inches (12.5 cm) of garden soil. Keep the entire plot moist. As these layers "cook" down, they will enrich and aerate the soil and keep weeds at bay. Once planted up, mulch the garden with straw or grass clippings.

NOURISH YOUR GARDEN

Fertilizing your garden helps to increase your crop yields and encourages the growth of strong, healthy plants that have better resistance to pests and diseases.

The most basic definition of a fertilizer is a substance that is added to soil to improve the supply of nutrients, which encourages plant growth. Many gardeners believe the best time to fertilize is the spring, when plants are at their peak growing cycle—leafing out, flowering, or putting out new growth. This is also when increasing soil temperatures allow plants to uptake nutrients at the proper rate.

Use a soil test to determine the type of fertilizer you require for your garden plots. This indicates the nutrients and minerals lacking in your soil. Each plant's needs differ, so it is also important to know the nutrient requirements of specific varieties. There are also fertilizers geared to certain plant species, such as tomatoes. On the other hand, all-purpose fertilizers provide the basic nutrients and minerals most plants need and are a good option in many cases.

FEEDING THE KITCHEN GARDEN
Fertilizing vegetables, berries, and melons is a must if you wish to get the highest yields and best-quality produce. A soil test can determine what specific fertilizers are needed. The most common recommendations for vegetable gardens are nitrogen and phosphorus, but these aren't the only nutrients a healthy garden requires. Plants are composed primarily of carbon, hydrogen, and oxygen, nutrients absorbed from the air and water, but a fertile garden must have more than 14 additional macro- and micronutrients for healthiest growth. As with any garden, there are two types of fertilizer for edible gardens: synthetic and natural. Most produce needs a balanced fertilizer, such as a 10-10-10, but some need additional potassium. Leafy greens often require only nitrogen.

MICRONUTRIENTS
Those three bold numbers featured on packages of fertilizer, such as 10-10-10 or 5-2-6, are known as "fertilizer grade." Each number represents the percentage of three key macronutrients found in the mix: nitrogen, phosphorus, and potassium (potash), or N-P-K.

Nitrogen
Nitrogen is part of all living cells and is a necessary part of all proteins, enzymes, and metabolic processes involved in the synthesis and transfer of energy. It is a constituent of chlorophyll, the green pigment responsible for photosynthesis, and it helps with rapid growth and increased seed and fruit production.

Phosphorus
Phosphorus is an essential part of photosynthesis and is involved in the formation of all oils, sugars, starches, etc. It helps transform solar energy into chemical energy, aids proper plant maturation, and encourages blooming and root growth.

Potassium
Potassium is absorbed by plants in larger amounts than any other mineral element, except nitrogen, and, in some cases, calcium. It helps to build protein, aids photosynthesis, enhances fruit quality, and reduces diseases.

Secondary nutrients
There are three secondary nutrients necessary for plant growth.
- Calcium is essential for proper cell-wall structure and the transport of elements.
- Magnesium is critical for photosynthesis and activating growth enzymes.

Growing organic vegetables in a raised bed, full of mature compost. Compost, whether homemade or purchased, is ideal for vegetable plots, with all the vital nutrients required for strong growth released to the plants over a long period.

- Sulfur is essential for the production of protein, vitamins, and developing enzymes.

MICRONUTRIENTS

There are seven elements defined as micronutrients.

- Boron aids sugar transport, cell division, and the production of amino acids.
- Chlorine is necessary for photosynthesis and root growth.
- Copper activates enzymes.
- Iron aids in producing chlorophyll and in photosynthesis.
- Molybdenum is involved in nitrogen metabolism.
- Manganese assists iron in chlorophyll formation. It also serves as an activator for enzymes in the growth process.
- Zinc is a component of several enzymes and is important for hormone balance.

Some micronutrient lists also include nickel, which is required to complete the life cycle of a plant and its viable seed.

CHOOSING FERTILIZER

When shopping for fertilizer, consider how the capabilities of each nutrient relate to which vegetables you are growing. Higher percentages of nitrogen encourage vigorous leafy growth and rich green color and work best for foliage plants and grasses. Phosphorus ensures healthy roots, blooms, fruits, and seeds in flowering plants and vegetables.

Potassium keeps plants healthy by enhancing overall growth, while regulating root and top growth.

Natural fertilizers

Organic fertilizers contain only natural ingredients, those digested by soil microorganisms that then release the nutrients in a form available to plants. Natural fertilizers contain healthful microorganisms such as biological compounds, fungi, algae, or bacteria, all of which help your plants thrive. These microorganisms need a soil temperature of at least 50°F (10°C)—often higher—to work their magic, which is why it makes sense to fertilize in spring.

Natural fertilizers are available in three forms.

- Single-ingredient options include cow and horse manure, poultry manure, seaweed, blood meal, bone meal, feather meal, cottonseed meal, alfalfa meal, leaf litter, compost, bone, wood ash, and worm castings.
- Granular blends use a mix of the animal, plant, and mineral ingredients listed above; they usually offer an N-P-K ratio of 4-5-4 or 3-3-3.
- Liquid fertilizers may have fewer macronutrients, but they also contain trace nutrients, amino acids, and vitamins. These fertilizers include liquid kelp, fish emulsion, and fish hydrosylate.

You can work both granular fertilizer and liquid fertilizer into the soil surface. Another option is to add a time-release fertilizer that allows for slow uptake and continuous feeding of plants like vegetables and ornamentals.

Synthetic fertilizers

Synthetic, or inorganic, fertilizers contain no natural ingredients. They are water-soluble and are almost immediately taken up by plants. Although this provides a

Animal manure is a good source if you want to add phosphorus to soil.

quick boost of nutrients and rapid greening, the color won't last long. You must regularly reapply synthetic fertilizers to keep the results from fading. Synthetic fertilizers do little to stimulate soil life, improve soil texture, or promote long-term fertility. They can also leach into waterways. Use synthetic fertilizers with caution—apply too much and it may burn your plants. They come in liquid, pellet, granule, and spike forms; their nutrients percentages are listed on their labels.

MORE INFO
Fertilizer, Amendments, and Plant Food

There may be some confusion among gardeners about the difference between amendments, fertilizers, and products called plant food. Simply put, fertilizers directly affect plant growth by increasing the supply of nutrients in the soil. Soil amendments improve soil's physical condition (e.g., soil structure, water infiltration), indirectly affecting plant growth. Plant food is a naturally occurring form of sustenance that plants produce themselves, in part through photosynthesis. Additives calling themselves plant food are more likely a type of fertilizer.

ENRICH WITH COMPOST

Whatever its current conditions, the addition of compost can transform your soil into a healthy growing medium for a thriving vegetable garden.

Made up of organic materials that break down in the soil, compost enriches the structure of soil and adds essential nutrients. Think of the natural decomposition process found in nature: wooded areas are filled with trees, leaves, and other organic materials. Over time, they slowly decompose with the help of micro-organisms and earthworms. Once decomposed, they turn into humus, an essential element in the production of rich, fertile soil. This process is similar to garden composting. Once decomposition has taken place in the compost pile, the result should be similar to that of humus with a dark, crumbly, soil-like material.

COMPOSTING BASICS

Compost can be worked into the soil by hand or tilling or added as top-dressing to improve the quality of garden soil. It also makes suitable mulch. Numerous benefits are associated with the use of compost. It enhances soil, building up its structure and texture; increases airflow and water retention; stabilizes pH levels and supports essential bacteria; and allows plants to effectively use nutrients for achieving healthier growth. The organic matter found in compost encourages earthworms, which also help aerate the soil. Other benefits include erosion control and the reduction of soil-borne diseases.

HOW TO MAKE COMPOST

Compost can be created by numerous means, but there are five commonly used methods: in holding units, turning units, by soil incorporation, vermicomposting, and through the creation of compost heaps, or piles.

The easiest and least expensive method for most people is heap composting. With this method, no structure is required, although you can use a compost bin. A compost heap or pile can be untidier than a bin, but for newbies, this method is the simplest. If you would prefer to camouflage an unsightly compost heap, surround it with tall flowering plants or decorative fencing. If you prefer to use a bin, enclosure, or compost container, you can find ones that vary in size, ranging between 5 to 7 feet (1.5 to 2 m) and 3 to 4 feet (1 to 1.2 m). For smaller a garden, a bin no larger than 3 by 3 feet (1 x 1 m) is best.

Kitchen scraps, such as vegetable and fruit peelings, act as "green" material, which will add nitrogen to garden soil, improving its ability to nurture healthy plants.

A gardener holds a clump of compost teeming with red wigglers. These worms can process half their body weight in kitchen scraps per day.

Autumn is the ideal time to start a compost heap, when both nitrogen and carbon materials are readily available. There are just a few necessary steps.

Determine the location

Choose an open, level area with good drainage—you do not want your compost to sit in standing water. Partial sunlight or shade is best: too much sun can dry the pile out, but too much shade can result in overly wet conditions. An important location consideration is siting the heap away from areas that can be reached by dogs or other meat-eating animals.

Figure out the size

Your compost heap should be no smaller than 3 feet (1m) high and 3 feet (1 m) wide and no larger than 5 by 5 feet (1.5 x 1.5 m). Too small, and it might not heat up efficiently, and anything larger might hold too much water and become difficult to turn. Start your pile on bare ground, rather than on asphalt or concrete. These hard surfaces might impede aeration and inhibit microbes. You can, however, place a wooden pallet underneath the pile

Add organic materials

A compost heap will need "green" and "brown" materials. Green items, such as grass clippings and kitchen scraps, add nitrogen to the compost. Brown materials add carbon to compost and consist of things like leaves, newspaper, and small woody materials.

When adding material to build the pile, layer the nitrogen/greens and carbon/browns, as you would when making lasagna. Lightly water each layer as it is added, firming it down, but do not compact it.

- Start by layering bulkier organic materials in the ground layer, such as twigs (less than ½ inch, or 1.25 cm, in diameter) or straw, to about a height of 4 to 6 inches (10 to 15 cm).
- Next, add in some green materials, such as kitchen waste and grass clippings, again about 4 to 6 inches (10 to 15 cm) thick. Additionally, animal manure and fertilizers serve as activators that accelerate the heating of your pile and provide a nitrogen source for beneficial microbes.
- Continue alternating layers of green and brown materials until you reach the top or run out.

Water and turn the compost

Compost should be frequently turned with a garden fork to aid in aeration, as well as to speed up decomposition. The pile should be moist, but not soggy. Rainfall, as well as the moisture in green materials, will supply most of the water, but you might need to water the pile on occasion. If the pile gets too wet, turn it more frequently to dry it, or add more brown materials to soak up excess moisture.

Once you turn the pile the first time, these materials will get mixed together and decompose more efficiently. Frequently turning the pile will help with aeration and speed up decomposition. Depending on the materials used and size of the compost pile, decomposition can take anywhere from weeks or months to a year.

Editor's Tip

Some material is better than others. Most kitchen scraps are welcome additions to a compost pile, but some things are simply no-nos. Never add meat, fat, and bone products to the pile, because they can introduce harmful parasites and attract hungry animals, as well as produce odors and bacteria buildup (of the unhealthy kind).

Do add:

- leaves
- garden plants
- newspaper
- straw
- grass clippings
- manure
- vegetable and fruit peelings
- eggshells
- coffee grounds

Don't add:

- meat or bones
- dairy products
- fat or oil
- carnivorous pet feces, such as dog or cat waste
- diseased plants
- weeds that have seeded
- human waste
- charcoal or coal ash (wood ash is okay, though)

GATHER YOUR TOOLS

Creating and tending an edible garden takes only a few essential tools, but there are many other kinds of equipment to make this work easier and more productive.

Maintaining a healthy, productive garden—preparing the soil, planting, weeding, watering, deadheading, and harvesting—depends on a dozen or so time-tested tools. Yet, even if you start out content with some hand tools and a shovel, you will soon find yourself progressing to power tools like rototillers and weed-eaters. And every few seasons, you might even need to rent a piece of really big equipment, like a skid steer or brush hog, to clear out some land for a new garden.

Once you have collected the right implements for your vegetable garden, the next step is making sure they stay in good working condition with frequent cleaning, oiling, and sharpening. Otherwise you will find yourself replacing them every few seasons. In addition to tools, you'll require yard equipment, like ladders and wheelbarrows.

THE RIGHT TOOL FOR THE JOB

There are many different types of tools for gardening, and each has a special purpose. Digging tools, like shovels and spades, can be used to cultivate, plant, or clear a plot. Long-handled shovels reduce the need to squat or kneel, but there is still no substitute for a hand trowel for up-close digging.

A hoe chops weeds and makes neat rows, while a spading fork breaks up soil clods and turns compost piles with ease. There are various types of cultivators that are useful in the vegetable garden as you get it ready for spring. Rakes come in the flexible style, useful for raking up leaves, or the hard rake option, which breaks up soil or thatches the lawn.

Most reputable garden centers can advise you about various tools and their purposes. They will also have a wide range of basic garden tools for beginners.

HAND TOOLS

These small tools do a lot of work for their size. These are the go-to tools that are easy to carry and perform essential tasks.

When choosing hand tools, examine how the implement is made. How the handle is attached to a digging tool can mean either a lifetime of use or instant breakage when you hit that first hard rock. The least-expensive tools will likely have a tang-and-ferrule attachment. These are cheaply made and usually separate after a short period of use. Solid-socket tools have a forged connection from handle to working end. These are more expensive but will provide a lifetime of service. The most expensive option offers a seamless solid-strap attachment that isn't going anywhere.

Another consideration is comfort. The grip is crucial when picking out hand tools. A padded grip will result in fewer blisters and aching hands. Non-slip grips are useful when working in the rain, while ergonomic grips reduce hand stress from

Vegetable gardeners need both large and small tools to make their tasks easier. Large handheld tools like hoes are a must, and no one should be without a wheelbarrow, which will facilitate moving heavy loads throughout the garden.

clasping too hard. Larger handles minimize strain and give a better grasp of the tool. Always test out an implement—pantomime the motion you will be repeating with the tool to see if it is the right length, grip, and weight for you. The length of the handle should allow maximum exertion with minimal effort. Longer handles allow for a two-handed grip and better leverage. These may also be helpful to a gardener with a physical disability or mobility issue.

Garden trowel

This indispensable small shovel-shaped handheld tool is used for digging out planting holes, weeding, and scooping up soil.

Hand transplanter

This trowel-like tool is used for digging, aerating, and transplanting smaller vegetables, fruits and other plants. It has a serrated edge to cut into the ground and depth measurements for easier use.

Hand garden fork

Often called a weeding fork, this tined tool is ideal for loosening soil and uprooting weeds in confined spaces. You can also use it to prepare planting holes, transplant seedlings, and aerate and mix additives into your soil. In addition, you can also use it to level around border edges.

Trowels, forks, and transplanters are some of the most commonly used hand tools.

A gardener uses a double-sided fork hoe to cut off the roots of a scallion.

Hand rake

Also called a cultivator, this large-tined, curved fork breaks up clumped or rocky soil, mixes in amendments, or loosens weeds.

Hand hoe

This flat-sided tool chops down through weed roots.

Double-side hand tools

Combining a hand hoe and a cultivator, a hoe, and a fork, or a trowel and fork, these dual-purpose tools work to break up clumpy soil and to weed between garden rows.

Bulb planter

The tube-shaped head removes a cylinder of soil, leaving behind a pocket for your bulb. It can be handy for planting onions or root vegetable like potatoes.

Knife

Use to cut string or twine for staking or to pry out small rocks. You can also use it to harvest certain herbs.

Scissors and shears

Gardening scissors and shears deadhead flowers and harvest tender herbs and produce.

MORE INFO *Effective weeding tools*

Weeds can quickly get out of control and crowd out desirable plants. High-quality, ergonomic weeding hand tools help you keep weeds in check while reducing stress on your back, knees, and wrists. But when it comes to choosing weeders, no single tool is right for everybody. Do you fight weeds with long taproots? If you don't get the root, the bits left behind will generate a new plant. You'll need a different tool for shallow-rooted weeds or those with runners or stolons. If you have trouble kneeling or bending, look for long-handled weeders. Quality weeding tools needn't be fancy, and they shouldn't break the bank. Still, quality tools may cost a little more, but they're worth it. Sturdy tools last longer, and they can be resharpened.

- **Stirrup hoe.** This useful tool features a stirrup-shaped blade that's sharp on both sides. When pushed back and forth, the blade chops off weeds at the base.
- **Japanese hori hori knife.** The smooth edge is made for cutting or slicing, while the serrated edge saws through roots and sod and prunes small branches. Or use it like a trowel for digging in small areas.

- **Japanese hand hoe.** The super-sharp blades of this knife power through small weeds when you scrape the hoe across the soil; it comes in various types and sizes. The pointy end pulls out stubborn weeds, cuts through compacted soil, or digs out trenches.
- **Fishtail weeder.** This easily plucks up tough weeds like dandelions, but also works well for those between crevices.

A gardener uses pruning clippers, or secateurs, to snip lima (aka butter) beans from the vine.

Secateurs/pruning clippers

Spring-loaded clippers harvest herbs and fruits and veggies with tough stems like tomatoes and peppers, prune small branches, deadhead flowers, cut through roots, and divide root balls. They are essential to manage the size and shape of individual plants. There isn't any significant difference between the two; which term you use mainly depends on where you live.

Garden snips

Use it to easily slice open soil bags and cut wire, netting, landscape fabric or plastic, and more.

LARGE TOOLS

No matter how small their planting beds might be, at some point most gardeners will require larger tools. A sturdy shovel comes to mind, as well as a leaf rake. The tools listed below are only a sampling of the many garden implements available at your local garden center, but they are the most useful.

Shovels and spades

These are the true workhorses of the vegetable garden. A long-handled garden shovel is typically bowl-shaped (concave) with a

The flattened shape and square edge of a spade slice through garden soil.

A garden shed features a purpose-built rack for storing large garden implements, including double-sided fork tools, leaf and soil rakes, garden forks, and shovels and spades.

rounded or pointed tip; use it to dig holes, turn soil, break up roots, and transport soil and mulch. A spade can be flat (or nearly flat) with a straight edge, and it is usually shorter than a shovel; use it to edge lawns, segment and remove sod, and slice through soil and roots.

Sharpshooter

Also called a tile spade, drainage shovel, or transplanting spade, this is a specific type of shovel with a long, narrow blade. It provides the necessary leverage and control to dig deeper, more precise holes.

Steel soil rake

Use this rigid rake to smooth out soil or work in amendments.

Leaf rake

This rake's springy tines pick up leaves, grass clippings, and other messy lawn debris.

Hoe

This ancient tool is used to cultivate soil or chop weeds.

Tree lopper

Trims errant branches from trees; some models have handles that extend to reach upper limbs.

Garden claw

This long-handed tool with a claw of twisted metal at the bottom is used to cultivate, loosen, and aerate soil, and to weed.

Forks

The are a few styles of long-handled garden forks, each with a different purpose. A manure fork, or pitchfork, with rounded, curved tines, is used to spread mulch or hay over beds. The spading fork has four narrow tines and is used to turn over soil and to gently lift perennials for replanting. The digging fork, with flattened tines, pries root vegetables from the soil. Garden forks can also be used to rake out weeds or large rocks.

Long-handled cultivator

A cultivator mixes up soil that is already loose and stirs in compost or fertilizer so that it is ready for planting. Many will know this as the Garden Weasel, which has detachable tines to help with cleaning and creating narrow garden trenches.

With a cultivator, you place the head on the ground and roll it back and forth so that the sharp rotary blades can break up and loosen hard soil.

MORE INFO
Cleaning and Sharpening Tools

Nothing is more frustrating, when you plan a few hours of spring gardening, only to discover that your trusty garden pruners rusted shut over the winter or the wooden handle of your favorite trowel has split. Properly caring for your tools will extend their life and save you money down the road.

- Every spring, place your tools on a tarp, and evaluate their condition. Check for rust, dull blades, and parched wood.
- Wash tools with mild detergent, and then dry them with a lint-free cloth. Fine-grained steel wool is effective against rust or other tough stains.
- Apply machine oil to all metal surfaces, especially moving parts, and reapply it after using the tools.
- With a mild bleach solution, wipe down cutting tools like saws, shears, or pruners to inhibit the possible spread of disease.
- Sharpen tools or shovel blades on a whetstone or with an all-purpose file, holding it at a 45-degree angle.
- Twice a season, sand wooden handles with medium-grit sand paper, and then rub in a protective coat of linseed oil. Never leave wooden tools outside after using them.

Walk-behind rototillers churn up and loosen garden soil in preparation for planting. Because they are used so rarely, these kind of garden machines can be rented.

Cultivator

These are best for churning up already-loosened soil; use them to aerate soil before planting or to stir in compost. Power versions of these tools can be corded, cordless, or gas-powered.

Leaf blower

This tool makes it a breeze to clean up the yard, helping to prevent disease and to gather organic material for compost.

A string trimmer makes fast work of eliminating weeds that crop up at the edges of raised vegetable beds.

String trimmer/weed whacker

This consists of a long handle and a rotating head that spins a string-like blade. It is indispensable when it's time to neaten up the garden, eliminate clumps of tall weeds, or trim back the plant borders and walkways. Robot versions are also available, which use height to differentiate between desirable plants and undesirable weeds.

Chainsaw

This is for the really tough trimming or lopping jobs; smaller versions are useful in any garden setting. These can be especially useful for pruning fruit trees or for keeping tree branches from casting too much shade over a vegetable plot.

Editor's Tip

Power tools can be dangerous if not used properly. Here are a few tips for handling these tools with care.

- Wear safety glasses, nonslip gloves, and sturdy, nonslip shoes whenever operating a power tool.
- Never carry a power tool by its cord.
- Correctly unplug corded power tools.
- Be sure to turn off tools before changing parts or adding accessories.
- Keep your cutting tools sharp. Dull blades can cause accidents.
- Look for power tools that come with working safety guards and switches.
- Carefully follow the manufacturer's cleaning and storage instructions.

POWER TOOLS

Most gardeners find that as their gardens or plantings expand, they come to rely on one or more of these power tools. Manufacturers typically offer tools with a choice of electric or battery power; some tools also run on gasoline. If possible, invest in brand names. You will get longevity and great performance and have a better chance at finding replacement parts and batteries.

Rototiller

A rototiller is a gas- or electric-powered machine designed with turning blades to break up and loosen soil. It can cut through hard, compact soil, which makes breaking ground in a new area much easier. Walk-behind versions come in various sizes, depending on your budget and your needs. As with many pieces of large power equipment, rototillers are often available as rentals for those who rarely need them.

TRACTORS AND ACCESSORIES

Few people with large yards ever regret this investment. Tractors can tow a garden cart or spreader or be fitted with a mower or auger attachment. You can accessorize a tractor for just about any job.

Plow attachment

A plow attachment does the arduous work of breaking up the ground and turning the existing vegetation over to decompose, preparing the soil for plantings.

Rotary tillers and disk harrows

Although they each work a bit differently, when it comes to tractor implements for gardening, rotary tillers and disk harrows achieve the same outcome—they break up those dirt clods left behind after plowing. This makes the dirt finer and easier to work with.

Garden bedders

This time-saving attachment runs through the soil to dig out rows for your vegetable plots with evenly spaced trenches on each side.

Spreader attachment

A spreader is used for uniformly distributing seeds and fertilizer. As a bonus, you can also use it to spread salt during an icy winter.

A small tractor can be fitted with numerous attachments that tear through heavy work. Here, a rotary tiller has been attached to effectively loosen soil in a large plot.

ESSENTIAL YARD EQUIPMENT

Gardeners and non-gardeners alike need to maintain their property, and this is where these basic yard-care pieces come in. The good news is that they are sturdy additions to your home's inventory and rarely need to be replaced.

Wheelbarrow

The indispensable king of the yard and garden; they are invaluable for bigger jobs like shuttling plants, pots, soil, amendments, edging

A yard cart or wagon helps transport items throughout the yard and garden.

stones, or bricks from place to place, as well as transporting pruning scraps, leaves, and grass clippings to the compost bin. Guaranteed to save your back!

Yard cart/trolley

Usually square shaped with two or four wheels, some push forward, others are drawn forward with a single handle. Used to transport wood, plants, soil, amendments—anything heavy or cumbersome. Certain models are able to dump their contents.

Small wagon

A child's metal or plastic wagon makes a great way to transport plant flats, pots, and heavy bags of soil or amendments.

No gardener should be without a wheelbarrow, which transports the first soil to a garden and the last of the harvest from it, and everything in between.

IRRIGATION TOOLS

Irrigation equipment, such as a long sturdy hose, is essential to keep your plants hydrated.

Hose

Choose from traditional rubber, vinyl, or a combination of the two. Some models are even expandable or retractable. Look into "quick connect" technology that replaces screw-on hose attachments with pop-off fittings. Many gardeners prefer watering wands over spray nozzles because they offer greater pinpoint control.

Soaker hose

This perforated hose seeps water into the ground along its entire length near the plants' roots for efficient, flexible irrigation that can be easily automated.

Water wand

This extension fits onto a garden hose to help direct and control the flow of water, reach farther, and precisely water small or difficult-to-access areas. Most have multiple settings, such as a fine mist spray or stronger, focused jets.

A water wand attaches to a garden hose to reach far spots in the garden. It also allows you to control the water flow, reducing the pressure without decreasing the volume.

Watering can

Old-fashioned watering cans are useful for spot watering, hydrating hanging baskets and containers, and adding diluted fertilizer to plants that require feeding. You'll need one if you grow plants indoors.

Spray bottle

Use for misting plants or spot-spraying insecticide.

OTHER HANDY ITEMS

There are also other items, such as totes and bins that make working in the garden a bit easier.

Seed or lime spreader

This simple push tool, designed to broadcast seed over turf lawns, works to spread dry amendments over garden soil.

Seed tape

A strip of biodegradable tape embedded with seeds at intervals makes handling and planting minuscule seeds much easier.

Plant markers

These identify seedlings or herbs. Markers and labels are easy DIY projects. For small seedling pots and trays, try Popsicle sticks. For larger pots or for outdoor plants, recycle corks, shells, bamboo skewers, plastic containers, cans, and broken terracotta pots.

Classic watering cans allow you to do spot watering of individual plants.

Seed tape lets you plant minuscule seeds in neat, evenly spaced rows.

Plant stakes and twine

Stakes act as vertical supports, with plants fastened to them with twine to help plants climb and grow upward. Staking is helpful for fruits and vegetables that can become too heavy to support themselves.

Tomato cages

Usually conical or square in shape, these structures protect tomato plants as they grow by spreading and supporting individual branches. They also make harvesting easier.

Roma tomatoes grow in a tomato cage.

Garden kneeler

These protect your vulnerable knees as you work in the garden. They can be as simple as a cushion to lay on the ground to more intricate folding models that feature a padded cushion set into a frame that flips to form a bench. Some come with tool organizers that drape over the sides of the frame to keep them in reach.

Avoid sore knees with a foam pad.

A canvas tote keeps tools in reach.

Garden tote

A sturdy, washable cloth or canvas bag with side pockets will hold and organize hand tools and other gardening aids.

Storage bench

This covered bin features seating above that flips upward to store garden supplies below.

Trug

This kind of flat, handled basket has been used for centuries to gather produce from the garden.

A garden trug holds harvested veggies.

Bucket

Whether traditional galvanized steel or plastic, a 5-gallon (20-L) bucket has numerous purposes, from hauling water, soil, fertilizer, or compost to serving as a container for growing vegetables.

Round plastic bin

This large, handled tote can hold tools, soil, gardening refuse, or kitchen scraps for composting.

Step ladder

Useful for getting to those high-up, hard-to-reach places. Choose aluminum over wood for durability. Consider purchasing a convertible model that turns into an extension ladder and a scaffold.

Chicken wire

This is one of the best materials for garden fencing and pest control. Its mesh structure can also serve as support trellises and planter walls and can be shaped to form cloches.

Chicken wire has scores of garden uses.

Editor's Picks

For gardeners who have trouble bending, a wheeled "scoot," often called a creeper, is a rolling seat that allows them to sit as they garden.

STORE YOUR EQUIPMENT

Gardening equipment requires housing to keep it safely stowed and out of the elements, so that it will all be easily found and in the proper shape to use when needed.

The storage solution most gardeners turn to is the shed—a smallish, sturdy, enclosed structure with a full-size door and sometimes a window or two. Sheds come in various sizes and materials, from small aluminum tool sheds to roomy wooden tractor sheds large enough to house all your hand and power tools. Some even provide a loft for storing holiday decor or other seasonal items. A shed is also a great place to maintain your tools, because you can perform any sharpening and cleaning right there in your garden before or after use.

MATERIALS

There is a wide range of materials that can be used to construct a shed.

Wood

Traditional wooden structures are the most common types of garden sheds, and they are often chosen for their rustic charm. These versatile sheds are typically constructed from treated timber for durability and can be customized to suit your specific needs. Although they are strong and durable, they do require some maintenance, such as painting or staining to prevent weathering.

Every bit of space is important. A small wooden shed is open to reveal its wall storage and interior shelving.

Metal

Metal sheds are durable and resistant to pests like termites. They are often made from galvanized steel and require less maintenance than wooden sheds. To many gardeners, however, they might not offer the same aesthetic appeal as a wooden shed and can be prone to rust if not properly treated.

Plastic, vinyl, and resin

Plastic, vinyl, or resin sheds are becoming increasingly popular due to their durability, low maintenance, and resistance to weather and pest invasion. They are typically easy to assemble and come in a wide range of sizes and styles.

Greenhouse sheds

These sheds combine the functionality and storage of a traditional shed with the benefits of a greenhouse, making them ideal for gardeners looking to start seeds early or grow sensitive plants.

A garden shed can be as utilitarian or as decorative as you desire. This rustic double-door shed features an insect hotel nailed to the exterior to lure pollinators to the garden.

SHED BENEFITS

Sheds have multiple benefits: they keep your tools organized and protected, and a locked shed can keep potentially hazardous garden supplies safely stored. They can also provide a small indoor space to perform garden chores.

Organize your tools

A shed offers you the perfect place to organize your collection of gardening tools. Any combination of shelves, drawers, bins, and wall hooks can help you lay out your tools and keep them in order, which will also help extend their lifespans and keep you from wasting time searching for the right tool.

Safety

A sturdy shed can help keep expensive equipment from being stolen, lost, or damaged by the weather. They are also a great way to keep potentially harmful chemicals like pesticides away from children and pets, as well as sharp or heavy tools that could pose a safety hazard if left lying around.

A potting shed includes a bench for messy work with soil and shelves for pots.

Process produce

Your shed can function as a processing station when it's time to harvest your produce in the autumn. A spacious-enough shed allows you to clean and sort your fruits and vegetables, set up a canning station or a drying rack for herbs, and even store produce, such as onions, for later use in the kitchen.

SHED MAINTENANCE

Keep your shed well-maintained. A wooden shed can be susceptible to rot if not properly treated and cleaned, as is the case with metal sheds and rust. Any dark, enclosed space can also quickly become a breeding ground for pests like insects and rodents if left uncleaned for too long, and dampness caused by lack of maintenance can lead to mold and mildew. Regularly clean the interior of your shed, check that the seals around any windows or skylights are secure, and clear away debris like leaves and branches from the roof and surrounding area to avoid trapping excess moisture.

POTTING SHEDS

A potting shed, as opposed to a storage shed, is an outdoor structure in which you can perform the messy jobs that often come with vegetable gardening, such as starting seedlings and re-potting plants. To qualify as a potting shed, it just needs a table to work at and storage for potting soil and an assortment of containers.

Dig Deeper

LEARN MORE AT GARDENING KNOW HOW

Sometimes, gardening tools end up being dropped where they were last used, not to be seen again for a long time. Organizing garden tools will give you a place to store them, making it easier to locate them while preventing rust or damage from harsh elements. To find out more about keeping your tools where you can find them, scan the QR code or follow this link.

"Garden Tool Organization – Ways To Organize Garden Tools"
LINK: *gkh.us/148412*

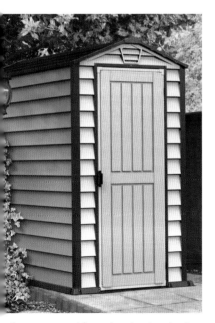

Easy to assemble and maintain, plastic, resin, or vinyl sheds can be economical and attractive alternatives to wood.

OUTFIT YOURSELF

Gardening is hard and often dirty work that requires hours spent in bright sunlight. Be sure to dress in comfortable clothes that can stand up to the challenge.

Gardening is good for the body, mind, and spirit, but nothing ruins a Zen moment in the garden like a painful scratch from a thorn or an itchy bug bite. Even though gardening is a fairly safe hobby, there are risks too. Consider the following hazards gardeners face on a regular basis.

- Sunburn and heatstroke
- Bug bites and stings
- Rashes
- Scratches and scrapes from twigs and thorns
- Accidents with pruning shears
- Pesticide and herbicide exposure
- Carpal tunnel syndrome

Protective garden clothing and healthful aids can help you avoid the worst of sunburn, bug bites, and scratches, keeping you safer outside. There are also some disease risks that come with working in the soil, including tetanus and Legionnaires' disease. Gardeners should always make sure they are up to date on their tetanus shots. To prevent rare but possible microbial diseases, wash your hands thoroughly after each gardening session.

HARMFUL SUNLIGHT
Considering what we now know about the cumulative dangers of

Pocketed overalls are practical garments for working in the garden.

sunlight, it is vital to keep covered up while gardening outdoors. But if long sleeves and long pants seem oppressive on really hot days, make sure to apply a good sunscreen to any exposed skin. Throughout the gardening year, choose fabrics that are known to block ultraviolet radiation. Unbleached cotton contains lignins, which absorb UV rays. Most fabrics with a tight weave—denim, linen, canvas, polyester, nylon, synthetic blends, and wool—also offer protection. Be aware, however, that any fabric that stretches can reduce UV blocking by up to 50 percent.

A gardener protects her clothes with a canvas apron while harvesting pepper plants.

CLOTHES AND ACCESSORIES
Gardening clothes should be comfortable and sturdy.

Overalls and coveralls
These hard-wearing farm standards, which can be slipped on over other clothes or worn alone, provide extra coverage and convenience. Made of durable fabric, most are designed with lots of pockets, so you can keep your seeds, secateurs and other essential items on hand.

Carpenter's half apron
This handy garment protects your clothing while you garden. Look for styles with lots of pockets to keep your gardening items and health aids at your fingertips. The more pockets, the better! They can be full or half style, and you can also use a carpenter's half apron to store tools.

Sturdy footwear
Protect your feet and ankles from sprains and sharp objects with a pair of sturdy shoes or work boots.

Rubber garden boots
"Wellies" are great for working in wet soil or if it's damp outside. It is also easy to hose off any dirt, mud, or other debris. Especially when worn with a thick pair of socks, they will also provide an extra layer of insulation when temperatures drop.

Rubber garden boots are easy to clean and protect your feet in sticky or damp soil.

A wide-brimmed hat keeps the sun off your face and neck, while gloves protect your hands. You can use a scarf as a ready towel to wipe away perspiration.

Gardening gloves
These should be thick enough to protect you from thorns and thistles but thin enough to allow you to work comfortably. Gloves also protect your hands from the sun and any chemicals you use.

Protective goggles
Be sure to cover your eyes while using any power tools in the yard.

Large bandanna or hand towel
Just a swipe keeps sweat off your face, head, and arms. A bandanna can also hold back long hair while you work.

Wide-brimmed hat
Worn as a sun shield, it should cover your scalp and shade your face.

Neck-cooling scarf
Use a damp scarf with expanding gel pellets inside to avoid heat exhaustion on a humid day. You can also wet down a regular scarf.

Thermal water bottle
Be sure to keep hydrated as you garden, and remember that sports drinks can replace lost electrolytes.

Insect spray or lotion
Protect yourself from biting flies, gnats, wasps, hornets, mosquitoes, and ticks on the buggiest days.

Sunscreen
Sunscreen is essential for protecting you from harmful UV rays as you toil in the garden. Use a minimum of SPF 30 on your face.

START FROM SEED

Starting your vegetable crops from seed is an awarding endeavor, one that can extend the length of your growing season, as well as save you money.

Starting plants from seeds can be a gratifying process. Not only is it cost-effective compared to buying mature plants, but it also gives you a broader variety of options, as well as an intimate understanding of the entire growth process. Whether you start seeds indoors to get a jump-start on the season or sow directly outdoors, here are tips to increase your chances of success.

STARTING SEEDS INDOORS

Starting your plants' life cycle indoors allows you to control their early environment and extend your growing season. This is particularly beneficial for plants with long growing seasons, like tomatoes, peppers, celery, and cauliflower.

1. **Choosing the right seeds.** Select seeds suitable for indoor starting and for your growing zone. Check the seed packet for instructions on the best time to start indoors relative to the last expected frost date in your area.

2. **Containers and soil.** You can start seeds in various containers such as seed trays, peat pots, biodegradable seed bags, or even repurposed egg cartons or other recyclable containers. Just ensure that the containers have good drainage and are deep enough for root development. Fill the containers with a sterile seed-starting mix that is light and well-draining.

3. **Planting.** Place a couple of seeds in each container, following the recommended planting depth on the seed packet. Lightly cover the seeds with soil, and gently water to avoid disturbing the seeds.

4. **Light and heat.** Most seeds need warmth to germinate, so place your containers in a warm location or use a seedling heat mat. After germination, seedlings require plenty of light. Position them near a sunny, south-facing window or under grow lights.

5. **Watering and feeding.** Keep the soil consistently moist but not waterlogged. Once the seedlings have developed their second

Fill the seed-starting tray with a sterile seed-starting mix.

Plant the seeds in the soil.

set of true leaves, you can start feeding them with a half-strength, water-soluble fertilizer every two weeks, if necessary.

6. **Transplanting.** Once the risk of frost has passed and the seedlings are strong enough, they can be transplanted outdoors. Acclimate them to the outdoor conditions by gradually increasing their exposure to wind and sun, a process known as "hardening off."

STARTING SEEDS OUTDOORS

Direct sowing is an excellent method for many vegetables and herbs, especially those that don't transplant well, such as carrots.

1. **Choosing the right seeds.** Check your chosen plant's compatibility with your area's climate and soil conditions. The seed packet will typically provide information on the best time for outdoor sowing.

2. **Preparing the garden bed.** Start with a weed-free, well-draining garden bed. Enrich your soil with compost or a balanced garden fertilizer, then rake it smooth.

3. **Planting.** Sow according to the packet instructions regarding depth and spacing. If you're sowing in rows, mark each row with a labeled stake.

4. **Watering and mulching.** Water the area gently but thoroughly after planting. Keep the soil consistently moist until germination. Once seedlings are up and growing well, a layer of mulch can help conserve soil moisture and suppress weeds.

5. **Thinning.** Once the seedlings have grown and developed a couple of sets of true leaves, thin them if they're becoming too crowded to allow remaining plants enough space, light, and nutrients to grow robustly.

MORE INFO
Common Problems

When starting your edible plants from seeds, you may run into the following issues that impede healthy growth. The solutions are often quite simple.

- **Poor germination.** This could be due to old or improperly stored seeds, incorrect planting depth, or unfavorable temperature and moisture conditions.
- **Leggy seedlings.** This is usually caused by insufficient light. Move seedlings to a brighter location, or invest in supplemental grow lights.
- **Damping off.** This fungal disease causes seedlings to wilt and die. Use clean containers and sterile soil, providing good airflow, and avoiding overwatering.

Dig Deeper

LEARN MORE AT GARDENING KNOW HOW

Discover fun and easy ways to start your favorite flowers, vegetables, and fruits from seed with the Seed Starting with Geoffrey Johnson workshop. This workshop is designed to help beginner's succeed and master gardeners to learn some new tricks about seed starting. Scan the QR code to sign up.

 "Seed Starting with Geoffrey Johnson"

Gently water the planted seeds.

SPOTLIGHT ON:

CHOOSING SEED-STARTING POTS

There are many choices for seed-starting trays, from the classic plastic to biodegradable peat. But why buy seed-starting pots and trays, when there are so many common household materials that you can easily transform into suitable containers to start your vegetables indoors? As well as a fun project for you to share with your children, it also benefits the environment, with many materials biodegradable. Here are a few options.

The standard for starting seeds indoors has for so long been commercially available plastic trays and pots. They do the job well, but there are many other eco-friendly options to try.

PEAT POTS AND TRAYS
Once seedlings appear, you can place the entire peat pot and plant in the soil, which reduces stress on the plant and avoids root shock.

PEAT PELLETS
These highly compressed discs expand to all-in-one net containers and medium. Transplant into larger containers or right into the ground.

TO-GO COFFEE CUPS
Paper cups can serve as starting containers. If the cups are coated, however, seedlings will need to be removed before planting.

COFFEE K CUPS
These tiny cups aren't recyclable, so why not give them a new purpose as seed-starting pots for tiny seeds? Be sure to poke holes in the bottoms.

PLASTIC BOTTLES
Cut down a plastic water bottle to make a seedling pot. Save the top to pop over the soil to form a mini greenhouse.

YOGURT CONTAINERS
Reuse any yogurt containers to start your seeds. Just poke a few small holes in the bottom of the pots for drainage.

EGG CARTONS
With cells the perfect size to start seeds, cardboard egg cartons can be cut apart and planted right into the soil, where they will degrade.

EGGSHELLS
Clean the shells before using. When its time for seedlings to go into the ground, lightly crush the shells to allow the roots to spread.

TOILET PAPER OR CUT-UP PAPER TOWEL ROLLS
Great for plants with sensitive roots, you can plant the entire roll in the soil. The cardboard breaks down, allowing the roots to spread.

NEWSPAPER
Easy to make and biodegradable, newspaper seed-starting pots can go into the ground with the seedlings, which can prevent root shock.

DIG A VEGETABLE PLOT

One benefit of creating a planting bed from scratch is that you can design it in any style you like—big or small, raised or flat—whatever strikes your fancy.

Before you work out a garden plan, take some time to look through gardening books for layouts you love, as well as the vegetable choices that appeal to you. That way you can look up the plants, and make sure they are right for your regional climate. The staff at a local garden center is an excellent source of information on which plants will thrive in your area and whether they need a lot of sun or not. Once you have a relationship with a garden center or nursery, it will become your go-to destination whenever you need advice or recommendations for plants.

ASSESS YOUR OPTIONS

Carving a vegetable garden out of a section of lawn or a patch of weeds may seem like an intimidating task. Where do you even begin? Before starting on any sort of plot or bed, you need to assess the landscape. Take a stroll around your property and note the available light and nearby structures, so that you can choose a suitable location.

It is also essential to determine the whereabouts of underground utility lines and the nearest water source—you don't want the garden dozens of feet or meters from the end of the hose. Location can make all the difference between bumper crops of vegetables versus a few weedy specimens even the woodchucks don't want to eat.

Choose your plants based on your garden's location—or chose the location based on the plants you intend to grow. Keep in mind that, although some plants simply require either full sun, partial sun, or full shade, many vegetables have more specific requirements. Some, like tomatoes and peppers, require sun by day and warm nights, while others, such as some lettuce varieties, enjoy shadier conditions and cooler weather.

SKETCH IT OUT

Before you start digging up your bed, it's a good idea to make several sketches of how the finished garden will look. This is important, because it allows you to play around with ideas, like the size and shape of the bed or whether you should add a path or seating area nearby. It will also make it easier when choosing plants, as these should always be compatible with your hardscape—buildings, walls, fences, etc. With vegetables, it is helpful to note that some species do well together, and others seem to clash. (For more information on companion planting, see pages 52 to 57.) Also be sure to place the taller plants to the north of the space, so they don't overshadow the smaller plants and block the sun. Sketching out a plan for your garden in advance will also help you prepare for crop rotation later down the line, and it will allow you to allocate space as needed for plants that will eventually take up a lot of room as they grow.

This vegetable garden uses an island layout of in-ground plots.

Two configurations are popular with many gardeners: border gardens and island gardens.

Border gardens

These are situated against a backdrop, such as a house, shed, fence, hedge, or walkway. This type of bed is worked primarily from one side. Typically, bed designs for borders feature tall plants at the back and mid-sized plants in the central area. Shorter plants, generally those measuring less than 10 inches (25 cm) in height, line the front of a plot.

Island gardens

These are positioned in the yard with no backdrop. They can be square, round, rectangular, or any other shape. Unlike borders, island gardens can be worked from all sides—and that also means they receive sunlight from multiple directions. The layout is similar to a border, except taller plants are located in the center of the island with plants that are smaller placed toward the outer edges of the bed.

LAY OUT THE GARDEN'S SHAPE

Once you have an idea of the garden shape you want, use a flexible hose, landscaping spray paint, or cooking flour to mark it out on the lawn. Then with a flat-ended shovel, dig out the grass all around the perimeter of your garden bed to establish a boundary. You are now ready to begin preparing the beds for planting.

There are two basic types of garden beds: those that are on or near the same level as the lawn and raised beds, which elevate the soil above ground level and are contained by some kind of wall. (For more information on aboveground beds, see pages 58 to 59.)

LEVEL BEDS

Once you know the location and shape of your garden bed, you're ready to excavate it. Depending on its location and size, starting a bed often begins with the removal of grass. There are several ways to accomplish this: dig it out, apply herbicide (make this one a last resort), or smother it with newspaper or cardboard. (For more information on no-dig plots, see the box on page 23.)

DIGGING OUT THE BED

If you choose to dig out the grass in your new bed, it will be easier to use a flat-ended shovel or spade. It is a four-step process.

Use a spade or flat-ended shovel to dig out grass in squared clumps that you can later use to fill in thin lawn areas.

1. After you have established a border by digging down about 4 to 5 inches (10 to 12.5 cm) around the bed's perimeter, you need to remove the grass. Cut the sod into small squares, and pry it from the planting area with the end of the shovel. (Excess sod can be incorporated into thin areas of your lawn and watered.)

2. Clear out any rocks or debris with a hoe or metal rake.

3. Loosen the soil with a pitchfork or spade. If it's a new garden, loosen to a depth of at least 8 to 12 inches (20 to 30 cm) so that roots can grow down. If it is a spring refresh, you probably won't have to dig so deep.

4. Add organic matter on a day when the soil is moist but not wet. Spread a minimum of 2 to 3 inches (5 to 7.5 cm) of compost or aged manure onto your soil. Some gardeners will dig the organic matter into the soil, while others have a no dig philosophy that exposes fewer weed seeds and does not disturb the soil structure. They leave the compost on the surface and let the worms do the digging in. The usual recommended ratio is 1 to 3 inches (2.5 to 7.5 cm) of organic amendments mixed into 6 to 8 inches (15 to 20 cm) of ground soil.

Working the ground with a pitchfork will loosen the soil so that roots can take hold.

IRRIGATE YOUR GARDEN

Plants, just like all living things, need water to survive and thrive. Knowing when and how much to water your edible garden is essential to maintaining healthy crops.

When it comes to watering their vegetable gardens, many people struggle over questions such as, "How often should I water my plants?" or "How much water should I give my garden at a time?" It's really not that complicated, but there are some factors that should be considered. These include the type of soil you are dealing with, the size of your garden or beds, the kinds of crops you are growing, and what your climate or weather is like. Naturally, seasonal rainfall makes a difference in a garden's water needs. A wet autumn followed by a snowy winter will start your spring garden off with good levels of ground moisture.

WHEN TO WATER

The general rule of thumb is about 1 or 2 inches (2.5 or 5 cm) of water each week using deep, infrequent watering as opposed to the more frequent shallow watering; however, when and how much to water really depends on a number of factors.

Consider soil type

This a primary consideration. Sandy soil is going to hold less water than heavier, more-absorbent clay soil. Therefore, it's going to dry out faster, while clay-like soil will hold moisture longer (and is more susceptible to overwatering). This is why amending the soil with compost is so important. Healthier soil drains better but allows for some water retention. Applying surface mulch is also a good idea, helping to keep moisture in the soil and reducing water needs.

Consider weather conditions

These determine when to water garden plants. If you're having a hot spell, for example, you'll have to water more often. Of course, in rainy conditions, little watering is needed. Most container plants need watering on a daily basis in hot, dry conditions—sometimes twice or even three times a day. Hanging plants also need more attention in prolonged periods of heat.

An automatic hose timer can set the duration of watering times. The splitter allows you to create separate water flows from the same source.

MORE INFO *Five watering mistakes*

There is a right way and a wrong way to water. The following are some errors vegetable gardeners should be aware of.

1. Avoid watering in bright sunlight; much of the water will evaporate.

2. Don't allow a strong overhead spray of water to pummel your tender plants; this practice also wastes water, which ends up on foliage instead of in the soil. Splashed-up soil can add the risk of disease to leaves.

3. Don't underwater or overwater the garden. Some dried organic bedding products, like peat, take time to rehydrate, so after the initial watering,

wait a bit, then check how far the water has gone down into the soil. If only 1 inch (2.5 cm) or so, then water again. Overwatering is often a problem with containers that have no drainage holes. The end result is root rot. In garden plots, signs of overwatering are yellowing and wilting foliage.

4. Never water all your plants the same way. In every garden there are plants with different water needs and at

different stages of development. Delicate seedlings need to be watered differently (soaker hose or hand watering) than hardy full-grown plants (irrigation or hose watering). Thirsty fruiting plants, like tomatoes, require more water than leafy greens.

5. Failure to mulch, a practice that helps retain soil moisture, can have serious repercussions, especially with crops like potatoes, where the yield goes way down if the soil dries out.

Consider plant varieties

These, too, dictate when and how often to water. Different plants have different watering needs. Larger plants need more water, as do newly planted ones. Many vegetables tend to have shallower root systems and also require more frequent watering, some daily—especially in temps over 85°F (30°C).

Consider the time of day

This also dictates when a garden should be watered. The most suitable time for watering is early morning, which reduces evaporation, but late afternoon or early evening are okay, too—provided you keep the foliage from getting wet, which can lead to fungal issues.

HOW MUCH WATER SHOULD I GIVE MY PLANTS?

Deep watering encourages deeper and stronger root growth; therefore, watering gardens to soak the soil about 2 inches (5 cm) or so deep, once a week, is preferable. Watering

Editor's Tip

If you are conservation-minded, you might consider setting up a water collection barrel under your gutter downspout or employing a child's wading pool to collect rainwater. Use floating mosquito dunks to prevent these insect pests from breeding in any standing water, and make sure there are a few bricks or rocks in the pool in case any small animals tumble in while drinking.

more often, but less deeply, tends to lead to weaker root growth and faster evaporation.

TYPES OF WATERING SYSTEMS

There are several methods of irrigating a vegetable garden, and some are better than others.

Overhead sprinklers are often frowned upon, except on lawns, because these lose more water to evaporation. Soaker hoses or drip irrigation systems set between the plant rows are always a better option, with water going straight to the roots, while keeping foliage dry. Both these systems can be fitted with automatic timers that make sure your plants are getting watered on a regular basis, even while you are away from home.

Of course, there are the old standbys—hand watering with a hose, wand, or watering can. Because the latter process is more time consuming, it's best reserved for smaller garden areas, container plants, and seedling trays.

HELPFUL TOOLS

There are a number of tools and gadgets that will quickly prove their worth at watering time.

- An automatic timer will turn on your soaker hose a set number of times a week. The timer will automatically shut off at the end of the time you've specified.
- A variable-pattern spray nozzle using quick-connect technology allows you to easily connect and disconnect hose attachments
- A hose-splitting device will allow you to place a soaker hose and timer on one connector and a regular watering hose with nozzle on the other.
- Hose-end sprayer receptacles allow you to spread fertilizer or other amendments around the garden while you water.

A raised-bed garden of brassicas and Swiss chard has been fitted with a drip irrigation system with hoses that run along the plants' bases. This system is both good for the environment and for your budget, possibly reducing water use by 30 to 50 percent.

CONTROL WEEDS

Weeds, plants growing out of place, can be more than a nuisance when you are cultivating a garden, competing with desired plants for sunlight, water, and nutrients.

Weeds are a fact of life for most gardeners. They may pop up in the heart of your garden, taking advantage of the healthy soil you've created for your chosen plants.

A light-hearted definition of a weed is "any plant growing where you don't want it." Yet true weeds, based on human value judgment, are the most costly category of agricultural pests. Worldwide, they cause more yield loss and add more to farmers' production costs than insects, crop pathogens, nematodes, or warm-blooded pests. In the United States, they are formally categorized as weed (such as crabgrass), noxious weed (field bindweed), and invasive weed (kudzu or English ivy). Elsewhere, they might be classified by their overall morphological features as grasses, sedges, and broadleaf weeds or grouped by their life cycle as annual, biennial, and perennial.

Whatever the categories, these weeds need to be recognized and controlled. Yet, weeds aren't inherently bad: many weeds stabilize the soil, add organic matter, and recycle nutrients. Some are edible to humans and provide habitat and food for wildlife. There might also be cases where you keep a "visiting" species. You may be thrilled to see charming, albeit aggressive plants, such as columbine. Several weeds are also edible, such as amaranth, chickweed, dandelion, and fennel.

If you see a seedling you don't recognize, use an app or search online for a match. You can opt to wait and see if the adult plant is one you want to preserve. Unfortunately, by that time, an objectionable plant might already be entrenched. If something is recognizable as a weed, remove it while it is young to prevent further spreading. Plants with deep taproots will also be easier to unearth when immature.

In general, you can minimize weeds with a thick layer of mulch around your plants, and any weeds that make it through are much easier to remove. Keep your garden clogs and weeding tools clean to prevent spreading any seeds. Be cautious with pre-emergence sprays, as these may prevent your veggie seeds from emerging. For an eco-friendly weed treatment, spread black plastic over an area in the autumn or early spring. Leave it for six to eight weeks to prevent weed seed germination.

WEED CONTROL METHODS

There are a number of methods for controlling weeds, depending on the weed and the gardener. Here are your options.

Cultural weed control

One of the easiest ways to control weeds is through cultural control, or, simply, prevention. Close planting in the garden can reduce weed growth by eliminating open space for them to take over. Cover crops are good for this as well. Adding mulch will prevent light from getting to weed seeds and prevents growth.

Mechanical weed control

Hand-pulling, hoeing, digging, or mowing (which slows growth and reduces seed formation), are safe ways to control weeds. These methods are effective, but can be time consuming.

Chemical weed control

No gardener wants to spray a toxic weed killer in an edible garden. Fortunately, there are now ways to prevent and control weeds without the use of toxic chemicals, which can be harmful to people, pets, beneficial insects, and other wildlife. Natural citrus-based weed killers can be highly effective when sprayed on young, tender weeds. To prevent weeds, corn gluten works by killing weed seeds before they sprout, but it can kill vegetable seeds as well. Still, many weeds can become aggressive to the point of taking over, so chemical control is sometimes necessary and used as a last resort. There are numerous herbicides available to help eliminate common weed plants.

Weeding by hand or with a hoe or fork is hard work, but it is the safest weed-control method for edible gardens.

COMMON GARDEN INVADERS

The particular species of weeds that might invade a vegetable garden varies by geographical region, but here is a small sampling of some of the most common weeds that crop up in home gardens, with tips on how to combat them.

Bindweed

This pretty but pernicious climber (*Convolvulus* spp.), often called wild morning glory, wraps thin threadlike vines around other plants. It has a large and hardy root system, so killing it may take several attempts. Start by pouring boiling water about 2 to 3 feet (60 to 90 cm) beyond the bindweed patch to reach as many of the roots as possible. You can also heavily apply an herbicide, and re-apply when the plant reaches 12 inches (30 cm). Adding plants that spread densely will force bindweed out of the bed.

Common chickweed

Common chickweed (*Stellaria media*) is an annual weed that grows in moist areas; without competition from other plants, it can produce roughly 800 seeds and can take up to eight years to eradicate. Fight back by pulling young plants before they flower and keeping soil at a low pH (acidic) level.

Hairy bittercress

Edible as a salad green, hairy bittercress (*Cardamine hirsuta*) has an exploding seedpod. Each plant can produce thousands of seeds, but they can be easily hand-pulled before seedpods form.

Nutsedge

Nutsedge (*Cyperus* spp.) is a grasslike weed that spreads via tubers on rhizomes in wet or poorly drained areas, competing with crops and suppressing growth via soil toxins. If you have a small patch, you can dig down at least 10 inches (25 cm) deep and 8 to 10 inches (20 to 25 cm) beyond the infested area to reduce its numbers.

Plantain

Its young leaves are edible, but plantain (*Plantago major* and *P. lanceolata*) can easily get out of control, producing up to 14,000 seeds per year. Control by hand-digging and mulching.

Shepherd's purse

Another edible wild plant, shepherd's purse (*Capsella bursa-pastoris*) gets its name from its triangular, purse-shaped seedpods. It spreads by seed (more than 30,000 per plant), but can be easily hand-pulled when young.

MORE INFO
Beneficial Weeds

Invasive weeds are well worth the hard work of removal. Some weeds, however, can be quite attractive in the garden, so why not consider allowing them to stay? This more-natural weed control method results in a lush native environment when weeds are given their own designated spot. Some of these "good weeds" include chicory (*Cichorium intybus*), Queen Anne's lace (*Daucus carota*), and Joe-pye weed (*Eupatorium* spp.). Dandelions (*Taraxacum officinale*), one of the first blooms of early spring, provide food for pollinators, and their flowers and greens are also edible for humans. Of course, which weed goes and which weed stays depends on the preferences of an individual gardener, although a little bit of information on weed types and control methods makes this decision easier. And always check for any regulations in your area about cultivating potentially invasive weeds.

CHOOSE YOUR MULCH

A valuable addition to a vegetable garden, an appropriate mulch can aid in weed control, conserve soil moisture, modify soil temperatures, and help to decrease disease.

To mulch or not is a personal choice. Some traditionalist gardeners do not mulch their plants or crops. They rely on the soil to insulate plants from heat and cold and to retain enough moisture to supply water to thirsty roots. Yet, increasing numbers of gardeners are realizing the many benefits of adding mulch to a garden plot.

One of mulch's most valuable properties is the ability to retain moisture in the soil. Its other advantages include the following.

- Organic mulches break down over time and contribute nutrients that increase soil health. This can be very helpful in areas with poor soil.
- Mulch piled around plant crowns can reduce winter injury and also help with weed control.
- Mulch is able to protect soil from wind or rain erosion.

- Mulch creates a visual barrier that protects plants from weed eaters and lawnmowers.

TYPES OF MULCH

Mulch for vegetable gardens differs from those used for flower beds and other ornamental purposes. The wood chips, pine bark nuggets, and other woody materials used with shrubs and perennials can actually harm a vegetable plot. These common types of mulch decompose slowly, rob nitrogen from the soil, and tend to be bulky, which can interfere with next spring's garden preparation.

The wide variety of mulches available at garden centers that are appropriate in an edible garden can be broken down into two main groups—organic and inorganic. Of course, the best mulch for your garden depends on your personal preferences and budget, but if you are interested in improving soil fertility, choose an organic mulch.

Organic

Organic, or natural, mulch tends to cost less than synthetic mulch, but it has to be replaced more frequently due to deterioration. The best types include the following.

- Hay is one of the best natural mulches for an edible garden plot. Look for weed-free salt hay to avoid introducing weed seeds into the garden. A typical hay bale can cover a 10-x-10-foot (3 x 3 m) garden to a depth of about 3 inches (7.5 cm).
- Grass clippings have the strong advantage of being readily available from your own lawn, although they can get moldy and might introduce weed seeds. Be sure the clippings

A gardener spreads straw mulch around planted seedlings to control weeds, improve the soil, and protect plants from drought.

A young tomato plant pokes through red plastic sheeting, a synthetic mulch.

are dry before adding them to a garden plot, and only use clippings from grass that has not been treated with herbicides.

- Leaves are a natural option, but they can easily mat down. Always use shredded leaves and not whole ones.
- Paper mulches, such as newspaper or rolls specifically made for garden use, act similarly to synthetic mulch. The advantages of paper mulch are that just a thin layer will effectively control weeds, and it is biodegradable. Any remaining paper can be turned into the soil at year's end. Disadvantages are the unsightly look of newspaper, and garden-specific rolls can be costly.
- Cocoa bean hulls are good for fruiting crops like tomatoes and peppers. Yet, keep in mind that this mulch can be toxic to dogs.

Inorganic

Inorganic, or synthetic, mulches tend to warm the soil, allowing for earlier crop yields.

- Plastic mulch comes in rolls or sheets and can be either clear or colored. It usually comes in strips 3 or 4 feet (1 or 1.2 m) in width. It should be laid over moist soil about one to three weeks before you plant seeds or transplants and secured by burying the edges in the soil. You can cut holes in the plastic to insert transplants into the ground, and some large-seed veggies, such as squash, cucumbers, and melons, can be seeded directly through the punched holes. The ideal way to water with plastic mulch is to place trickle tubes or soaker hosing under the plastic before laying it to directly water roots.
- Perforated or porous plastic is used like regular plastic mulch, but it tends to be highly expensive. It is cheaper to poke your own holes in plastic mulch.
- Landscape fabric is permeable to air and water, but it can allow some weeds to grow through it, and, like perforated plastic, it costs far more than black plastic.

Black garden fabric provides weed control around sweet pepper plants.

MORE INFO *Colors of plastic mulch*

Rolls of plastic mulch are increasingly found in farms and kitchen gardens, where "plasticulture" is used to modify microclimates and improve crops. Plastic mulch warms the soil, minimizes evaporation, limits nutrients leaching from soil, and results in earlier harvests. Perhaps the most interesting aspect is that different color mulches can impact various crops in different ways.

- **Black.** The most common and least expensive of the plastic mulching options, black is said to better suppress weeds, thanks to its opacity. It also raises soil temperature up to 5 degrees at a 2-inch (5 cm) depth.
- **Blue.** This color mulch is better than black if you are planting cantaloupes, summer squash, or cucumbers.

- **Red.** Plastic mulch in red works better for crops like tomatoes, which, in studies, yielded 20 percent more fruit when planted with red plastic mulch, while strawberries were sweeter and had a better fragrance.
- **Silver.** This color mulch increases photosynthesis by reflecting sunlight to the undersides of plants, leading

to rapid growth. It is great at keeping aphids and whiteflies away and also reduces populations of cucumber beetles and squash vine borer.

- **Brown and green.** These two mulches are available in infrared transmitting plastic (IRT). This warms up your soil better than regular plastic mulch at the start of the growing season.

FIND COMPANIONS

Help your plants to help each other grow. Understanding how plants, insects, and organisms work together can reduce or eliminate the need for inorganic remedies, increase your gardening successes, and influence your plant choices.

Companion planting is growing two or more plants close together for the benefit of one or all. Benefits of this method of garden planning include pest control, pollination, providing habitats for beneficial insects, maximizing use of space, and otherwise increasing crop productivity. For almost every vegetable, there is a companion plant that will increase soil nutrients, chase away pests, and help you get the most out of your garden. Here is a sampling of plants and their garden friends and foes.

MORE INFO *The Three Sisters*

A trio of Native American staples—corn, squash, and beans—are known as the Three Sisters. They not only taste great when served together, they also nutritionally complement one another. Try planting all three in the same plot: the corn stalks provide structures for the vining beans to climb, while the wide squash leaves spread over the ground, retaining moisture and deterring weeds. Bean roots host rhizobia, beneficial bacteria that absorb nitrogen from the air and transform it into usable nutrients for neighboring plants.

ASPARAGUS

Basil, parsley, and nightshade family members like tomato and eggplant protect the tender shoots of an asparagus plant against asparagus beetles. Basil and parsley will also attract pollinators. Coriander and dill repel harmful insect pests, such as aphids and spider mites. Marigolds and nasturtiums act as powerful natural insect-repellers.

- **Friends:** Basil, parsley, nightshades (like tomato and eggplant), coriander, dill, marigold, nasturtium
- **Foes:** Garlic, onion, potato

BASIL

Basil repels aphids, asparagus beetle, mosquitoes, and tomato hornworm. It also boosts tomato yields, and the flowers attract pollinators. A basil-asparagus combo appeals to ladybugs, which control aphids. Borage improves its growth and flavor. Flowering herbs like chamomile, chives, and oregano enhance its essential oils.

- **Friends:** Asparagus, beet, borage, carrot, chamomile, chives, marigold, oregano, pepper, radish, tomato
- **Foes:** Cucumber, fennel, rue, sage

BEANS (BUSH)

Beans provide nitrogen to the soil. Catnip can repel flea beetles. Potato plants and strongly scented marigolds deter Mexican bean beetles, and nasturtium and rosemary repel bean beetles.

- **Friends:** Beet, broccoli, Brussels sprouts, cabbage, carrot, catnip, cauliflower, celery, corn, cucumber, eggplant, kale, marigold, nasturtium, peas, potato, radish, rosemary, squash, strawberry, tomato
- **Foes:** Alliums (such as chives, garlic, onion, and shallots)

BEANS (POLE)

Beans provide nitrogen to the soil. Corn acts as a natural trellis, while providing shade. Squash shades the roots and repels pests.

- **Friends:** Broccoli, cabbage, carrot, catnip, cauliflower, celery, corn, cucumber, eggplant, marigold, nasturtium, peas, potato, radish, rosemary, squash, strawberry, tomato
- **Foes:** Alliums (such as chives, garlic, onion, and shallots), beets

BEETS

Composted beet leaves add magnesium to the soil. Members of the onion family can be natural insect repellents. Garlic improves the growth and flavor of beets, and marigolds will help destroy root-knot nematodes.

- **Friends:** Beans (bush), broccoli, Brussels sprouts, cabbage, cauliflower, garlic, kohlrabi, leeks, lettuce, onion, marigold
- **Foes:** Beans (pole)

BROCCOLI

Dill attracts predatory wasps that control pests. Rosemary repels cabbage flies. Celery, potato, and onion improve the flavor of broccoli.

- **Friends:** Basil, beet, celery, cucumber, dill, garlic, lettuce, marigold, mint, nasturtium, onion, potato, radish, rosemary, spinach, thyme
- **Foes:** Asparagus, beans (pole), corn, melons, pepper, pumpkin, squash, strawberry

BRUSSELS SPROUTS

Brussels sprouts are susceptible to a number of insect pests common to brassicas, including aphids, beetles, cabbage loopers, cutworms, leafminers, and squash bugs. Planting them near pungent companions, such as basil, garlic, onion, and mint, can repel these pests. Strawberry can inhibit the growth of Brussels sprouts.

- **Friends:** Basil, beans, beet, carrot, radish, garlic, mint, nasturtium, onion, peas, thyme
- **Foes:** Beans (pole), strawberry, tomato, other brassicas

CABBAGE

Marigolds and aromatic herbs, such as mint, rosemary, and thyme, repel cabbage moths. Dill, celery, garlic, mint, and onion enhance the taste of cabbage, and some will also deter insect pests. All members of the cabbage family do well when combined with mineral-enhancing beets.

- **Friends:** Beans (bush), beet, celery, chamomile, dill, mint, onion, oregano, rosemary, sage, thyme
- **Foes:** Beans (pole), mustard, strawberry, tomato

CARROTS

Beans fix nitrogen into the soil. Chives improve growth, flavor, and texture of nearby carrots. Onion, parsley, rosemary, and sage deter carrot flies. Dill may stunt the growth of carrots. Combine with leeks, which will deter carrot flies, while the carrots with return the favor by repelling leek moths. Marigold helps deter carrot rust flies.

- **Friends:** Beans, chives, lettuce, onion, pea, pepper, radish, rosemary, sage, tomato, leek, marigold
- **Foes:** Dill, parsnip

CORN

One of the Three Sisters, corn works well with beans and squashes. The tall stalks of the corn plants will provide shade and are natural trellises for climbing pole beans. Corn is a heavy feeder, so plant alongside beans and peas to add nitrogen to the soil. Marigolds repel Japanese beetles.

- **Friends:** Beans, cucumber, marigold, melon, parsley, peas, potato, sunflower, winter squashes (such as pumpkin)
- **Foes:** Celery, tomato

CUCUMBER

Cucumbers grow poorly when planted near potatoes or sage. Dill will attract beneficial insects that feed on pests, such as the cucumber beetle. Nasturtium deters aphids and beetles while improving growth and flavor. Radish repels pests, including cucumber beetles and rust flies.

- **Friends:** Beans, cabbage, cauliflower, corn, dill, lettuce, marigold, nasturtium, peas, radish
- **Foes:** Aromatic herbs (except dill), potato, tomato

DILL

Dill discourages pests, such as aphids, cabbage loopers, and spider mites. It also attracts beneficial insects, such as bees, hoverflies, ladybugs, and parasitic wasps. Be careful planting it too close to other members of the celery family, Apiaceae: dill cross-pollinates with its relatives, such as cilantro and carrot.

- **Friends:** Broccoli, Brussels sprouts, cabbage, corn, cucumber, lettuce, onion
- **Foes:** Cilantro, carrot, tomato

EGGPLANT

Other *Solanums,* or nightshade, relatives, such as pepper, potatoes, or tomatoes, can make eggplant more susceptible to blight disease. Catnip repels flea beetles, a common vegetable pest that can target eggplants. Eggplant is a heavy feeder; beans and peas fix nitrogen into the soil. Marigold deters nematodes.

- **Friends:** Beans, catnip, marigold, peas, pepper
- **Foes:** Other nightshades (such as pepper, potatoes, and tomatoes)

GARLIC

Garlic keeps away a wide range of pests, including ants, aphids, cabbage loopers, fungus gnats, Japanese beetles, onion flies, snails, and spider mites. Chamomile improves garlic flavor. Rue repels maggots. Summer savory and yarrow also benefit garlic. Garlic can stunt the growth of asparagus, beans, parsley, peas, and sage.

- **Friends:** Beet, brassicas, dill, eggplant, kohlrabi, pepper, potato, spinach, tomato
- **Foes:** Beans, parsley, peas, sage

KALE

Kale plants are heavy nitrogen feeders. Plant them near beans or peas, which add nitrogen to the soil. Avoid planting kale near other brassicas to prevent the spread of disease. Members of the *Allium* genus can deter common pests.

- **Friends:** Beet, beans, celery, cucumber, dill, garlic, lettuce, mint, onion, peas, pepper, potato, rosemary, sage, spinach
- **Foes:** Other brassicas (such as broccoli, Brussels sprouts, and cauliflower)

LETTUCE

Basil improves lettuce's flavor while repelling mosquitoes. Beets supply minerals to the soil that lettuce needs to thrive. Chives and garlic deter aphids. Mint repels cabbage moths and slugs. Some sources say to avoid planting lettuce near brassicas. Results may vary. Cabbage, celery, and parsley may inhibit lettuce growth.

- **Friends:** Asparagus, basil, beans, beet, carrot, chives, corn, cucumber, eggplant, garlic
- **Foes:** Cabbage, celery, parsley

MINT

Mint is a natural pest deterrent. It repels flea beetles, which chew holes in the leaves of cabbage, cauliflower, kale, and radish. It also discourages aphids, carrot root flies, mealy bugs, onion flies, and spider mites. It attracts beneficial insects such as hoverflies, ladybugs, and predatory wasps that feed on pests.

- **Friends:** Beet, broccoli, Brussels sprouts, cabbage, cauliflower, eggplant, kale, kohlrabi, lettuce, peas, squash
- **Foes:** Chamomile, parsley

ONION

Onion repels brassica pests including cabbage loopers, cabbage worms, and cabbage maggots. It also deters aphids, carrot flies, and Japanese beetles. Don't plant near other alliums, such as garlic, leek, and shallots to avoid spreading onion maggots or rust.

- **Friends:** Beet, broccoli, Brussels sprouts, cabbage, carrot, chamomile, lettuce, pepper, strawberry, tomato
- **Foes:** Asparagus, beans, peas, sage, other alliums

PEAS

Pea plants are good companions to many other vegetables because they increase the availability of nitrogen in the soil. Members of the *Allium* genus, such as chives, garlic, onion, and shallots, can stunt the growth of peas.

- **Friends:** Beans, carrot, celery, corn, cucumber, eggplant, lettuce, marigold, parsley, potato, radish, spinach, strawberries, tomato, turnip
- **Foes:** Alliums (such as chives, garlic, onion, and shallots)

PEPPERS

Basil deters aphids, spider mites, and thrips, and improves the flavor of peppers. Dill and coriander repel aphids and encourage beneficial insects. Parsley attracts predatory wasps. Alliums repel aphids, beetles, slugs, and spider mites.

- **Friends:** Basil, beans, beet, carrot, chives, coriander, cucumber, dill, eggplant, garlic, lettuce, parsley, onion, spinach, tomato
- **Foes:** Brassicas (such as broccoli, Brussels sprouts, cabbage, cauliflower, kale, and kohlrabi)

POTATOES

Beans repel Colorado potato beetle. Horseradish increases disease resistance. Many herbs enhance potato flavor. Cucumber, raspberry, and tomato attract harmful insects. Avoid planting near other nightshades. Asparagus, carrot, fennel, onion, and turnip can stunt potato growth.

- **Friends:** Beans, cabbage, corn, herbs, horseradish, lettuce, marigold, peas, radish, spinach,
- **Foes:** Other nightshades, asparagus, carrot, tomato, turnip

RADISHES

Use radish as a "trap plant" to lure pests, such as root maggots and flea beetles, away from other vegetables. It also repels cucumber beetles and squash bugs. Chervil deters aphids and slugs. Chervil and nasturtium improve growth and flavor. Hyssop stunts the growth of radish.

- **Friends:** Beans, carrot, chervil, cucumber, lettuce, melon, nasturtium, peas, spinach, squash
- **Foes:** Brassicas (such as broccoli, Brussels sprouts, cabbage, and cauliflower), hyssop

ROSEMARY

The pungent scent of rosemary repels many typical vegetable garden pests, including bean beetles, cabbage loopers, cabbage moths, carrot root flies, slugs, snails, and weevils. The flowers of rosemary will attract necessary insect pollinators. Rosemary improves the flavor of sage when planted nearby.

- **Friends:** Beans, broccoli, Brussels sprouts, cabbage, carrot, cauliflower, kale
- **Foes:** Pumpkin, squash

SUMMER SQUASH

Borage attracts insect pollinators and improves growth and flavor. Nasturtium deters aphids and squash bugs and improves growth and flavor. Radish and tansy repel squash bugs. Potato will compete for nutrients. Pumpkin, which is a type of winter squash, can cross-pollinate, affecting seeds saved for the next year's crop.

- **Friends:** Beans, borage, corn, marigold, nasturtium, peas, radish, tansy
- **Foes:** Potato, pumpkin

STRAWBERRIES

Never place plants susceptible to verticillium wilt, such as nightshade members, nearby. Alliums repel predatory insects. Borage attracts pollinators and repels pests while increasing disease resistance. Caraway attracts beneficial insects. Planting with lettuce and spinach can enhance productivity.

- **Friends:** Beans, borage, caraway, chives, garlic, lettuce, onion, sage, spinach, thyme
- **Foes:** Brassicas, eggplant, melon, pepper, potato, tomato

TOMATOES

Plant near asparagus to repel asparagus beetles; asparagus can also repel nematodes. Basil improves growth and deters pests. Borage improves growth and flavor and repels tomato hornworms. Don't plant tomatoes near dill or brassicas; they can stunt growth. Corn attracts tomato hornworms.

- **Friends:** Asparagus, basil, borage, carrot, celery, chives, cucumber, garlic, lettuce, marigold, mint, onion, parsley
- **Foes:** Brassicas, corn

MORE INFO

Universal Companions

Some flowering plants and herbs team up well with just about any vegetable you might want to grow. Plant them throughout a garden bed—some will add bright color and others lovely scents, while helping to reduce pests, increase crop yields, and improve the flavor of their veggie companions.

Perennials
- mints
- thyme

Annuals
- basil
- borage
- calendula
- marigold
- nasturtium
- zinnia

OPPOSITE PAGE: A row of marigolds (*Tagetes* spp.) planted between rows of tomato and lettuce plants helps encourage healthy specimens.

USE ABOVEGROUND BEDS

Are you looking for a vegetable garden that eliminates a lot of the work required by other gardens? Consider growing your plants in raised boxes.

Because they are elevated above the level of the walkways, these beds require less bending, making them easier on your knees and back. If you live in a colder region, consider that a raised garden bed can help wet, cold soils dry out and warm up more quickly in spring. They allow you to match soil type to the plants you wish to grow: slightly acidic for cauliflower? No problem.

A raised vegetable garden is also an excellent alternative for growing plants on difficult sites, such as hillsides. Here, depths can be easily adjusted to fit the slope of the hill. They are useful if your soil is poor or if there's some other reason you can't readily dig into the soil. They also save on space and allow plants to grow closer together, resulting in more moisture for the crops. Their tight plantings also reduce the presence of weeds, and their accessibility makes invasive insects easy to remove or discourage.

Elevated gardens are also easier to maintain because they are accessible from all sides. With raised beds, you have the option of creating a plot as small as you like, and then adding onto it as time, experience, and your individual needs require. Finally, you can cover your raised beds before planting with black plastic or cardboard to block light against weeds and protect them from snow, rain, and erosion.

DESIGN A RAISED GARDEN

Depending on your specific needs, raised beds can take many forms. Nearly any material that holds soil and retains its shape can be used to edge a raised garden bed. Wood, concrete blocks, bricks, stones, or logs are easily available and inexpensive. A galvanized steel container with drainage holes or a water trough will also work well. Wood is the most common material used, but you should stay away from any lumber that has been pressure treated, because the chemicals that are used to treat the wood can leach into the soil and harm plants.

Raised garden boxes are typically laid out in a rectangular shape approximately 3 feet (1 m) in width. This width measurement allows all areas of the bed, including the center, to be easily accessible. The length of a raised vegetable garden depends on your personal choice, but the depth of the raised garden boxes should be at least 6 to 12 inches (15 to 30 cm) to allow for the proper root development of plants.

Creating paths between the beds makes maintenance easier and looks attractive, too. You can create paths by spreading a weed

Raised beds allow you to control the type of soil you use for each type of vegetable.

MORE INFO
Positioning Raised Garden Beds

The optimal place to locate a raised garden bed will be based on a host of factors, including the following.

- Available sunlight
- Soil porosity
- Soil texture
- Soil nutrient levels
- Soil pH
- Wind exposure
- Moisture availability
- Previous pest issues
- Distance from house
- Proximity to trees

barrier of plastic or other gardening fabric between each bed and covering it with a suitable mulching material, such as gravel or pebbles. The pathways should be wide enough for easy accessibility to the beds with additional room for a wheelbarrow. Generally, a width of 2 to 3 feet (60 cm to 1 m) is sufficient.

Don't forget to locate the plot near a water source—a spigot, pump, well, or cistern. When applying water to raised gardens, it is better to use soaker hoses that can be placed directly on the bed; sprinklers work, but they are more likely to spread diseases if the foliage stays excessively wet. The use of organic mulches, such as straw or hay, can also help these beds to retain moisture.

SOIL FOR RAISED BEDS

When you are ready, fill your new boxes with commercial soil. For older beds, mix the existing soil with compost or manure. As you build up soil levels, keep adding compost to further improve its structure and drainage. When you begin planting crops, place taller varieties to the north to prevent shading of the smaller varieties.

If you are planting in a flat bed using ground soil, you will likely need to increase the quality with amendments (see pages 22 to 23). With raised beds, one of the

A raised bed built to tabletop or waist height makes it easier to work your garden, saving you from backaches. It is also great for wheelchair-using gardeners.

benefits is that you fill the boxes with fresh soil, either compost you have created or amended soil purchased from a garden center.

There are several types of soil sold in garden centers, which might prove confusing to gardening novices. Topsoil is considered soil, while some potting soils and all peat mosses are "soil-less."

Topsoil

This rich soil, taken from the top layers of a field, is sand or clay (ground-up rocks) mixed with organic materials, such as compost. It is meant for in-the-ground planting. Topsoil is heavy and holds a lot of water, keeping plant roots moist. It is dense and packs down easily.

Peat moss

This growing medium is completely soil-less. You can use straight peat moss as your potting mix, but be careful not to overwater. Peat moss all by itself can stay wet for a long time after plants are watered.

Potting soil

This soil is ideal for planting in containers. It provides the proper texture for plants in a small space, whether they are grown indoors or

out. Potting soil is a mixture of peat moss and other organic materials like coco coir or coconut husks, vermiculite, shredded bark, and composted sawdust. It allows water to drain easily and the roots to dry out quickly. It is mostly air, so it is light and fluffy and can be difficult to pack down.

The recommended combination of mediums for raised beds is 60 percent topsoil, 30 percent compost, and 10 percent potting soil, but gardeners often noodle with the percentages until they find the combination that works best for their conditions.

A raised bed is surrounded by woven willow in an edible kitchen garden.

Modern brick raised beds can work perfectly in an urban vegetable garden.

PROTECT WITH COLD FRAMES

A cold frame allows you to lengthen the growing season, harden off seedlings, start seedlings earlier, and overwinter tender dormant plants.

Easy-to-construct cold frames are structures used to capture solar energy and create an insulated microclimate. Vegetables, especially leafy green ones like arugula, kale, lettuce, spinach, and cabbage, along with broccoli, beet, green onion, and radish, do well in a cold-frame environment.

COLD FRAME STYLES

There are many styles of cold frames. Some fit directly over an existing raised bed, while others are placed directly on the ground. They typically have one hinge and open from the top, but designs can vary. Traditional brick-built cold frames are often attached to a greenhouse, coming off a walled side. Wooden-sided cold frames help keep the warmth of the day inside the structure overnight. Aluminum and glass allow more light to enter but don't hold the heat as well overnight. There are also thin-walled plastic models that cover a steel or wooden frame. Some are zippered so that multiple units can be connected end-to-end to create a continuous row of coverage. The zippered windows allow easy access to the plants while still controlling temperature and humidity.

Some free-standing units come with a polycarbonate top panel to protect plants from chilly temperatures and wind that can slide out to reveal screening when the weather warms up. The screen keeps out most insects, slugs, and wildlife, while allowing air to circulate—and you can water right through the screen.

Cloches are low enclosures used to cover plants. Many can function in a manner similar to a cold frame. They can be made of glass, plastic, and other materials.

Cold frames are also prefect DIY projects. You can build them out of plywood, concrete, tile, bricks, or even hay bales, and then cover the structure with old windows or plastic or Plexiglas sheeting.

GROWING IN A COLD FRAME

Whatever materials you choose, if you are using cold frames to protect tender plants from winter temps, cut the plants back as much as possible before the first autumn frost. If they aren't already in pots, put them in large plastic containers, and fill them with soil. Pack the cold frame with the pots. Fill in any large air gaps between pots with leaves or mulch. Water the plants.

Thereafter, you will need to monitor the conditions inside the cold frame. Keep the soil inside it damp, but not wet. Cover the frame with a white plastic cover or the like to keep out most of the light. Too much light will encourage active growth, and it isn't yet the right season for that. The white plastic will also keep the sun from overheating the cold frame.

Seedlings can be transferred to the cold frame or started directly in it. If sowing directly into the cold frame, have it in place two weeks before seeding to warm the soil. If you start them inside and transfer them to the frame, you can start those six weeks earlier than normal. Keep an eye on the amount of sun, moisture, temperature, and wind within the frame. Seedlings benefit

Cold frames are great up-cycling projects. Here, plywood frames filled with a crop of leafy salad vegetables are covered with recycled door frames hinged to lift open.

from warmer temps and moisture, but winds, heavy rain, or too much heat can kill them.

MONITORING TEMPERATURES

Growing plants in a cold frame requires the constant monitoring of temperature, moisture, and ventilation. Most seeds germinate in soil that is around 70°F (21°C), although some crops like it a little warmer or cooler. Air temperatures are also important.

- Cool-season crops prefer temps around 65°F to 70°F (18°C to 21°C) during the day and 55°F to 60°F (13°C to 15.5°C) at night.
- Warm-season crops like temps 65°F to 75°F (18°C to 24°C) during the day and not lower than 60°F (15.5°C) at night.

Careful monitoring and response are important. If the frame is too warm, vent it. If the cold frame is too cold, cover the glass with straw or another padding to conserve heat. To vent the cold frame, raise the sash on the opposite side from which the wind is blowing to protect tender, young plants. Completely open the sash or remove it on warm, sunny days. Close the sash in the late afternoon once the danger of excess heat has passed and before the evening air turns chilly.

WATERING IN A COLD FRAME

Water plants early in the day so the foliage has time to dry before the frame is closed. Only water the plants when they are dry.

For transplanted or direct-sown plants, very little water is necessary because the cold frame retains moisture, and temperatures will remain cool. As temperatures increase and the frame is open for longer periods, introduce more water. Allow the soil surface to dry out between waterings, but do not wait until the plants wilt.

Gardeners stretch greenhouse film over steel-tubed frames to create a cold frame. The covering will also keep out plant invaders, like hungry deer. In warm weather, the film can be replaced with mesh screening to protect the plants from insects.

Link to the Experts

READ MORE AT GARDENING KNOW HOW

To find out more about cold frames, follow these links.

- "Cold Frame Construction: How to Build a Cold Frame for Gardening"
  LINK: gkh.us/19795
- "Cold Frames and Frost: Learn About Fall Gardening in a Cold Frame"
  LINK: gkh.us/124333
- "Keeping Plants in a Cold Frame – Using Cold Frames for Overwintering Plants"
  LINK: gkh.us/124421

A vintage wood-framed glass cloche acts as a cold frame that can move around the garden, protecting vulnerable plants as needed and acting as a mini greenhouse.

FIGHT DISEASES AND PESTS

It often feels as if gardens are magnets for problems. In spite of all the hard work you put into your plots, some invader, pest, or disease is always just looming on the horizon.

Gardeners once felt free to use toxic chemical sprays against these threats. But now a new era of planetary stewardship is upon us, and we are much more careful about how we fight back, seeking out organic solutions before resorting to the chemical sprayer. Weeds can be controlled by pulling or using boiling water. Biological controls for insect pests include ladybugs, praying mantids, ground beetles, aphid midges, braconid wasps, damsel bugs, and green lacewings. Other safer solutions include neem oil, pyrethrin, and good old soapy water. Chamomile tea is a cure-all for fungal diseases, while a mix of garlic cloves, water, and liquid soap can thwart fungal, viral, and bacterial diseases.

Sunken, dark spots are a common symptom of the fungal disease anthracnose.

Editor's Tip

When plants display symptoms of disease, it's a good idea to prune out the diseased, damaged, or dead plant tissue. Be aware, though, that disease pathogens can catch a ride on your pruners or other gardening tools, possibly infecting the next plant you use them on. Sterilizing tools between uses can help prevent the spread of diseases.

To find out how to keep your tools sterile, scan the code or follow the link to:

 "Sterilizing Pruning Tools: Learn How to Sterilize Pruning Tools"
LINK: gkh.us/121835

FIGHT PLANT DISEASES

If your vegetable garden is flourishing, that means your plants are healthy—and healthy plants are better able to resist disease. Yet, the cool moist spring and autumn weather typical of many temperate regions can promote the ideal conditions for the spread and development of plant diseases. This is why it's important to space plants properly and provide good air circulation to keep diseases at bay. Commercial disease-control products are all protectants, which means they must be applied before the problem occurs. Therefore, it pays to be vigilant throughout the growing season and frequently check leaves, stems, buds, flowers, and fruit for any signs of infection.

COMMON PLANT DISEASES

Here are several plant diseases that commonly affect vegetables.

Anthracnose

More than a dozen species of *Colletotrichum* are collectively known as the fungal disease anthracnose, which can quickly destroy a harvest. It often affects pepper, bean, tomato, eggplant, cucumber, muskmelon, watermelon, pumpkin, spinach, and pea crops. Look for fruits and pods with small, dark sunken spots, which will show pinkish spores in the center during wet weather. To control, apply liquid copper or neem sprays, beginning applications just as leaf buds break in the early spring. It is best to destroy severely affected plants.

Bacterial leaf spot

This affects tomatoes, peppers, lettuce, and cabbage-family crops. The leaves of infected plants will show small, dark water-soaked spots that dry up and drop out leaving "shot holes." Fruits may show small, sunken dark spots or cracks. Because there is no cure, you can only control its spread by applying copper or sulfur-based fungicides at the first sign of this disease and then weekly thereafter. You should also limit the use of high-nitrogen fertilizers and rotate crops. Heavily infected plants should be destroyed.

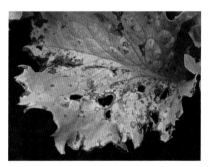

Bacterial leaf spot cuts holes in lettuce.

Clubroot

This severe disease infects brassica crops and leads to swollen and distorted roots and stunted growth. Fungicides will not treat it, but it can be reduced (but not eliminated) by raising soil pH through liming.

Chinese cabbage shows the deforming effects of clubroot disease.

Botrytis mold covers a snap bean.

Botrytis

Also called gray mold, botrytis is a fuzzy fungus that develops on dead and dying plant tissue but spreads to healthy tissue in wet conditions. Tomatoes grown in greenhouses are susceptible, as are strawberries. Control with disease-resistant cultivars, and discard garden debris and refuse in autumn. Grow susceptible plants in sunny areas with good air circulation, and water only at the base of plants. Remove infected leaves and fruit. Fungicides rarely control this disease.

Downy mildew presents as browning on the leaves of a cucumber plant.

Downy mildew

This grows in moist environments and attacks cold-season vegetables, such as brassicas and cucurbits, and might cause the loss of your whole harvest. Symptoms begin with irregular yellow patches on leaves, which then turn light brown. A fluffy white fungus will start to grow on the undersides of leaves. Cabbage, cauliflower, and broccoli can develop dark spots. Severe infections can kill young plants. Control with good air circulation and spacing and a copper fungicidal spray, and clean up garden debris where spores hide.

Early blight infects a potato plant.

Early and late blight

Early and late blight are fungal diseases that attack nightshade members. Early blight (*Alternaria solani*) appears as dark brown or black leaf spots with concentric rings on stems and large, black, leathery, sunken spots on fruit. During wet years, infections occur in spring. Late blight (*Phytophthora infestans*) forms irregular greenish black blotches first on older leaves or stems, then quickly spreads to fruit. It may not appear until August in wet years, but can destroy entire plants overnight. Control early blight by spacing and pruning, avoid overhead watering, pick off infected leaves, and apply a copper spray every 7 to 10 days. For late blight, remove entire plants, and bag immediately. Do not compost.

Late blight destroys tomatoes.

The leaves of an eggplant are infected with tobacco mosaic virus.

Mosaic
This is a group of viruses that affect numerous plants. Tomato mosaic virus affects tomatoes, peppers, potatoes, apples, pears, and cherries; tobacco mosaic infects eggplants, tomatoes, peppers, cucumbers, beets, and lettuce. Symptoms include distorted leaves mottled with yellow and green, stunted growth, malformed fruits, and reduced yield. No chemical solutions are available, so remove infected plants, right down to the roots, and destroy them; do not cultivate susceptible plants in the same area for two years.

Powdery mildew
This is caused by many different species of fungi in the order Erysiphales. It is very host-specific, but vegetables that share a family—such as melons and pumpkins—can be affected by the same species. Look for white, powdery growth on leaves and shoots that develops during warm days with cool nights. Control by choosing disease-resistant varieties, and avoid planting in shady or crowded spots. Start a fungicide spray program before the disease is advanced. Destroy infected leaves. Prevention includes spraying a copper- or sulfur-based fungicide every 10 days from spring to autumn.

Rust
Rust refers to a large family of fungi, with each type infecting only specific plants. Most rust diseases begin as small orange, red, or brown spots on the underside of leaves that then turn brown in summer. Susceptible plants include beans; fruit trees, such as pears and apples; alliums, such as garlic and leeks; and leafy vegetables like spinach or cabbage. Control with resistant cultivars, remove infected leaves, and spray every 10 days with a copper- or sulfur-based fungicide.

A chili pepper plant shows the killing effects of fusarium wilt.

Verticillium and fusarium wilt
These serious fungal diseases affect potato, tomato, eggplant, and pepper plants by invading roots and moving upward to plug up the plant's transportation system. Symptoms start with yellowing, wilting, and dying of young twigs and branches, often on one side. It gets worse from year to year. Control is all prophylactic; there is no treatment for infected plants. Remove dead and dying plants, infested roots, and soil; replant with resistant species. After pruning each plant, sterilize tools with rubbing alcohol, Lysol, or a 10 percent household bleach solution.

Rust disease marks broadbean plants.

Powdery mildew has begun to infect the leaves in a patch of pumpkin plants.

A gardener inspects the leaves of an eggplant to identify an aphid infestation.

Link to the Experts

READ MORE AT GARDENING KNOW HOW

To learn more about insects in the garden, follow these links.

- "What Bug Is This — Basic Tips on Identifying Garden Pests"
  LINK: gkh.us/134520
- "Getting Rid of Bad Bugs with Beneficial Insects"
  LINK: gkh.us/261

Red larvae of the Colorado potato beetle eat through potato plants.

CONTROL INSECTS

Experts estimate that there are up to 30 million species of insects on the planet, so it is no wonder that identifying garden pests can be tricky. Yet recognizing insect pests helps you distinguish between beneficial bugs and bug pests so that you can encourage the former and discourage the latter. It also allows you to tailor pest control to the particular culprits involved.

If you actually see an insect on a plant, note its appearance and habit –size, color, body shape; flying or crawling; alone or in a group—plus the damage it did and the type of plant it targeted. Insects usually damage plants either by sucking or chewing. Sap-feeding pests insert slender, needle-like mouthparts into the leaves or stems of plants and suck out the sap. This results in browning or wilting or a sticky substance called honeydew on the foliage. If the leaves are spotted, you likely have mesophyll feeders that suck out individual plant cells of leaves and stems. Here is a list of common insect pests and how to identify and treat them.

Aphids

Aphids are teensy pear-shaped bugs that suck the sap out of leaves and stems. Signs include sticky honeydew, wilted or yellowed leaves, or black sooty fungus residue. Treat them with a soapy water solution or neem oil.

Cabbage maggots

Adults are tiny gray-brown flies. Females lay eggs at the roots of brassicas, and the larvae gorge themselves on the roots, killing the plants. Signs are wilting foliage and stunted growth. To treat, cover young cabbages with row covers until after egg-laying season; destroy any eggs you find. (For more on row covers, see page 149).

The root of a cabbage plant shows the damage caused by cabbage maggots.

Colorado potato beetles

These pests enjoy all nightshade plants. They eat foliage, cause stunted growth, and decimate young plants. Signs are feeding beetles and defoliated plants or leaves speckled with holes. Hand pick them off, and drown them in soapy water. Destroy any eggs.

A cutworm crawls on an eggplant leaf.

Cutworms

These moth larvae feed at night, and cut through stems of young plants. Collar stems with segments of paper towel tubes, fitting them snugly into the ground. Diatomaceous earth or coffee grounds can also deter them.

Flea beetles

These pests eat the foliage of cabbage family and nightshade plants. The larvae feast on roots. Signs are small black beetles and small round holes in foliage. Dust leaves with talcum powder, or mix 1 part alcohol, 2½ parts water, and 1 teaspoon liquid dish soap.

A flea beetle munches on a mustard leaf.

Mexican bean beetles

These look like ladybugs but are more orange-yellow, with 16 black spots. Both the larvae grubs and adults devastate foliage. Fight back at the earliest stage—dust diatomaceous earth on foliage to kill the bright yellow eggs and larvae. And be sure to move your beans the following season.

A Mexican bean beetle eats it way through a cucumber leaf.

A slug eats through a zucchini.

Slugs

Slugs feed at dusk and dine on your vegetable plants until dawn. Signs include jagged holes in leaves and slimy trails. Hand pick off or deter with diatomaceous earth, eggshells, or coffee grounds sprinkled around plants. Do not use poison baits; other wildlife can eat the dead slugs.

A yellow summer squash plant is infested with squash bugs.

Squash bugs

Brown and slightly flattened, they suck the sap from zucchini, summer squash, winter squash, and pumpkins, along with cucumbers and melons. Look for yellowing or browning leaves. Scrape eggs from the underside of leaves. Adults overwinter in vines, so compost or burn any autumn garden debris.

Thrips

Thrips are minute, slender little insects with fringed wings and asymmetrical mouthparts. They feed mostly on plants by puncturing and sucking up the contents. Look for tiny rice-like flecks on foliage, deformed growth, and discolored spots. Blast with a garden hose or saturate the plant with a solution of dish soap and water.

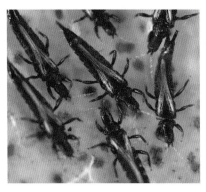

Minute thrips gather on a leaf.

Tomato hornworms

These fascinating creatures are larval sphinx moths, an unusual moth that should be protected, but they do love to eat tomatoes. Signs are the larvae themselves, plus holes in the leaves. Do not kill them, but do remove them to a distant spot with lots of greenery.

The tomato hornworm blends in with the tomato plants it loves to eat.

Try offering garden visitors snacks like carrots set away from the vegetable garden.

THWARTING ANIMAL PESTS

Hungry animals can be a menace to any garden, but doubly so when you're growing produce. They can threaten plants on two levels: below the ground and above the ground. Burrowing voles will eat roots, bulbs, and tubers. Mice love seeds like corn and sunflowers, so they can threaten a newly planted garden. Browsing deer, along with rabbits, woodchucks, and other small mammals will eat foliage, flowers, or fruit—sometimes all three. One aspect of having a garden is enjoying the wildlife that comes into the space, but not when they decimate your cabbage crop or help themselves to your entire strawberry harvest.

Fortunately, gardeners have come up with a variety of ways to humanely foil these wily intruders.

Alternative snacks
Offer critters alternative food sources, like cut-up veggies in small buckets, placed away from the garden.

Scarecrow
To keep birds away from newly seeded plots, you can always resort to a trusty scarecrow. It can also deter other animals from eating or otherwise disturbing seeds, shoots, and fruit in your garden.

Cloches
Place wire cloches over growing plants to protect their delicate leaves. You can also recycle large plastic bottles to place over plants to protect them from critters.

Chicken wire
Chicken wire or other fencing—sunk several inches into the ground and high enough to thwart deer—will safeguard the kitchen garden.

Hot pepper mixture
Spray this hot pepper mixture on your plants. Mix 1 ounce (30 ml) of hot pepper sauce, 4 drops of natural dish soap, and 1 cup (128 g) of aromatic marigold leaves. Add eggs and garlic for an extra ick factor.

Undesirable plants
Plant species that animals dislike—marigolds keep rabbits away, and mint and lavender will keep small pests at bay. Garlic and onions can be effective at deterring deer.

Specialized repellents
Check out store-bought repellents geared to specific pests; these include predator urine for deer.

Milk soap spray
Add a splash of milk and 4 drops of dish soap to the water in a spray bottle to keep deer away.

Soap bars
Stop deer and squirrels from munching on young plants with bars of soap raised up on skewers.

Noise
Use noise to scare off shy animals like deer and rabbits. Place a large wind chime in the garden or leave a battery-operated radio on overnight tuned to heavy metal rock.

A scarecrow protects a vegetable patch from unwanted visitors.

ROTATE YOUR CROPS

Crop rotation is an age-old gardening practice that involves changing the type of crops grown in a particular area over sequential seasons to promote healthy soil.

Crop rotation is an effective method of maintaining soil health, enhancing crop yield, and managing pests and diseases. This strategy can be as simple or as complex as you wish, depending on the size of your garden and the variety of crops you intend to grow.

The principle behind crop rotation is that different plants have varying nutrient needs and pest problems. Some plants, like legumes, enrich the soil with nitrogen, while others, like tomatoes and corn, are heavy feeders that deplete soil nutrients. By rotating crops, you can balance nutrient demands, replenish the soil, and disrupt the life cycle of destructive pests and diseases.

PLANNING CROP ROTATION

A successful crop rotation starts with good record-keeping and planning. Sketch a map of your garden, noting the location of

Year one   Year two   Year three

OPPOSITE PAGE: A sign explains the crop rotation schedule of the vegetable garden at Royal Horticultural Society Harlow Carr in Harrogate, North Yorkshire, England.

each crop. Keep track of what was planted where, year after year, to guide your rotation plan.

A basic rotation plan might involve a three-year cycle for a single plot or bed, such as the following rotation schedule that cycles through three plant types.

1. Year one
Plant heavy feeders, such as corn, cabbage, tomatoes, broccoli, beets, eggplant, Brussels sprouts, lettuce, and other leafy crops.

2. Year two
Plant light feeders, such as carrots, garlic, onions, peppers, potatoes, radishes, rutabagas, sweet potatoes, Swiss chard, and turnips.

3. Year three
Plant soil builders, such as peas and beans, or cover crops like clover.

BENEFITS OF CROP ROTATION

A schedule of crop rotation can help you maintain an edible garden that lasts through many years of harvest.

Enhanced soil fertility

Different crops contribute to or draw from soil nutrients in diverse ways. Legumes enrich the soil with nitrogen, while other plants may add organic matter or improve soil structure. Rotating these crops can help maintain a balanced nutrient profile in your soil.

Pest and disease management

Many pests and diseases are specific to certain plant families. By rotating your crops, you disrupt their life cycles and reduce the buildup of these harmful organisms.

Weed suppression

Certain crops with dense foliage, such as potatoes or squash, can effectively outcompete weeds, reducing their numbers in the next planting season.

Improved crop yield

Crop rotation promotes healthy soil and reduces competition and pest presence, which can lead to stronger plants and better yields.

Editor's Tip

For small home vegetable gardens, implementing an ideal crop rotation schedule can be quite challenging due to space constraints. If you have limited garden space, consider grouping together related plants and rotating those groups. You might not be able to achieve a perfect rotation, but even a little bit of shifting can be beneficial.

For container gardens or raised beds, replacing or amending the soil can be an alternative or complement to true crop rotation.

PLANT IN SUCCESSION

Succession gardening is a planning method that maximizes the use of garden space and time to ensure a steady harvest throughout the growing season.

This strategic approach involves planting a new crop in the same space as soon as the previous one is harvested. Understanding and implementing succession gardening can lead to more efficient use of your garden and a continuous supply of fresh produce.

WHAT IS IT?

At its core, succession gardening is about timing. You're coordinating the life cycles of multiple crops so that as one finishes, another begins. This involves considering the length of each crop's growing season, its preferred growing conditions, and how its needs and impacts fit with those of other crops.

There are three main types of succession planting.

Same crop

Here you plant the same crop in intervals. For example, you could plant lettuce every two weeks to ensure a continuous harvest, rather than having it all mature at once.

Different crop

This involves planting a new crop in place of the harvested one. For example, after harvesting spring peas, you could plant heat-loving beans in the same spot.

Relay planting

This involves planting a new crop before the existing one is completely harvested, often in the spaces in between. For example, you could plant autumn cabbage seedlings in the same bed as summer squash before it has finished producing.

PLANNING YOUR SUCCESSION GARDEN

Good planning is the cornerstone of successful succession gardening. Here are some steps to consider.

Know your crops

Understand the life cycle of each crop: how long it takes to mature, its temperature and space preferences, and its soil nutrient needs.

Consider timing

Look at the growing season of your region and how the needs of your plants fit into this timeline. Use the "days to maturity" listed on seed packets to plan your schedule.

Prepare your soil

Succession planting can deplete soil nutrients faster than single crop planting, so replenishing your soil is crucial. Fertilize in between plantings to maintain soil health.

Start transplants

For quick turnover, start the next crop in pots or seed trays so that a ready-to-plant seedling is available as soon as a spot opens up.

BENEFITS

Here are some of the key benefits of succession plantings.

Maximize yield

This method can dramatically increase the total yield from your garden, providing a steady harvest throughout the growing season.

Efficient use of space

This method is particularly advantageous for small gardens where space is at a premium.

Pest and disease management

Similar to crop rotation, the practice of changing crops in a given area can disrupt the life cycle of pests and diseases.

Weed suppression

Regular planting and harvesting can help suppress weeds by reducing the amount of open soil and light available for weed growth.

With the relay method, you plant a new crop before the previous one is harvested.

MAKING A SUCCESSION PLAN

Here's an example of a succession planting plan for a cold-winter climate worked out in a spreadsheet format for a single planting year.

In early spring, plant cool-weather crops like lettuce, radishes, or peas. In late spring to early summer, after harvesting the cool-weather crops, plant warm-weather crops like tomatoes, peppers, summer squash, or eggplants. In late summer to autumn, after the summer crops are done, plant autumn crops, like carrots, garlic, and low light greens.

FEB	MAR				APR				MAY					JUN					JUL					AUG				SEP				OCT			
3 4	1	2	3	4	1	2	3	4	1	2	3	4	5	1	2	3	4	5	1	2	3	4	5	1	2	3	4	1	2	3	4	1	2	3	4

last frost date ➡

EARLY SPRING TO AUTUMN GARDEN

⬅ first frost date

- Beets (APR) / Beets (JUN)
- Broccoli (early crop) (APR) / Broccoli (autumn) (JUN) / Broccoli (overwinter) (JUL)
- Cabbage (MAR)
- Brussels sprouts (JUN)
- Cauliflower (APR) / Cabbage (JUN)
- Carrots (MAR) / Carrots (JUL)
- Chard (APR) / Cauliflower (autumn) (JUN) / Cauliflower (overwinter) (JUL)
- Collards (MAR) / Chard (JUL)
- Fennel (APR) / Collards (JUN)
- Fava (FEB) / Radicchio (AUG)
- Kale (MAR) / Fennel (JUL)
- Kohlrabi (MAR) / Kale (JUN)
- Onion (APR) / Leek (JUN)
- Pea (FEB) / Mustard (AUG)
- Potato (early) (MAR) / Parsnip (JUN)
- Radish (MAR) / Potato (late) (JUN)
- Spinach (MAR) / Radish (winter) (JUL)
- Turnip (FEB) / Rutabaga (JUN)

LATE SPRING AND SUMMER GARDEN TO LATE PLANTING

- Beans (MAY) / Arugula (SEP)
- Broccoli (main) (MAY) / Carrots (SEP) (overwinter)
- Corn (JUN) / Greens (SEP) (overwinter)
- Cucumber (JUN) / Lettuce (SEP)
- Carrots (MAY) / Garlic (SEP)
- Eggplant (MAY) / Mâche (SEP)
- Peppers (MAY) / Radish (SEP)
- Potato (MAY)
- Summer squash (MAY)
- Tomato (APR)
- Winter squash (MAY)

CULTIVATE ORGANICALLY

Organic gardening is a holistic approach to cultivating plants that emphasizes the health of the entire ecosystem.

Rather than relying on synthetic fertilizers and pesticides that can negatively impact the environment, organic gardeners use more natural practices and solutions to build soil health, encourage biodiversity, and maintain ecological balance. Organic gardening can yield nutrient-rich fruits, vegetables, and herbs, while also fostering a sustainable and harmonious relationship with nature.

ORGANIC PRINCIPLES

Organic gardening is based on a few key principles.

Soil health

Healthy soil is the foundation of organic gardening. Organic gardeners focus on building rich, fertile soil through the addition of compost and other organic matter. This improves soil structure, retains moisture, and provides nutrients for plant growth.

Biodiversity

Encouraging a variety of plant and animal life helps maintain the health and resilience of the garden. Different plant species attract a range of beneficial insects and organisms that aid in pest control and pollination.

Sustainable practices

Organic gardening aims to conserve resources and minimize waste. This can involve using water

Organic gardeners use a variety of techniques to cultivate a sustainable vegetable garden that yields a bountiful harvest.

efficiently, recycling garden waste, and choosing locally sourced and renewable materials when possible.

Natural pest and disease control

Rather than resorting to potentially harmful synthetic pesticides, organic gardeners use techniques such as crop rotation, companion planting, and encouraging beneficial insects to manage pests and diseases. (For more information, see pages 62 to 67.)

TECHNIQUES

There are many techniques used in organic gardening, but here are some of the most important.

Fertilizing

Fertilizing with natural products that feed your vegetable plants and contribute to your overall soil health is a basic tenet of organic gardening. (For more information, see pages 24 to 25.)

Composting

Creating compost from kitchen scraps, garden waste, and other organic material recycles nutrients and reduces waste. Compost adds organic matter to the soil, feeding soil organisms and providing nutrients for plants. (For more information, see pages 26 to 27.)

Mulching

Mulch, made from organic materials like straw, shredded leaves, or newspaper, is spread on the soil surface to conserve moisture, suppress weeds, and add organic matter to the soil. (For more information, see pages 50 to 51.)

Crop rotation

Changing the location of crops each year disrupts the life cycle of insect pests and harmful diseases, reduces soil nutrient depletion, and can help improve your soil's structure and fertility. (For more information, see pages 68 to 69.)

Homemade manure tea and compost tea are organic alternatives to chemical fertilizers and are part of the sustainable practices of organic fertilization.

Cover crops and green manure

Cultivating cover crops and green manures, like clover or vetch, can improve your soil's health by adding organic matter, preventing erosion, and fixing nitrogen in the soil. (For more information, see pages 74 to 75.)

Companion planting

Planting certain crops together can deter pests, improve pollination, and enhance crop productivity. For example, marigolds can deter nematodes and other pests, while beans can provide nitrogen that benefits neighboring plants. (For more information, see pages 52 to 57.)

BENEFITS

Organic gardening offers several benefits, not only for the gardener but also for the environment. This practice is believed to encourage healthier produce, because fruits, vegetables, and herbs grown organically are free from synthetic pesticides and fertilizers, leading to healthier, nutrient-rich produce. Organic gardening practices also contribute to biodiversity, conserve water, reduce waste, and help to maintain healthy soil and ecosystems. Due to their diversity of plants and beneficial insects, they also tend to be more resilient to pests and diseases.

Link to the Experts

READ MORE AT GARDENING KNOW HOW

To learn how to make organic manure or compost tea for enhancing the soil quality of your edible garden, follow these links.

- "Manure Tea on Crops: Making and Using Manure Fertilizer Tea"
  LINK: gkh.us/3422

- "Compost Tea Recipe: How to Make Compost Tea"
  LINK: gkh.us/3441

PLANT COVER CROPS AND GREEN MANURE

Cover crops and green manure are essential tools in sustainable gardening and farming, helping to maintain and improve soil health to promote thriving, bountiful crops.

Cover crops and green manure represent a class of plants specifically grown to improve soil health, suppress weeds, and manage pests and diseases. Whether you're cultivating a large vegetable garden or a small raised bed, integrating these beneficial plants into your planting schedule can substantially enhance your gardening success.

CHOOSING THE CROPS

Cover crops are primarily grown to protect and improve the soil. They cover the ground, thereby reducing soil erosion, improving soil structure, and enhancing water retention. Some common cover crops include clover, rye, winter wheat, and buckwheat.

Green manure is a type of cover crop that is grown and then, rather than harvested, turned into the soil to improve its fertility. Legumes are often used as green manure due to their ability to fix nitrogen from the air and store it in their roots, thereby enriching the soil. For nitrogen fixation, consider legume crops like clover, alfalfa, vetch, peas, or beans. For improving soil structure, especially heavy clay soils, deep-rooted crops like daikon radish or cereal rye can be beneficial. If weed suppression is your primary goal, fast-growing crops like buckwheat or rye can form a dense canopy that hinders weed growth. Mustard plants can also serve as green manure if no cruciferous crops have been grown in that spot for the previous three years.

Once you've determined the best crops for your needs, follow these basic steps for growing these plants.

Sowing

Prepare your bed by removing weeds and spreading compost if necessary. Then spread the seeds evenly over the soil. Lightly rake the area to cover the seeds with soil, and water thoroughly.

Growing

Allow the cover crops time to grow. The length of time will depend on the particular crop, as well as your specific goals. Some gardeners might leave cover crops in the ground for just a few weeks in the off-season, while others may leave them in for several months.

Incorporating green manure

Turn green manure crops into the soil about three to four weeks before you intend to plant your main crops. This interval allows time for the green manure to decompose and release nutrients into the soil. You can chop the green manure crop at its base and then till it under, or simply dig it into the soil.

OPPOSITE PAGE: A gardening uses a fork to turn a crop of green manure into the soil of a vegetable patch. This practice can improve the quality of the soil, thereby promoting healthy plants.

MORE INFO *Benefits of cover crops and green manure*

Any extra effort and work involved with planting cover crops and turning green manure into the soil are well compensated by the benefits these kind of plantings provide, including improving soil fertility, controlling soil erosion, helping to suppress weeds, and helping to inhibit pests and disease.

- **Soil fertility.** Cover crops and green manure contribute to soil fertility. They add organic matter, which improves soil structure and water retention. Leguminous green manures also add nitrogen, an essential nutrient for plant growth.
- **Erosion control.** Cover crops can effectively protect the soil from erosion by wind and rain. The roots of these crops hold the soil together, and their foliage protects the surface of the soil.
- **Weed suppression.** Cover crops, such as certain grains, can outcompete weeds for light and nutrients, thereby reducing the need for labor-intensive weeding.
- **Pest and disease control.** Some cover crops can help manage pests and diseases. For example, certain types of marigolds can deter nematodes, rye can suppress various soil-borne pathogens, and buckwheat attracts a wide array of beneficial insects.

GROW IN A GREENHOUSE

The controlled environment of a greenhouse offers home gardeners a unique opportunity to experiment and broaden their horticultural horizons.

A greenhouse can be a wonderful addition to your gardening toolkit, enabling you to extend the growing season, protect your plants from harsh weather conditions, and even cultivate species not usually suited to your climate. At its most basic, a greenhouse is a structure with walls and a roof made primarily of transparent material, such as glass or plastic. This structure traps heat from the sun, creating a warmer microclimate within. This warmth, combined with humidity control, can create an optimal growing environment for a wide array of plants, regardless of the conditions outside.

CHOOSING THE RIGHT ONE

When selecting a greenhouse for your home, size matters. Ideally, your greenhouse should be large enough to house the plants you intend to grow while leaving room for future expansion. If space is limited, mini-greenhouses or growhouses—often not much larger than a bookshelf—can work wonders.

Greenhouses come in many shapes and sizes, from traditional freestanding structures to lean-tos that can be attached to your house or garage. They can be frame-based or hoop-based, with the former offering greater durability and the latter being more cost-effective.

The choice of the material for the frame and the covering is also critical. Frames are typically made from aluminum, steel, or wood, each with its pros and cons. Aluminum is lightweight and resistant to rust, steel is stronger and more durable, and wood can be cheaper and more aesthetically pleasing but requires regular maintenance to prevent rot.

For the covering, long-lasting glass is the traditional option, but it can be expensive and fragile. Polycarbonate, polyethylene, and Plexiglas sheeting are less costly and more durable choices, but they might need replacement over time. Plastic film is an especially affordable option, if somewhat flimsy.

SETTING UP YOUR GREENHOUSE

Once you've chosen the right greenhouse for your needs, it's time to set it up. Position it in a spot that receives at least six hours of sunlight per day, ideally with a north-south orientation to maximize sunlight exposure throughout the day. The site should also have easy access to a water supply and electricity, if required for heating, cooling, or lighting systems.

Inside your greenhouse, consider installing benches or shelving units to maximize space usage. You can also use plant hangers for climbing or vining plants. An efficient layout allows optimal airflow and access to all plants and tools for easy care and regular maintenance.

The greenhouse floor can be left as bare earth, covered with gravel for drainage, or even paved, depending on your preferences and the plants you're planning to grow.

A spacious, traditional glass greenhouse sits at the edge of a vegetable garden.

GREENHOUSE MAINTENANCE

Maintenance is vital to keep your greenhouse in proper shape and the plants within it thriving. This includes regular cleaning to prevent the buildup of pests and diseases, ensuring the transparent coverings are clear to allow maximum light penetration, and checking the structure for any damage, especially after severe weather.

Temperature control is crucial in a greenhouse. On sunny days, even in winter, temperatures can rise dramatically, which can harm your plants. Ventilation—either through manual vents or automated systems—can help regulate the temperature. In contrast, during cold nights or in the colder months, heating may be required. This can range from a simple space heater to more complex radiant heating systems.

Humidity and watering are also essential factors. Too little humidity can stress plants, while too much can encourage fungal diseases. A good rule of thumb is to water the plants in the greenhouse in the mornings so that excess moisture can evaporate throughout the day.

A small metal-framed polycarbonate greenhouse. Its advantages include high light transmission, thermal insulation, and impact resistance.

A wood-frame and glass greenhouse shows an efficient use of space, with shelving for plant pots, cabinetry for extra storage, and a support system for climbing plants.

Editor's Tip

When planting in a greenhouse, consider the space each plant needs, the compatibility of different species, and their individual light, temperature, and humidity requirements. You can group together similar plants to make environmental control easier.

Starting seeds in your greenhouse can give you a head start on the growing season, while tender plants like tomatoes, peppers, and cucumbers can benefit from the extended warmth a greenhouse provides.

Moreover, remember to rotate crops in your greenhouse, just as you would in an outdoor garden, to prevent the buildup of pests and diseases and maintain soil health.

PLANT A CONTAINER VEGETABLE GARDEN

Creating a container garden can be an ideal solution for those with limited space, poor soil conditions, or who simply want a more manageable gardening project.

A container edible garden can accommodate a wide range of fruits, vegetables, and herbs, lending a splash of color and life to your balconies, patios, or indoor spaces, such as a windowsill, while also serving a practical purpose.

MAKE A PLAN

Every thriving garden begins with a good plan. First, determine the location for your container garden. Consider factors such as available sunlight, proximity to a water source, and the aesthetics of your chosen area. Most fruits, vegetables, and herbs need at least six hours of sunlight per day, so place your containers in a sunny spot.

Next, consider what you want to grow. Are you a fan of fresh basil, or do you prefer home-grown tomatoes? The size of your containers will depend on the plants you choose. Larger vegetables like tomatoes or peppers will need a deep container to accommodate their expansive root system. Herbs and smaller vegetables like lettuce or radishes can thrive in smaller pots.

CHOOSING THE RIGHT CONTAINERS

When it comes to picking a container, you have a multitude of options. Traditional pots, window boxes, barrels, or even unconventional choices like old buckets or repurposed crates can all work. The crucial thing is that your chosen container should have ample drainage holes to prevent waterlogged soil and root rot.

Materials for containers range from plastic, resin, ceramic, and terracotta to wood, stone, or metal.

Terracotta and ceramic pots filled with tomatoes, leafy greens, and other plants form a movable edible garden on a home deck.

A balcony railing gives an urban gardener space to grow colorful chili peppers and a variety of herbs in a sturdy plastic window box planter.

Plastic pots are cheap, lightweight, and retain moisture well, while classic terracotta pots are heavier, breathable, and provide excellent drainage. Wood containers can be a charming rustic choice, but you should ensure that the wood is not treated with harmful chemicals or prone to rotting. Metal pots can get very hot in the sun and may not be suitable for heat-sensitive plants.

SELECTING AND PREPARING THE SOIL

Container gardening requires a different soil approach than traditional plot gardening. Garden soil can be too dense for container use, and it might contain weed seeds, insects, and fungal diseases. Instead, use a high-quality potting mixture that is lightweight, yet rich in organic matter.

Many commercial potting mixes already contain slow-release fertilizers and moisture-retaining pellets. If not, consider adding a slow-release organic fertilizer at planting time. Additionally, adding compost to your potting mix can provide a nutrient boost to your plants and improve soil structure.

PLANTING AND MAINTENANCE

Once your containers, location, and soil are prepared, you're ready to plant. Follow the seed packet or plant label instructions for planting depths and spacing. Overcrowding can lead to poor air circulation and increase the likelihood of disease.

Regular watering is critical in container gardening because potted plants dry out faster than their in-ground counterparts. Water your plants when the top 1 inch (2.5 cm) of soil feels dry to the touch. Remember, it's better to water deeply and less frequently than to often give your plants just a little water.

Remember that plants in containers are entirely dependent on you for their care. Monitor them closely for signs of distress, such as yellowing leaves or slow growth. Additionally, rotate your pots every few weeks to ensure even sunlight exposure. Nutrients also get depleted more quickly in containers, so regular feeding is essential. Use an organic liquid fertilizer every two weeks or as per the product's instructions.

A wine barrel has been cut in half to up-cycle it into a container for a tomato plant.

CULTIVATE AN INDOOR EDIBLE GARDEN

For those living in apartments or with limited or unsuitable outdoor space, an indoor garden is possible, with a wide variety of vegetables and herbs that will do well inside.

Indoor gardening is a fantastic way to grow your own fruits, vegetables, and herbs, regardless of the size of your living space or the weather outside. With a little preparation and care, you can cultivate a thriving indoor garden that yields fresh, flavorful produce year-round.

Indoor gardening allows you to extend the growing season, grow plants that wouldn't normally thrive in your region, and have fresh produce at your fingertips year-round. Moreover, tending to your indoor garden can be a relaxing and fulfilling pastime. It brings a bit of nature into your home, purifies the air, and can even improve your mental well-being. Whether you live in a tiny apartment or a large home, you can create an indoor garden that's just right for you and enjoy the fruits (and vegetables and herbs) of your labor throughout the year.

UNDERSTANDING INDOOR GARDENING

Growing plants within an indoor environment, such as your house or a greenhouse, provides a controlled environment where temperature, light, and humidity can be adjusted as needed, offering you a great opportunity to grow a wide variety of plants that might not otherwise thrive in outdoor conditions.

Growing strawberries indoors keeps this delicious fruit away from any hungry deer that want to dine in your garden.

Indoor gardening can range from a few pots on a sunny windowsill to elaborate setups with grow lights and hydroponic systems. The scale of your indoor garden will depend on your space, resources, and the type of plants you want to grow.

ESSENTIAL ELEMENTS OF INDOOR GARDENING

Here are some key considerations for a successful indoor garden.

Light

Plants need light for photosynthesis. Ensure your plants get enough light, either through a sunny window or with artificial lighting, such as fluorescent or LED grow lights.

Temperature

Most fruits, vegetables, and herbs prefer temperatures between 65°F and 75°F (18°C and 24°C). Keep

Sprouted onions thrive on a windowsill in DIY pots made from paper milk bottles.

plants in a location with consistent temperatures and avoid drafts or sudden temperature changes.

Humidity

Indoor environments can often be dry, which is less than ideal for many plants. Consider placing a tray with water near your plants or using a humidifier to increase humidity.

Soil and containers

Use a high-quality potting mix that drains well, and choose containers with drainage holes to prevent waterlogging the soil.

Watering

Indoor plants don't lose as much water to evaporation as outdoor ones, so they generally require less frequent watering. The watering frequency depends on the plant type and its growing conditions, but always let the top 1 inch (2.5 cm) or so of the soil dry out between waterings to avoid overwatering.

CHOOSING INDOOR PLANTS

When it comes to indoor gardening, the right plant choice is crucial. Many fruits, vegetables, and herbs can grow indoors, but they may have different requirements.

Peppers and tomatoes

With enough light, peppers and dwarf or patio varieties of tomatoes can be grown successfully indoors.

An indoor edible garden features homegrown young vegetables, such as cucumber, snow peas, and peppers, growing in a variety of up-cycled pots on a kitchen table.

Leafy greens

Leafy greens like lettuce, spinach, and kale don't require as much light as some other vegetables, which makes them a suitable choice for indoor gardening.

Fruits

Strawberries can be grown in hanging baskets or pots. Some dwarf varieties of fruit trees, like figs and citrus, can also be grown indoors under the right conditions.

Herbs

Many herbs will thrive as indoor plants. Basil, parsley, chives, thyme, and oregano are all great choices for and indoor edible garden.

They're compact, have a relatively short growth period, and can be continually harvested throughout their growth.

Editor's Tip

Here are a few useful tips for successfully cultivating an indoor edible garden.

- Provide enough light. Ensure your plants receive at least six hours of sunlight each day, or provide supplemental light with grow lights.

- Rotate your plants. Rotating them every few days can help them grow more evenly, because they'll stretch toward the light source.

- Don't overwater. This is a common problem in indoor gardening. Let the soil dry out between waterings to avoid root rot.

- Feed your plants. Use organic fertilizers to provide your plants with the necessary nutrients. Compost tea, fish emulsion, and seaweed extract are all great options.

MORE INFO *Hand pollination*

Most fruiting plants grown indoors require manual pollination, which is the transfer of pollen from the stamen, or male part of the flower, to the pistil, or female part. A highly effective method is to pollinate by hand. A bit labor-intensive, this method calls for using a very small, soft paintbrush or cotton swab to collect pollen. Be sure the utensil is clean, and lightly swab the center of a flower, starting from the deepest part and working upward to the stamen. Move from flower to flower, which will transfer pollen from flower to flower and plant to plant. You can repeat the process every few days throughout the flowering season.

LEARN ABOUT HYDROPONICS

Hydroponics is a soil-less form of gardening that offers a precise, efficient, and sustainable way to cultivate plants, including fruits, vegetables, and herbs.

Hydroponics works by delivering nutrients directly to plant roots through a water-based solution, which allows for faster growth, higher yields, and often superior-quality produce compared to traditional soil-based gardening.

The term *hydroponics* comes from the Greek words *hydro* ("water") and *ponos* ("work"), essentially meaning "working water." In hydroponics, plants are grown in a nutrient-rich water solution instead of soil. This method provides plants with the precise nutrients they need.

Hydroponic systems can be set up indoors or outdoors and can vary widely in size and complexity. From a simple lettuce raft in a bucket to a large, fully automated vertical garden, this system provides a range of options for home gardeners and commercial growers alike.

TYPES OF SYSTEMS

There are several types of hydroponic systems, each with its own advantages and unique considerations. Here are some of the most common.

Deep water culture (DWC)
In a DWC system, plant roots are submerged in a nutrient solution, with an air pump providing oxygen to the roots.

Nutrient film technique (NFT)
In NFT systems, a thin film of nutrient solution continuously flows over the roots of the plants, which are supported by a slight slope.

Ebb and flow
Also called "flood and drain," this system periodically floods the plant roots with nutrient solution, then drains it back, allowing the roots to absorb oxygen.

Kratky system
One of the simplest systems and one you can build yourself: you just need a container, some growing media, and plants like leafy greens and fresh herbs. It's a cost-effective method to learn hydroponics.

Wick system
Simple to set up and maintain, a wick system uses a wicking material to grow plants in containers. The wicking material absorbs water and nutrients from the reservoir and delivers it to the roots of the plants.

Drip system
This system relies on an automated watering system that slowly and regularly drips water and nutrients onto the roots of the plants.

Vertical or wall garden
You can use any hydroponics system in a vertical layout, which is ideal for apartment dwellers and those with limited space.

A small hydroponics unit can fit on a kitchen countertop to grow herbs like basil.

KEY ELEMENTS OF HYDROPONIC GARDENING

Hydroponic gardening requires a somewhat different set of considerations than traditional soil gardening. Key elements include the following.

Nutrient solution

A balanced hydroponic nutrient solution supplies all the elements that plants would normally obtain from the soil. It's crucial to monitor the solution's pH and nutrient levels.

Light

If growing indoors, artificial lighting, such as LED grow lights, might be required. The amount of light needed will depend on the type of plants you're growing.

Air circulation

Good air movement is important for plant health and to prevent the spread of diseases. This can be achieved with fans in an indoor setup.

Temperature and humidity

Like all plants, hydroponic plants have preferred temperature and humidity ranges. Maintain a suitable environment for the specific plants you're growing.

A vertical hydroponic system is set up in wall-mounted pipes to grow lettuces.

The roots of cos lettuce extend out of a slotted pot in a reservoir wick system.

BENEFITS OF HYDROPONICS

Hydroponics offers a number of advantages, including the following.

- Because the nutrient solution is recirculated, a hydroponic system uses significantly less water than soil gardening—good for the environment and your budget.
- By growing plants vertically or in closely spaced containers, hydroponics makes efficient use of available space. This makes it ideal for crowded urban environments or indoor settings.
- Hydroponics gives the grower a high level of control over the plants' conditions, including nutrient levels, pH, and lighting, which can lead to higher yields and faster growth.
- Hydroponics is typically cleaner than soil gardening, as it reduces issues with pests, weeds, and soil-borne diseases.

MORE INFO
Challenges of Hydroponics

Hydroponics has many advantages, but there are also challenges to consider. Namely, this system requires a more significant investment of time and money for the initial setup than standard gardens; it also needs a fair amount of monitoring and technical knowledge. The nutrient solution needs to be checked and adjusted often to ensure your plants are getting what they need, and understanding plant nutrient requirements, maintaining the right pH balance, and operating systems for lighting and pumps can be daunting for beginners.

PRESERVE AND STORE YOUR HARVEST

Storing produce offers many benefits, chiefly prolonging the shelf life of fruits, vegetables, and herbs so that you can enjoy the fruits of your labor well past the growing season.

Proper storage methods help retain flavor and nutritional value, ensuring that you can savor the taste of fresh garden produce throughout the year. Certain preservation techniques, such as fermenting or pickling, can even enhance flavors and nutritional content. Additionally, having a well-stocked larder reduces waste and provides a sense of food security, as you have access to healthy, home-grown food even during off-seasons or unexpected circumstances.

SHORT-TERM STORAGE

Many fruits, vegetables, and herbs can be stored for a short period without any special treatment. Keep in mind that each fruit or vegetable has an ideal temperature and humidity for storage. As a general rule, cool and dark locations, such as a pantry or a cellar, are best for most vegetables, while most fruits generally do well at room temperature. Here are some guidelines to help you to effectively manage short-term storage.

Fruits

Most fruits do well in a cool, dry place. Some fruits, like apples and pears, last longer when refrigerated. Remember to keep them in a breathable bag or container to prevent moisture buildup.

Vegetables

Root vegetables like potatoes, onions, and garlic do well in cool, dark, and dry conditions. Leafy greens, on the other hand, require refrigeration in a slightly damp environment to stay crisp.

Herbs

Fresh herbs can be stored in a jar of water on your countertop or wrapped in a slightly damp paper towel in your refrigerator.

LONG-TERM STORAGE

For long-term storage, there are various methods to preserve your harvest, including freezing, drying, canning, and pickling.

Freezing

Freezing is one of the easiest methods to preserve fruits, vegetables, and herbs. Most vegetables will need to be blanched first to deactivate enzymes that cause deterioration. Then, cool them quickly in ice water, drain, and pack into freezer-safe containers. Fruits can usually be frozen directly, though you may wish to pit, core, or slice them first. Herbs can also be frozen (for more information on freezing herbs, see pages 154 to 155).

Preparing a selection of fruits and vegetables to freeze. Many kinds of vegetables, fruits, and herbs do well in the freezer, as long as they are in airtight containers.

Sealing filled jars to prepare them for the water bath method of canning. A good seal and thorough sterilization of containers are essential for safe canning at home.

Drying

Drying removes water from the produce, slowing the growth of bacteria and mold. Herbs can be air-dried or dried in a dehydrator or oven. Vegetables and fruits can be dried using a dehydrator or an oven set at a low temperature.

Canning

Canning involves placing fruits or vegetables in jars and heating them to a temperature that destroys microorganisms and inactivates enzymes. This heating and subsequent seal also creates a vacuum, eliminating oxygen, which is needed for spoilage.

Canning is a popular and practical way to preserve a variety of foods at home. There are two primary methods: water bath canning and pressure canning. Each is best suited to different types of foods.

Water bath canning is generally used for high-acid foods, such as fruits, pickles, jams, jellies, and chutneys. Here are the basic steps.

1. **Prepare your jars.** Sterilize the jars, lids, and bands by washing them in hot soapy water, then boiling them in a large pot of water for about 10 minutes.
2. **Prepare the food.** Follow your specific recipe to prepare the food that you will be canning.
3. **Fill the jars.** Pack the prepared food into the sterilized jars. Leave some headspace at the top of the jars to allow for expansion of the food during processing.
4. **Seal the jars.** Wipe the rims of the jars with a clean cloth to ensure a good seal. Place the sterilized lids on top, then screw on the bands. Do not overtighten; they should be just tight enough to hold the lids in place during processing.
5. **Process the jars.** Place the jars in a water bath canner or large pot. The jars should be covered by at least 1 inch (2.5 cm) of water. Bring the water to a boil, and start your processing time, as specified by your recipe.
6. **Cool the jars.** Once the processing time is up, turn off the heat, and very carefully remove the jars from the hot water. Allow the jars to cool completely.
7. **Check the seals.** After the jars have cooled, check the seals by pressing down on the center of each lid. If the lid doesn't pop back, it's sealed. If it does pop back, it's not sealed properly and should be refrigerated and used soon.

Pressure canning is used for low-acid foods like vegetables. The process is similar to water bath canning, but requires a specialized piece of equipment called a pressure canner.

1. **Prepare your jars and food.** As with water bath canning, start by sterilizing your jars and preparing your food according to your specific recipe.
2. **Fill and seal the jars.** Again, fill your jars with food, leaving the recommended headspace. Wipe the rims, apply the lids and bands, and tighten them as per the guidelines.
3. **Process the jars.** Place the jars in the pressure canner, following the manufacturer's instructions for securing the lid. Heat the canner over medium-high heat until it reaches the pressure specified in your recipe, then start your processing time.
4. **Cool the canner and jars.** When the processing time is up, turn off the heat. Allow the canner to cool and depressurize before opening it. Then, carefully remove the jars and let them cool completely.
5. **Check the seals.** As with water bath canning, check the seals once the jars have cooled.

Pickling

Pickling is an excellent way to preserve and add flavor to a wide variety of fruits and vegetables. Traditional pickling methods use a brine of water, salt, and sometimes sugar, while quick pickling often involves vinegar. Below is a simple guide to start pickling at home using the quick pickling, or refrigerator pickles, method, a fast and simple way to preserve your produce. It doesn't require special canning equipment or techniques. You need only the following list of basic ingredients and tools.

- Fresh fruits or vegetables
- Vinegar (white, apple cider, rice, or any other type of vinegar, according to your preference)
- Water
- Salt
- Sugar
- Pickling spices (dill, garlic, mustard seeds, etc., depending on the specific recipe)
- Saucepan
- Wooden spoon
- Ladle
- Measuring spoons
- Canning jars with lids

A wide variety of vegetables, such as cucumbers, cauliflower, and carrots, as well as savory fruits like tomatoes and peppers, can be preserved by pickling them.

Once you've gathered your materials, follow these steps for a quick pickling of produce.

1. **Prepare the produce.** Thoroughly wash your chosen fruits or vegetables. Cut, slice, or chop them, if needed.
2. **Prepare the brine**. In a saucepan, combine equal parts water and vinegar. Add salt and sugar (usually 1 to 2 tablespoons (15 ml to 30 ml) of each per cup of liquid), and bring the mixture to a boil.
3. **Add spices and produce.** In your canning jars, add the desired spices and herbs. Pack the produce into the jars, and then pour the boiling brine over top, leaving about ½ inch (13 mm) of headspace.
4. **Seal and refrigerate.** Wipe the rims of the jars, then place the lids on top and screw on the bands. Allow the jars to cool to room temperature, then store them in the refrigerator. Wait at least a day before eating to let the flavors develop.

Fermented pickles rely on the natural bacteria present on the produce and in the air to create a tangy, flavorful pickle. Follow these steps for traditional fermentation.

1. **Prepare the produce.** Choose fresh, high-quality fruits or vegetables. Many types of produce can be fermented, including cucumbers, carrots, beans, and cabbage.
2. **Prepare the brine.** Dissolve salt in water to create a brine. The exact amount will depend on your recipe, but a general guideline is 2 to 3 tablespoons (30 ml to 45 ml) of salt per 1 quart (1 L) of water.
3. **Pack the jars.** Add your choice of spices and herbs to your jars, then pack in the produce. Pour the brine over the produce, ensuring that it is completely submerged. You may need to use a weight or a smaller jar to keep the produce under the brine.
4. **Ferment.** Loosely cover the jars with a lid or a cloth, and store them at room temperature out of direct sunlight. Allow the produce to ferment for several days to a few weeks, depending on the temperature and your taste preference. Check the jars daily to make sure the produce is still submerged and to skim off any foam or mold that may form on the surface of the brine.
5. **Store.** Once the pickled produce has reached your desired level of tanginess, secure the jars' lids, and store them in the refrigerator.

Air Drying

This method works best with herbs and hot peppers. Simply bundle your herbs or peppers together, hang them upside down in a warm, dry, well-ventilated location away from direct sunlight, and leave them until they are completely dry.

Oven drying

If you don't have a food dehydrator, you can use your oven to dry fruits and vegetables. Here's how:

1. **Prepare the produce.** Wash your fruits or vegetables thoroughly. Slice them thinly and uniformly to ensure they dry at the same rate.
2. **Blanch the produce** (optional). Some vegetables, like carrots, beans, and potatoes, should be blanched before drying to stop enzyme activity and maintain color and flavor. Blanching involves boiling the vegetables for a short time, then cooling them rapidly in ice water.
3. **Arrange the produce.** Arrange the produce in a single layer on a baking sheet. You can line the sheet with parchment paper for easier cleanup.
4. **Dry the produce.** Set your oven to the lowest possible temperature, ideally no higher than 200°F (93°C). Place the baking sheet in the oven. Keep the oven door slightly open to allow moisture to escape.
5. **Check the produce.** Drying can take several hours, depending on the type of produce and your oven. Regularly check the produce to prevent over-drying or burning. The produce should be pliable and no moisture should be visible on the surface.

Cherry tomatoes have been arranged on baking sheets to dry in a home oven.

Using a Dehydrator

Food dehydrators are designed specifically for drying food, such as herbs, fruits, and vegetables, and they allow for more consistent results and easier temperature control than an oven.

1. **Prepare the produce.** Wash and slice your fruits or vegetables as you would for oven drying.
2. **Blanch the produce** (optional). Again, some vegetables and fruits may need to be blanched before drying.
3. **Arrange the produce.** Place the slices of fruit or vegetable on the trays of your dehydrator, ensuring that they don't overlap.
4. **Dry the produce.** Set the temperature according to the instructions that came with your dehydrator, and let it run. It may take several hours or even a full day to fully dehydrate the produce, depending on moisture content.

Storing dried produce

Once your produce is dried, allow it to cool before packing it into airtight containers. Store in a cool, dark, and dry place. Properly stored dried produce can last for months, but check periodically for any signs of moisture or mold.

Onions, beets, carrots, bay leaf, and pumpkin have been preserved by drying in a food dehydrator, and then stored in glass jars with airtight lids for future use.

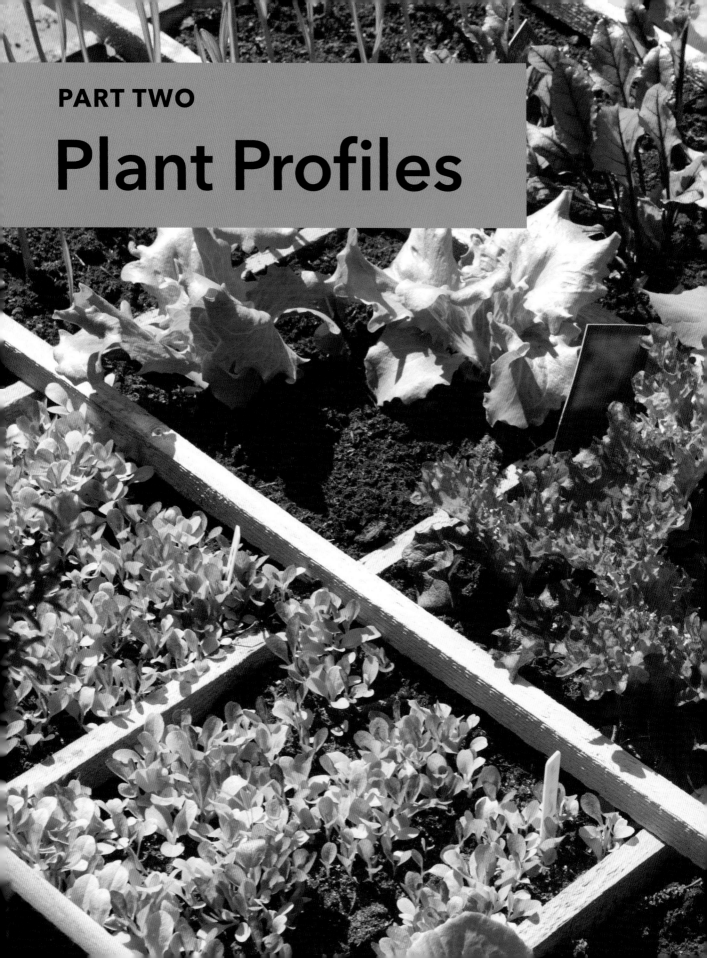

PART TWO
Plant Profiles

CHAPTER TWO
FRUITS AND VEGETABLES

Once you've learned what you need to know about creating a vegetable garden, your next step is choosing which plants to cultivate in it. The following pages feature a wide range of common vegetable and fruit plants that are suitable for growing in a home garden. Included are instructions for planting, tending, and harvesting these plants, along with a quick "essentials" guide that provides a rundown of the pertinent facts, such as when to plant, when to harvest, what kind of soil it will thrive in, how often you need to water, and how much space you need for it, so that you can make an informed decision about which plants will work best for your area and your needs.

KNOW YOUR VEGETABLES

Choosing which plants to include in your garden depends on many factors, including their growth habit, length of growing season, and what you will ultimately use them for.

There are various ways to categorize vegetable garden plants, including their life cycles (annual, biennial, or perennial), parts harvested for food (which determines whether they are a vegetable or a fruit), and broad family or generic categories (such as the *Brassicas* or *Alliums*).

ANNUAL, PERENNIAL, OR BIENNIAL?

Vegetables and fruits, like other plants, are divided into annual, biennial, and perennial crops. In simple terms, the difference between the three categories comes down to how many years they live: annuals live for one year, biennials live for two years, and perennials live more than two years —from three years to hundreds. The difference is not so simple, however. Depending on where you live, a tender perennial that is not winter hardy will be treated as an annual. Many biennial food crops are grown as cool-weather annuals.

Most of the vegetables that we buy are annuals. These vegetables complete their life cycles—from germination to flowering and fruiting to the production of seeds—within one growing season, and then they die. The length of the growing season or period in which these stages take place varies according to geographical location. The bulk of the vegetables in our modern diet—corn, potatoes, tomatoes, peppers, soybeans, and spinach—are all grown as annuals. In regions with shorter growing seasons, certain vegetables will perform better under those restrictive conditions. These include beans, beets, broccoli, cabbage, cauliflower, carrots, and cucumber.

> **MORE INFO**
> ## Fruit or Vegetable?
>
> Just about everyone knows the debate about whether a tomato is a fruit or a vegetable, but what makes a plant one or the other? Technically, a fruit is a plant's developed ovary that comes from a flower and contains one or multiple seeds. The much broader term "vegetable" refers to any part of a plant we use for food, including the roots, tubers, stems, and leaves. We know lots of fruits that are typically treated as veggies in the kitchen, such as eggplant, pepper, and cucumber. Rarer are the vegetables, such as rhubarb, that are treated as fruit.

When planting annual vegetables and fruits, it is essential to start seeds indoors or sow outdoors at the right time. It helps to keep a garden diary, indicating month-by-month when plants should go into the ground (often determined by the date of your last predicted frost). Depending on your local climate, correct planting dates will differ. If you are uncertain, contact an agricultural authority in your area.

Biennial plants grow big the first year, then seed the second, if we still have them. Some biennials, such as certain root vegetables are generally grown as annuals because they are harvested for their edible roots.

Perennials continue to produce for more than two years. These plants don't need to be started from scratch each year, and if well tended,

The main ingredients for the classic French ratatouille—zucchini, squash, eggplant, bell pepper, and tomato—are all actually fruits that are used as savory vegetables. This is just one of the healthy meals you can create from the harvest from a home vegetable garden.

Link to the Experts

READ MORE AT GARDENING KNOW HOW

To learn more about tending a vegetable garden, from how you can thwart pests to getting a garden ready for winter, follow these links.

- "Common Pests in Vegetable Gardens – Tips on Treating Vegetable Pests"
  LINK: gkh.us/50283
- "Perennial Vegetable Plants – How to Grow Perennial Vegetables"
  LINK: gkh.us/80195
- "Edible Perennial Plants – Growing a Perennial Food Garden"
  LINK: gkh.us/166341
- "Cleaning the Garden in Autumn – Getting Your Garden Ready for Winter"
  LINK: gkh.us/2523
- "Self Sowing Veggies: Reasons for Planting Vegetables That Self Seed"
  LINK: gkh.us/131985
- "Patio Garden Plants – Small Fruits and Vegetables"
  LINK: gkh.us/166338

Learning all you need to know about the different plant types, whether vegetables or fruits, can ensure a diverse harvest of fresh produce in nearly every season.

they can provide years of harvesting. They are generally eaten more in the form of fruit—such as berries, apples, and oranges—but there are also a number of perennial vegetables we enjoy on a regular basis. Some of the better-known include asparagus, artichoke, and garlic. In certain cases, perennials like potatoes are treated as annuals and sown anew each year in alternating locations to reduce pest problems and the possibility of devastating disease.

VEGETABLE GROUPS

Vegetables are also divided by families or which part is used in cooking. Some, such as crucifers, fall into more than one category.

- Alliums, members of the large and varied genus *Allium*, give us such staples as onion and garlic.
- Cruciferous, or brassica, vegetables are members of the family Brassicaceae and include a wide variety of healthy veggies like cabbage, Brussels sprouts, cauliflower, and broccoli.
- Stem vegetables are harvested for their edible stems or stalks, such as asparagus, celery, and rhubarb. Crucifers like broccoli also have edible stems.
- Leafy green vegetables, high in vitamins, minerals, and fiber, include veggies eaten either raw or cooked, such as lettuce, spinach, kale, and Swiss chard.
- Root vegetables are the staples such as carrots, potatoes, sweet potatoes, turnips, parsnips, beets, ginger, and radishes that are harvested for their edible underground parts.

- Squashes are edible members of the gourd family, Cucurbitaceae. Although used as vegetables, the part of a squash plant used in cookery is actually the fruit of the plant (squash flowers are also edible). Examples include, pumpkin, cucumber, and zucchini. This group is also known as marrow vegetables.

Dig Deeper

LEARN MORE AT GARDENING KNOW HOW

Scan the QR code or follow this link for several informative articles that help you get the most from a vegetable garden.

Vegetable Growing Guide
LINK: gkh. us/160774

ASPARAGUS

Scientific name: Asparagus officinalis

A new shoot of purple asparagus peeks up from the soil, ready for harvest. This spring vegetable is a prized variety, often boiled or steamed and drizzled with Hollandaise sauce to serve as a side dish or appetizer.

The Essentials

planting time early spring

light full sun

soil well-draining heavy, medium, or sandy soils

pH level pH 6.5 to 7.0

water 1 inch (2.5 cm) per week

size 6 to 12 inches (15 to 30 cm) tall; 1 to 3 feet (30 cm to 1 m) wide

harvest in 2 to 3 years

Asparagus (*Asparagus officinalis*), also called garden asparagus or sparrow grass, are the tender young shoots of a perennial flowering plant native to most of Europe and western temperate Asia. Formerly grouped in the lily family, since the early 2000s, the species has been classified in a family of its own, the Asparagaceae, along with yucca, bluebell, and hosta.

This is a long-lasting perennial—it is so long-lived, in fact, that some types of asparagus survive for as long as 20 to 30 years. Asparagus takes three years to grow before it is ready to harvest, but it can then be cultivated and harvested season after season for several decades.

Asparagus plants can be either male or female. There are some similarities between the two, but most farmers and gardeners choose to produce only male asparagus; male asparagus does not expend energy producing fruit, so it produces as many as three times more spears than female plants. Male asparagus also tends to live longer and start producing spears earlier in spring, making it generally more valuable.

Growing and caring for the plants

To start, buy one-year-old, healthy asparagus crowns. Dig a trench 8 to 10 inches (20 to 25 cm) deep and wide enough to accommodate the growing asparagus roots. If you're planting a larger crop with multiple rows, space the trenches 4 feet (1.2 m) apart.

Apply about 1 pound (500 g) of triple superphosphate (0-46-0) or 2 pounds (1 kg) of superphosphate (0-20-0) to the soil for every 50 feet (15 m) of trench. Place the crowns 18 inches (45 cm) apart, right on top of the fertilizer. Work liberal amounts of organic material into the dug soil, then use this soil to backfill the trench to a depth of 2 inches (5 cm).

As the asparagus grows, backfill with more soil every time you see another 2 inches (5 cm) of the tender new stalks. Care must be taken to protect these delicate shoots. Once the trench is filled, the bulk of the hard work is done. Weed the bed thoroughly in early spring to avoid competition for nutrients, and feed the growing asparagus annually with a 10-10-10 granular fertilizer.

Harvesting asparagus

In the third year of growth, after planting one-year-old crowns, asparagus spears will be ready for harvesting. During this initial harvest year, harvest during the first month only. Removing the spears for more than a month during this important year of growth will weaken and possibly kill the plants.

Asparagus spears are ready to harvest when they are about 5 to 8 inches (12.5 to 20 cm) long and as big around as your finger. Asparagus that grows too long will quickly become woody and bitter; you will want to harvest it early enough in the season so that it is still tender, while allowing smaller spears to continue growing. Carefully cut or break the spears from the point closest to their attachment to the fibrous roots. Excessive disturbance of the area can result in damage to spears that have not yet broken ground.

Dig Deeper

LEARN MORE AT GARDENING KNOW HOW

Scan the QR code or follow this link to learn more about growing this delicious early spring vegetable.

"Planting Asparagus: How to Make an Asparagus Bed"
LINK: gkh.us/575

BEET

Scientific name: Beta vulgaris

Freshly rinsed beets show off their color. By staggering your crops, you can ensure that you have a steady supply of both roots and greens during harvest season.

The vegetable beet, one of several cultivated varieties of *Beta vulgaris* grown for its edible taproot and leaves, is called beetroot in British English and is also known as the table beet, garden beet, red beet, golden beet, or dinner beet. This healthy and tasty veg has been cultivated since ancient times and during its long history has been used as both a culinary and medicinal plant.

The bulbous root can be served boiled, roasted, or raw, and the leafy portion, called beet greens, can be added raw to salads when young and boiled or steamed when mature. Pickled beetroot is a traditional food in many countries. As well as a culinary staple, the deep purple root is also used as a food colorant, adding its bright tones to tomato paste, desserts, jams, ice cream, candy, breakfast cereals, and other foods and beverages.

Along with the well-known purplish red beet, there are also golden, white, and red-ringed varieties. Golden and white beets have a sweeter taste than the earthier reds.

Growing and caring for the plants

When considering how to grow beets in your garden, remember that they do best in backyard or raised-bed gardens, because they don't require much room.

First consider your soil's composition. Beets thrive in deep, well-drained soil. Sandy soil is best; clay is the worst because it is too heavy for large roots to grow. Mix clay soil with organic matter to help soften it. Hard soil can cause the roots to be tough, but if you plant beets in autumn, use a slightly heavier soil to help protect against any early frost.

When to plant a beet crop is another consideration. Beets can be grown all winter long in many southern areas, but in northern soils, you shouldn't put them in the ground until the temperature of the soil is at least 40°F (4°C). Beets like cool weather, and they grow well in the chillier temperatures of spring and autumn and do poorly in hot weather.

Plant the seeds in a row, spacing them 1 to 2 inches (2.5 to 5 cm) apart. Lightly cover the seeds with loose soil, and then sprinkle it with water. Plants should sprout in 7 to 14 days. If you want a continuous supply, plant your beets in several plantings, about three weeks apart from one another.

You can plant beets in partial shade, but you want their roots to reach a depth of at least 3 to 6 inches (7.5 to 15 cm), so don't plant them under a tree where they might run into the tree's roots.

Harvesting beets

You can harvest beets seven to eight weeks after the planting of each group. When the taproots have reached the desired size, gently dig them up from the soil. Beet greens can be harvested as well: pick these while a beet is young and the root is small.

The Essentials

planting time spring

light full sun to partial shade

soil well-draining, moist, and loamy soil

pH level 6.0 to 7.0

water 1 inch (2.5) per week

size 12 to 18 inches (30 to 45 cm) tall; 18 to 24 inches (45 to 60 cm) wide

harvest in 50 to 60 days

Editor's Tip

A root or earth cellar was once a common place to store vegetables like beets and potatoes long-term. Lacking one doesn't mean you can't preserve your surplus crop.

- Keep beet greens in the refrigerator in a plastic bag for up to one week.
- Store beets in your fridge's crisper for one to three weeks.
- Store in a cold, moist place (40°F to 50°F, or 4°C to 10°C) for up to three months.
- Freeze beets for up to a year by first cutting off the leaves, cleaning off the soil, and then gently boiling them for 30 minutes. After cooling them in an ice bath, cut them into uniform pieces, and place in freezer bags.

A Gallery of
PEPPER VARIETIES

Along with tomatoes and eggplants, peppers (*Capsicum* spp.) are members of the nightshade family. The genus includes thousands of cultivars that produce a wide array of heat levels, from the sweetly mild to the searingly hot. *Capsicum annuum* includes bell peppers, cayennes, jalapeños, and serrano; *C. chinense* includes the fiery peppers, such as the habaneros, Scotch bonnets, and Carolina Reapers. You'll probably want to include at least one or two varieties in your vegetable garden. These easy-to-grow plants not only look great, they also produce right up until the first frost of autumn.

Editor's Tip

When deciding which peppers to grow, keep in mind that varieties range in heat from mild to scorching. Scoville heat units (SHU) are a good guide to help you choose the level you are comfortable with. Remember, the higher the number, the hotter the pepper. Here is a sampling of some of the many garden pepper varieties and their SHU range.

SHU	Pepper Variety	
0 to 100	• Bell pepper	• Pimiento
100 to 1,000	• Banana pepper	• Cubanelle
1,000 to 10,000	• Ancho • Poblano	• Jalapeño
10,000 to 100,000	• Serrano • Chile de árbol	• Cayenne • Chipotle • Malagueta
100,000 to 350,000	• Habanero	• Scotch bonnet
350,000 to 800,000	• Red Savina	• Chocolate habanero
800,000 to 3,200,000	• Ghost pepper • Trinidad Scorpion	• Carolina Reaper • Dragon's Breath

BELL PEPPER
0 SHU
Also known as the sweet pepper or green pepper, the heatless bell pepper comes in a range of colors, including red, yellow, orange, green, white, chocolate, candy cane striped, and purple. For more information, see page 98.

BANANA PEPPER
0 to 500 SHU
This mild and tangy pepper, also known as the yellow wax pepper, is a medium-sized variety of *C. annuum* with a curved shape. It is typically bright banana yellow, but can change to change to green, red, or orange as its ripens.

PIMIENTO
100 to 500 SHU
The sweet, succulent pimiento (aka pimento or cherry pepper) is large, heart-shaped *C. annuum* that is usually bright red but can also be yellow, green, and maroon. These mild peppers are typically used fresh or pickled.

CUBANELLE
100 to 1,000 SHU
Widely used in Italy and Cuba, this sweet variety of *C. annuum* is also known as the Cuban pepper or the Italian frying pepper. Its long, tapered fruit first appears in a yellowish green color; if allowed to ripen it will turn a bright red.

POBLANO
1,000 to 1,500 SHU
A mild *C. annuum,* the poblano is a chubby pepper famously stuffed and roasted in the popular *chiles rellenos* dish. Chile ancho, the most widely used pepper in Mexican cuisine, is its dried form and is often used in traditional mole sauce.

JALAPEÑO
4,000 to 8,500 SHU
A medium-sized and medium-heat cultivar of *C. annuum,* the jalapeño has become widely popular for its use in fast-food Mexican. It is picked and consumed while still green. Chipotle peppers are smoke-dried ripe jalapeños.

SERRANO
10,000 to 23,000 SHU
The second-most-used chili in Mexican cuisine, this meaty *C. annuum* variety is usually picked while green, but will ripen to brown, orange, or yellow. Typically eaten raw, its bright and biting flavor is perfect for *pico de gallo* and salsa.

CHILE DE ÁRBOL
15,000 to 30,000 SHU
A small and potent Mexican variety, chile de árbol is also known as bird's beak chile and rat's tail chile. The fruits start out green and turn a bright red as they mature. They can be used fresh or dried or ground to use as a spice.

CAYENNE
30,000 to 50,000 SHU
Familiar to many in its dried form, this long, waxy-skinned red chili is the favored spice of Creole and Cajun cuisine. Thin-walled and skinny, a cayenne matures to a wrinkled shape, with its heat level rising the longer it stays on the plant.

MALAGUETA
60,000 to 100,000 SHU
This small, tapered pepper is a medium-heat variety of *C. frutescens* widely used in Brazil, the Caribbean, Portugal, Angola, Mozambique, and São Tomé and Príncipe. Initially green, it takes on a deep red color at maturity.

HABANERO
100,000 to 350,000 SHU
Once touted as the world's hottest, this fiery South American pepper has since been supplanted by other, even hotter varieties of *C. chinense*. Most commonly orange or red, it has a flavor described as sweet, fruity, tropical, and smoky.

SCOTCH BONNET
100,000 to 350,000 SHU
Also called the Bonney pepper, or Caribbean red pepper), this *C. chinense* gets its name from its resemblance to a tam o' shanter. Small but fiery, it originated in Jamaica and packs a punch in cookery all over the Caribbean.

RED SAVINA
350,000 to 577,000 SHU
This habanero cultivar has been bred to be more potent, as well as heavier and larger, than the original. Its wrinkled fruit resembles a Chinese lantern in shape and ripens to a distinctive, dark red color.

CHOCOLATE HABANERO
425,000 to 577,000 SHU
A habanero cultivar, this chili has been bred to produce a more potent fruit that is spicier, heavier, and larger. Black habanero is an even darker version. Just small slivers of these peppers will raise the heat of any dish they is used in.

GHOST PEPPER
1,041,427 SHU
Also called bhut jolokia, this fiery hot pepper is a hybrid of *C. chinense* and *C. frutescens,* cultivated in northeast India. Ripe peppers are 2½ to 3½ inches (6 to 9 cm) long and have bumpy skin in red, yellow, orange, or chocolate.

TRINIDAD SCORPION
1,000,000 to 1,463,700 SHU
C. chinense cultivars are among the hottest peppers in the world. "Scorpion" in the names of the Trinidad Moruga Scorpion and the Trinidad Scorpion Butch T peppers refers to their pointed ends, said to resemble a scorpion's stinger.

CAROLINA REAPER
2,200,000 SHU
Red with a bumpy texture and small pointed tail, the gnarled Carolina Reaper is a cultivar of *C. chinense* developed by American breeder Ed Currie. In 2017, Guinness World Records declared this variety the hottest chili pepper.

MORE INFO
Dragon's Breath Pepper

With its staggeringly high SHU measurement of 2,480,000, the fiery Dragon's Breath pepper stands to take the title of world's hottest pepper, although it has not yet been officially recognized as such (the Carolina Reaper still held the title as of 2023). Never grow this pepper in a home garden: experts warn that swallowing one might cause death by choking or anaphylactic shock.

BELL PEPPER

Scientific name: *Capsicum annuum*

Ripening bell peppers. How long you keep them on the vine will determine their color.

Like most gardeners, when you're choosing veggies, you'll probably want to include bell peppers (*Capsicum annuum*). These members of the nightshade family are warm-weather crops that produce fruit popular for eating both raw and cooked. Crunchy, sweet bell pepper plants lack capsaicin, the active component in hot peppers that gives them their heat.

Growing and caring for the plants

Bell peppers are fairly easy to grow, but plant care in the early stages is critical. Temperature is an important factor to consider. Unless you live in a hot climate, always start seedlings indoors; the seeds need the warmth to germinate. Fill a seed tray with seed-starting soil or a well-draining potting soil, placing one to three seeds in each container. Place the tray in a warm location or use a warming mat to keep them between 70°F and 90°F (21°C to 32°C)—the warmer the better. It can be helpful to cover the tray with plastic wrap. Water droplets will form on the underside of the plastic to let you know the baby seeds have enough water. If the drops stop forming, it's time to give them a drink. You should begin to see signs of plants popping up within a couple of weeks.

When your little plants get to be a few inches tall, gently transfer them separately into small pots. As the weather begins to warm, harden off the seedlings by putting them outside for a bit during the day. This, along with a little fertilizer now and then, will strengthen them in preparation for outdoor life.

Editor's Tip

Pepper plants are considered to be fairly sturdy specimens, but, on occasion, the weight of developing fruit has been known to break their stems. The best way to stake peppers is to drive a wooden or metal stake next to the plant or every 3 to 4 feet (1 to 1.2 m) per row. Then, loosely tie the main stem and branches of the plant to the stake using torn sheets or pantyhose. Continue to add ties as needed while the plants are actively growing.

Bell peppers thrive in warm seasons, so wait for the nighttime temperatures in your region to rise to 50°F (10°C) or higher before transplanting them to the garden, making absolutely certain that the chance of frost is long gone. A frost will either kill the plants altogether or inhibit pepper growth, leaving you with bare plants. When the weather has warmed up and your young plants have grown to about 8 inches (20 cm) tall, they can be transferred to the garden.

Before putting them into the ground, amend your soil as necessary. Peppers prefer a rich, well-draining, sandy or loamy soil with a pH of between 6.0 and 7.0. Space the plants from 18 to 24 inches (45 to 60 cm.) apart. They'll enjoy a spot near your tomato plants.

Harvesting peppers

Healthy plants should produce fruit throughout late summer. Begin to pick the peppers once they are 3 to 4 inches (7.5 to 10 cm) long, and the fruit is firm and green. If they feel somewhat thin, they aren't ripe. If they feel soggy, it means they've been left on the plant too long. After you harvest the first crop, feel free to fertilize the plants to give them the energy they need to form another crop.

If you prefer the red, yellow, or orange shades of bell peppers, allow the fruit to stay longer on the vine to mature. They'll start out green, but you'll notice they have a thinner feel. Once they begin to take on color, they will thicken and become ripe enough to harvest.

BROCCOLI

Scientific name: Brassica oleracea

Broccoli's large and leathery blue-green leaves surround its mass of flower heads.

The Essentials

planting time spring

light full sun

soil moist, well-draining loamy soil

pH level 6.0 to 7.0

water 1 to 1½ inches (2.5 to 3.5 cm) per week

size 18 to 30 inches (45 to 75 cm) tall; 12 to 24 inches (30 to 60 cm) wide

harvest in 55 to 100 days

Nutrient-rich broccoli (*Brassica oleracea*) is a stout, thick-stemmed plant with large flower heads, usually dark green, branching out from the thick, lighter green stalk. In cookery, it can be eaten raw, lightly sautéed, or used in stir fry, soup, pasta, and rice-based entrées.

Growing and caring for the plants

For a midsummer harvest, start broccoli indoors six to eight weeks before the last frost date. Sow seeds ¼ to ½ inch (6 to 13 mm) deep in a seed-starting mix or soil pellets. Seeds generally germinate within four to seven days when ambient temperatures remain between 45°F and 85°F (7°C and 30°C). For an autumn crop, direct seed into the garden in midsummer.

When growing seedlings indoors, provide plenty of light to prevent plants from becoming leggy. If long stems develop, try repotting the seedlings deeper (up to the first leaves), and then provide more light. Wait until frost-free weather has arrived before transplanting spring seedlings in the garden. Harden off plants by gradually exposing the seedlings to direct sunlight and wind.

When planting outdoors, choose a spot that provides a minimum of six to eight hours of direct sunlight daily. Broccoli prefers an organic, rich soil

that is slightly acidic. Space plants 12 to 24 inches (30 to 60 cm) apart. Fertilize seedlings and young transplants to maintain steady growth. Use a balanced fertilizer—too much nitrogen promotes excessive leaf growth, while potassium and phosphorus encourage bloom development. Water regularly; broccoli grows best in moist, but not soggy, soils. Mulch to control weeds and retain soil moisture levels. To prevent disease and control pests, plant in an area of the garden where you haven't grown Brassicaceae crops for four years. Row covers can protect transplants from cold snaps, pests, and deer.

Harvesting broccoli

The edible part of the plant is the unopened flower. Harvest the central head when it's fully developed, but before the individual buds open into small, yellow flowers. Harvest-ready broccoli will have a tight head, about 4 to 7 inches (10 to18 cm) in diameter, with large, dense flower buds. If the buds begin to open, harvest immediately. If the plant has bolted, it's too late to pick it.

Use a sharp knife to remove the central flower head. Leaving the plant in the ground encourages side shoots to develop. Though smaller

than the central head, these allow you to continue harvesting for a longer period. To maintain the quality of fresh-picked heads, harvest during the cool morning hours, and refrigerate as soon as possible. Unwashed heads can be stored in the refrigerator for three to five days. Blanched broccoli freezes well and maintains its quality for up to 12 months.

SIMILAR PLANTS
Broccolini

Broccolini is a hybrid of European broccoli and Chinese *gai lan*. In Italian, the word *broccolini* means "baby broccoli," hence it's common name. Broccolini has very small florets and a tender stem with large, edible leaves. It has a subtle sweet/peppery flavor. To find out more about broccolini, scan the QR code or follow this link.

"Broccolini Information – How to Grow Baby Broccoli Plants"
LINK: *gkh.us/108839*

BRUSSELS SPROUTS

Scientific name: *Brassica oleracea* var. *gemmifera*

Brussels sprouts are the miniature cabbage-like buds that develop on the plant's stem.

Brussels sprouts (*Brassica oleracea* var. *gemmifera*) have gotten a bad rap. These nutritious, flavor-packed cole crops have too often been vilified, yet these edible buds are extremely tasty if eaten freshly picked. Forerunners of the vegetable we grow today were cultivated at least as far back as ancient Roman days, but the name we now know them as comes from the Belgian city of Brussels, where they have long been popular.

A member of the cabbage family, the sprouts look like miniature cabbages dotted up and down long stems that reach 2 to 3 feet (60 cm to 1 m) in height. Brussels sprouts are the hardiest of the cabbages, and in some regions, such as areas of the Pacific Northwest, growing them over winter is a common practice.

Growing and caring for the plants

Growing Brussels sprouts is much like growing cabbage, kale, or many other members of the cabbage family, which tend to thrive in cool temperatures and do best when the range is between 45°F and 80°F (7°C to 27°C). Because they take so long to mature, your best bet is to plant them in early to late summer, depending on your climate, so that they reach full maturity in the cooler autumn months.

Plan to put them in your garden about three months before the first frost for your area. You will likely have more success growing them from transplants, rather than from seeds planted straight into the garden. This will allow the seedlings to develop in a cooler, shaded environment, which gives them a greater chance of surviving warmer weather outside.

Choose a site for your plot that gets plenty of sun and has well-draining, nitrogen-rich soil. Brussels sprouts are a great candidate for a raised bed, which can help the plants better withstand any temperature fluctuations. If planting from seed, plant the seeds around a ½ inch (1.25 cm) deep and about 3 inches (7.5 cm) apart. When they reach 6 inches (15 cm) on height, thin the plants to about 18 to 24 inches (45 to 90 cm) apart. For larger transplants, place them about 36 inches (90 cm) apart.

Growing Brussels sprouts need plenty of nutrients and water. Once the seedlings reach around 6 inches (15 cm) tall, you can apply an organic fertilizer high in nitrogen, and reapply throughout the season. Water is vital to a good crop, so never let your Brussels sprouts bed become too dry, as this will stress the plants and result in a poor harvest.

The Essentials

planting time early to late summer

light full sun

soil well-draining, loamy soil

pH level 6.0 to 7.0

water 1 to 1½ inches (2.5 to 3.5 cm) per week

size 2 to 3 feet (60 cm to 1 m) tall; 12 inches (30 cm) wide

harvest in 80 to 110 days

Expect to give them about 1 to 1½ inches (2.5 to 3.5 cm) of water per week, depending on your area's rainfall.

Harvesting Brussels sprouts

A mature plant resembles a tall green tower with knobs and leaves—the knobs, or buds, will be the veggie you eat. Once the buds have reached about 1 to 1½ inches (2.5 to 3.5 cm) wide and are firm when you squeeze them, they are ready to harvest.

Use a sharp knife and cut the ready buds off the vertical main stem. Work from the bottom of the plant up; the bottom sprouts will be ready first. You can also twist and pull buds from the stalk if you first remove the leaf below each sprout (after a first harvest, you might see a second crop at the base of the stem). Avoid washing sprouts until you are ready to use them. Fresh-picked Brussels sprouts last for about five days in the refrigerator.

Dig Deeper

LEARN MORE AT GARDENING KNOW HOW

Scan the QR code or follow this link to learn why your Brussels sprouts plants might not be producing.

"Reasons for No Brussels Sprouts on Plants"
LINK: gkh.us/201183

BUSH BEANS

Scientific name: Phaseolus vulgaris

Kidney bean plants, a bush bean variety, mass together in a kitchen garden.

There are two types of garden beans: bush and pole. Bush beans grow up to 2 feet (60 cm) tall and don't need support to stay upright. Pole beans, on the other hand, can grow up to 12 feet (3.7 m) and need a pole or some other support to stay upright (for info on growing pole beans, see page 127).

In general, bush beans take less time than pole beans to produce a crop. Their seeds can be planted within 6 inches (15 cm) of other bush bean plants and will also take up less room in a garden. Some beans have varieties in both bush and pole categories, such as the green bean and pinto bean.

Bush beans can be further broken down into three types: snap beans (where the pods are eaten), green shelling beans (where the beans are eaten green), and dry beans, (where the beans are dried and then re-hydrated before eating).

Growing and caring for the plants

Bush beans grow best in well-drained soil that is rich in organic material, and they need full sun to produce best. Before you start planting bush beans, you should consider amending the soil with bean inoculant, which contains bacteria that help the plants produce better. Your bush beans will still produce if you do not add inoculants to the soil, but it will help you get a more abundant crop.

Plant bush bean seeds about 1½ inches (3.5 cm) deep and 3 inches (7.5 cm) apart. If you are planting more than one row, the rows should be spaced 18 to 24 inches (45 to 60 cm) apart. You can expect beans to germinate in about one to two weeks.

If you would like a continuous harvest of bush beans through the season, plant new bush bean seeds about once every two weeks. Once bush bean plants have started growing, they need little care. Make sure that they get at least 2 to 3 inches (5 to 7.5 cm) of water a week, either from rainwater or a watering system. If you like, you can add compost or fertilizer after the beans have sprouted, but if you started out with organic-rich soil, they will not need it.

Bush beans do not normally have any issues with pests or disease, but on occasion they will suffer from bean mosaic, anthracnose, bean blight, and bean rust. Pests such as aphids, mealybugs, bean weevils, spider mites, and bean leaf beetles can be a problem too. Control is fairly uncomplicated. For example, if you see spider mites, use a hose to spray a hard stream of water on infested leaves. To control bean leaf beetles, it is best to delay planting until mid- to late June. If beetles appear, handpick beetles off the beans and place in a pail of soapy water.

The Essentials

planting time spring to early summer

light full sun

soil well-draining clay or silt loam

pH level 6.0 to 7.0

water 2 inches (5 cm) per square foot per week

size up to 2 feet (60 cm) tall; up to 18 inches (45 cm) wide

harvest in 50 to 55 days

MORE INFO *Bush bean varieties*

- **Lima.** These flat, creamy white beans have a buttery-rich flavor and are ideal for soups, stews, or casseroles. Look for varieties like 'Fordhook', 'Henderson', or 'King of the Garden'.

- **Kidney.** Named for their shape, these reddish-brown beans are often one of the main ingredients in chili con carne. Choose from light red varieties like 'Pink Panther' and 'Blush' or dark red kidney beans such as 'Red Hawk' and 'Fiero'.

- **Northern.** The favored legume for Boston baked beans, great northern beans easily absorb the flavors of spices and other foods in which they are cooked. Check out varieties like 'Orion' or 'Beryl'.

- **Pinto.** Popular in Mexican and Tex-Mex cuisine, the flavor of this oval-shaped bean is best described as earthy or nutty. Uncooked pinto beans have mottled brown and beige skin, which turns all brown when cooked. Select a variety like 'Quincy' or 'Burke' to star in your next batch of refried beans.

- **Black.** Also known as turtle beans, these small, black-skinned beans have a sweet, earthy flavor. Black beans retain their dark color when cooked and add contrast in soups, salads, and pizza. To prevent color bleed, rinse cooked beans before adding to dishes. Popular varieties include 'Eclipse' and 'Black Coco'.

 To find out more about these beans, scan the QR code or follow this link.

"Top 5 Dry Bean Varieties: Grow and Dry Beans at Home"
LINK: gkh.us/171472

A Gallery of
CRUCIFEROUS VEGETABLES

Cruciferous vegetables have recently generated a lot of interest in the health world due to the cancer-fighting compounds they have been found to contain. This has led many gardeners to wonder if they can grow them in their gardens. Good news! You probably already grow at least one type (and more likely several types) of crucifer.

These nutrient-rich and antioxidant-rich vegetables belong to the Cruciferae/Brassicaceae/mustard family, which is mainly made up of the multitudinous *Brassica* genus, but which does include a few other genera. In general, cruciferous vegetables are cool-weather crops with flowers that have four petals, so that they somewhat resemble a cross (*crucifer* means "cross-bearer" in Latin). In most cases, it is the leaves or flower buds of cruciferous vegetables that are eaten, but there are a few examples in which the roots or seeds are also consumed.

As with most vegetables that belong to the same family, crucifers are susceptible to identical diseases and pests, so it's vital not to replant them in the same spot the following season. Allow at least two years before returning them to the original site. Diseases include anthracnose, bacterial leaf spot, black leaf spot, black rot, downy mildew, peppery leaf spot, root-knot, white-spot fungus, and white rust. Insect pests may include aphids, beet armyworm, cabbage looper, cabbage maggot, corn earworm, cutworm, diamondback moth, and nematodes.

This large family is made up of many popular vegetables . . . and then there is broccoli. An American president famously said he "hated it," and many people concurred. Yet it is one of the most versatile of vegetables, which can be steamed, roasted, grilled, riced, added to soups and stir-fries, and eaten raw. Some of broccoli's crucifer brethren are shown here.

BROCCOLI RABE
Broccoli rabe (*B. rapa*) is also known as rapini. This green vegetable's leaves, buds, and stems are all edible. Rapini is associated with Mediterranean cuisine, and it has a somewhat bitter taste. It is, however, a good source of vitamins A, C, and K, as well as iron.

BRUSSELS SPROUTS
Part of the Gemmifera Group of *B. oleracea*, this flavorful leaf vegetable is grown for its edible buds. The sprouts resemble mini cabbages. This is another veggie that people either adore or strenuously avoid. For more information, see page 100.

CABBAGE
Cabbage (*B. oleracea*) is round, compact, and leafy green in color. Smooth-leafed, firm-headed green cabbage is the most common, followed by smooth-leafed purple and crinkle-leafed savoy in both colors. For more information, see page 104.

CAULIFLOWER
Cauliflower is part of the Botrytis Group of *B. oleracea*. The head is composed of a white inflorescence meristem that also comes in hybrids of orange or purple. In the garden, it can be more demanding than its cousins. For more information, see page 106.

CHINESE BROCCOLI
Part of the Alboglabra Group of *B. oleracea*, Chinese broccoli is also known as *gai lan* or Chinese kale. It has thick, flat, glossy blue-green leaves with thick stems and florets similar to broccoli. The taste is strong and bitter. Broccolini is a hybrid between *gai lan* and broccoli.

CHINESE CABBAGE
B. rapa includes two cultivar groups used in Chinese cuisine: Pekinensis (napa cabbage) and Chinensis (bok choy). Napa has broad green leaves that form a compact head; bok choy has smooth, dark green leaf blades that form clusters similar to celery.

COLLARD GREENS
A member of the Viridis Group of *B. oleracea,* this cultivar, with its large, slightly bitter, dark-green leaves, is eaten as a vegetable all over the world. It contains substantial amounts of vitamins K, A, and C, and it is a good source of iron, vitamin B_6, and magnesium.

DAIKON
Also called winter radish, daikon (*Raphanus sativus* var. *longipinnatus*) is a white root vegetable shaped like a large carrot, but it is flavored like a mild radish. It is grown in many Asian countries and is the most popular vegetable in Japan.

HORSERADISH
Horseradish (*Armoracia rusticana*) is a perennial root vegetable used as a spice and condiment. When it is cut or grated, enzymes from within the plant cells digest sinigrin to produce volatile mustard oil—responsible for the piquant taste. For more information, see page 173.

KOHLRABI
A member of the Gongylodes Group of *B. oleracea,* this stout cultivar with a swollen, nearly spherical shape is also called German turnip. The mild, sweet taste of kohlrabi is similar to a broccoli stem or cabbage heart. It can be eaten raw or cooked.

KOMATSUNA
Komatsuna (*B. rapa* var. *perviridis*) is a hardy leafy green. A versatile cool-weather plant, it can be eaten raw, pickled, stir-fried, or boiled, and it can be used fresh in salads or added to soups. The leaves can also be prepared and consumed at all stages of growth.

MIZUNA
Mizuna (*B. rapa* var. *niposinica*)—also known as Japanese mustard, spider mustard, or kyona—is a feathery crucifer with glossy dark green leaves that is eaten cooked or raw. Its mild mustard flavor is peppery, much like arugula, and it is slightly bitter, like frisée lettuce.

MUSTARD
The edible leaves, stems, and seeds of the brown mustard (*B. juncea*) appear in numerous world cuisines. Spicy brown mustard comes from this plant's seeds. The thin, tender leaves have a peppery and slightly bitter flavor. For more information, see page 187.

ROMANESCO BROCCOLI
This cool-season plant features upright, spiraling chartreuse fractals on its cauliflower-like head. The flavor, however, is similar to that of broccoli—mild, nutty, and sweet. It is actually an edible flower bud of *B. oleracea* that was first cultivated in 16th-century Italy.

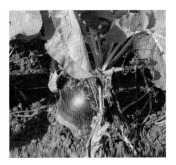

RUTABAGA
Also known as a swede, Swedish turnip, neep, rwden/rwdins, and turnip, this root veggie should not be confused with the related white turnip. Rutabaga (*B. napus*) originated as a hybrid between a cabbage and a turnip. For more information, see page 136.

TURNIP
Also called white turnip, the turnip (*B. rapa* subsp. *rapa*) is a fleshy root vegetable grown in most temperate climates. It has white skin, except for the pink or green part that can protrude above the ground. For more information, see page 146.

WASABI
Wasabi (*Eutrema japonicum* or *Wasabia japonica*), also called Japanese horseradish, is a bog plant found along stream beds in Japan's river valleys. A green paste made from the ground rhizomes is a pungent condiment for sushi and other foods.

Dig Deeper

LEARN MORE AT GARDENING KNOW HOW

Scan the QR code or follow the link to find out more about growing cruciferous vegetables.

"Types of Cabbage – Different Cabbages to Grow in Gardens"
LINK: gkh.us/134704

CABBAGE

Scientific name: Brassica oleracea var. capitata

A healthy white cabbage is ready for a summertime harvest. Also called Dutch cabbage, this variety is a green cabbage with pale-colored, tightly packed leaves.

Cabbage (*Brassica oleracea* var. *capitata*) is a cool-season crop suited to both summer and autumn harvests. A biennial typically grown as an annual, garden-grown cabbage isn't too fussy—knowing when to plant it and the conditions it likes best will reward you with an amazing vegetable that is great in salads, stir-fries, and countless other recipes.

The leaves of cabbage tightly wrap around one another, forming round, flattened, or pointed heads. In the center of the head is a short, thick stem or core. Available in a variety of green shades, as well as white, purple, or red, its shapes and textures vary widely. There are many different types, so be sure to choose one that's suitable for your growing region.

Growing and caring for the plants

Cabbage needs rich, fertile soil, plenty of water, and good fertilization. Choose a spot where you have not grown cabbage, broccoli, cauliflower, turnips, rutabaga, or Brussels sprouts for the last four years. It will do well in full sun or partial shade, as long as it gets about six hours of full sunlight each day. Several

varieties are available with different maturity times, which will determine when you should plant. For a summer harvest, start seeds indoors, sowing about four to eight weeks before the last spring frost. Early cabbage should be transplanted as soon as possible, so that it can mature before summertime heat. For an autumn harvest, in most areas you can direct-sow late cabbage seeds outdoors (or plant transplants) in mid- to late summer.

To start seeds indoors, plant at a depth of ¼ inch (6 mm). Keep seeds moist, and thin young seedlings to give them space to grow. When the first true leaf appears, apply fertilizer, using a half-strength starter solution once a week. In about three weeks, you can begin the hardening-off process. Hardened plants can be very tolerant of frosts.

When transplanting into your garden, space seedlings 12 to 24 inches (30 to 60 cm) apart to give them plenty of room to develop large heads. Early varieties will grow up to 3 pounds (1 kg). Later varieties can produce heads that weigh more than 8 pounds (4 kg).

Fertile soil gives cabbage a good start. Adding nitrogen after the plants are well established will help them mature. Its roots grow at a fairly shallow level, but it's important to keep the soil moist so that your vegetables will be juicy and sweet.

Harvesting cabbage

When a cabbage head has reached the size you like, cut it at the base. Don't wait until the head splits—a split head will attract disease and pests. After harvesting, remove the entire plant, including its root system, from the soil.

Harvested cabbage needs cold, moist conditions that are cooler than your fridge's. If you have a root cellar that maintains a temperature between 32°F and 40°F (0°C to 4°C) with 95 percent humidity, they can keep for months. Another solution for using your excess harvest is to ferment cabbage in tasty recipes like sauerkraut or kimchi.

CARROT

Scientific name: *Daucus carota sativus*

Harvest-ready carrots break through the garden's soil. These super-healthful veggies offer a sweet taste with a crisp texture that's delicious whether eaten cooked or raw.

The Essentials

planting time spring to late summer

light full sun to partial shade

soil well-draining soil that has a good mixture of clay and sand

pH level 5.5 to 7.5

water 1 to 2 inches (2.5 to 5 cm) per week

size 1 foot (30 cm) tall; 9 inches (23 cm) wide

harvest in 50 to 80 days

A domesticated form of the wild carrot (the European and southwestern Asian native *Daucus carota*), the garden carrot (*D. carota sativus*) is a root vegetable. Although we most often associate a bright orange color with this vegetable, purple, black, red, white, and yellow cultivars exist. Originally cultivated for its leaves and seeds, it is now most often harvested for its taproot, although the plant's stems and leaves are also edible. The carrots available today have been selectively bred to produce bigger, less woody, and tastier taproots than their wild progenitor.

The carrot is a biennial member of the umbellifer family, Apiaceae, which is most notably distinguished by the characteristic inflorescence of tightly aggregated flowers in an umbrella-like shape. The plant first appears as a rosette of leaves while it builds up an enlarged taproot. It can mature as quickly as 90 days after sowing the seed or as long as 120 days. The mature taproot is prized for its high quantities of alpha- and beta-carotene, as well as its vitamin A, vitamin K, and vitamin B$_6$ content.

Growing and caring for the plants

Carrots grow best in cool temperatures. The night temperature should be dropping to about 55°F (13°C), and the daytime temperatures should be averaging 75°F (24°C) for optimum growth. Carrots grow in small gardens, and they can accept a little bit of shade.

Before planting, clear soil surfaces of trash, rocks, and large pieces of bark. Finer pieces of plant material can be mixed down into the soil for enrichment. The soil should be a sandy, well-drained loam. Heavy soils cause carrots to mature slowly, and the roots will end up unattractive and rough. Rocky soil leads to poor-quality roots.

Till or dig up the area to soften and aerate the ground to make it easier for the roots to grow long and straight. Fertilize the soil with 1 cup (128 g) of 10-20-10 for every 10 feet (3 m) of row you plant. You can use a rake to mix the soil and fertilizer.

Plant in rows that are 1 to 2 feet (30 to 60 cm) apart. Plant the seeds about ½ inch (1.25 cm) deep and 1 to 2 inches (2.5 to 5 cm) apart. When deciding how many carrots to plant, assume you will get about 1 pound (0.5 kg) of carrots from each 1-foot (30-cm) row.

When the plants are 4 inches (10 cm) high, thin them to 2 inches (5 cm) apart. You might find that some of the carrots are already large enough to eat. Keep your plants free of weeds, which is especially important when they are small. Weeds will take away nutrients from the roots and cause poor development.

Harvesting carrots

Carrots grow continuously after you plant them. They also don't take very long to mature. You can start the first crop in mid-spring, after threat of frost has passed, and continue to plant new seeds every two weeks for continuous harvest through the autumn. You can begin to harvest carrots when their taproots are about finger sized. You can, however, allow them to stay in the soil until winter, if you mulch the garden well. To check the size of your carrots, gently remove some dirt from the top of the root. To harvest, gently lift the carrot from the soil.

Editor's Tip

Parsnip (*Pastinaca sativa*), another member of the carrot family, can be mistaken for a white carrot because of its similar size and shape. Consider growing this root veggie with your carrot crop. Often used in the same recipes, the spicy bite of the parsnip complements the sweeter taste of the carrot. For information on growing parsnips, see page 125.

CAULIFLOWER

Scientific name: Brassica oleracea var. botrytis

Cauliflower is finicky about its growing temperatures, which makes it a challenge for beginners. The extra care is worth the effort to enjoy this versatile vegetable.

The Essentials

planting time spring; midsummer

light full sun

soil rich, well-draining soil

pH level 6.5 to 7.5

water 1 to 2 inches (2.5 to 5 cm) per week

size 12 to 30 inches (30 to 75 cm) tall; 12 to 24 inches (30 to 60 cm) wide

harvest in 50 to 100 days

Cauliflower (*Brassica oleracea* var. *botrytis*) is a cool-season annual of the Brassicaceae family, which includes broccoli. In fact, cauliflower is often referred to as "heading broccoli." But unlike broccoli, which produces multiple side shoots, cauliflower only produces a single head—which means you have one chance to get it right. With its reputation as one of the more temperamental crops, many gardeners don't bother growing this vegetable, yet knowing the best time to plant and when to harvest cauliflower means you up your chances of success.

Growing and caring for the plants

Of all the cole crops, cauliflower is the most sensitive to temperature. It thrives in temperatures of around 60°F to 65°F (16°C to 18°C) and no higher than 75°F (24°C). When temperatures exceed 75°F, the plants have a tendency to button (prematurely develop heads) or bolt (go to seed). The best time to plant most varieties of cauliflower is in the spring so that they grow and produce their flower heads before summer's

hottest days, although some varieties have been developed that are suited for midsummer planting for an autumn harvest. Early-maturing varieties are more susceptible to buttoning than later-maturing cultivars.

For spring-sown cauliflower, start seed indoors in April. For autumn crops, start seed in July, either sown indoors or direct-sown into the garden. Do not transplant any earlier than two to three weeks prior to the average frost-free date for your area. This can be rather tricky, in that it is important to start cauliflower early enough so that it matures before the heat arrives but not so early that cold spring temperatures damage the plants.

Sow seeds ¼ inch (6 mm) deep in peat pots or in furrows in well-draining potting soil. Once the seeds have germinated, continue to grow them in an area of direct sun or under grow lights, and maintain a temperature of 60°F (16°C). Keep the seedlings moist.

Harden off seedlings for five days to a week before transplanting them outside by setting them in the shade,

and then gradually exposing them to longer periods of sun. Transplant on a cool, cloudy day or late in the afternoon to avoid stressing the plants. Plant the seedlings 2 feet (60 cm) apart in rows that are 30 to 36 inches (75 cm to 1 m) apart. Fertilize at transplanting with a liquid fertilizer according to the manufacturer's instructions and again when the plants are established, side dressing with nitrogen-rich compost. Keep the plants moist but not soggy. Mulch around young plants to help retard weed growth and retain moisture.

Green, orange, and purple cultivars need sun to develop their colors, but white cauliflower should be blanched to prevent it turning yellow and protect it from sun-scald. It will also keep it from developing a bitter taste. To blanch, watch until the cauliflower head reaches golf-to-tennis-ball size (about 3 inches, or 7.5 cm, in diameter). Then, tie the outer leaves loosely over the developing head with a soft cloth or nylon.

Harvesting cauliflower

Cauliflower is ready to harvest a week or two after blanching. Harvest when the heads are more than 6 inches (15 cm) across, but before the flower parts begin to separate. Cut the head from the plant with a large knife, leaving at least one set of leaves to protect it.

Store harvested heads in a plastic bag in the refrigerator, where they should last for about a week. For long-term storage, you can also freeze or pickle the heads.

CELERY

Scientific name: Apium graveolens

A row of healthy celery plants shows their bright green stalks and leaves. Celery is a finicky grower, however, and only thrives if all its exacting needs are met.

The Essentials

planting time early spring

light full sun

soil well-draining, compost-rich soil

pH level 5.8 and 6.8

water 1 to 2 inches (2.5 to 5 cm) per week

size 8 to 15 inches (20 to 38 cm) tall; 6 to 12 inches (15 to 30 cm) wide

harvest in 130 to 140 days

Harvesting celery is easily done by cutting the stalks below where they are joined together. You can also harvest the leaves for use as a flavoring in soups and stews. A few plants can be left to flower or go to seed, if desired, for use in recipes and propagation of future crops.

Celery (*Apium graveolens*) is generally considered to be a very challenging vegetable to grow. It has a very long growing season but a very low tolerance for both heat and cold, making it difficult to keep alive through changing seasons while protecting it from the elements. It has been cultivated for thousands of years, although it was first valued for medicinal rather than culinary uses.

Growing and caring for the plants

Celery has a very long maturity time, so unless you live in an area with long growing seasons, start celery seeds indoors at least 8 to 10 weeks before the last frost date in your region.

The seeds are tiny and tricky to plant. If you have trouble handling them, mix them with sand, and sprinkle the sand-seed mix over the potting soil. Cover the seeds with just a little bit of soil—celery seeds like to be planted very shallowly. Once the seeds have sprouted and are large enough, either thin the seedlings or separate them out to their own pots.

Once the temperatures outside are consistently above 50°F (10°C), you can begin transplanting your celery seedlings into the garden. Remember that celery is very temperature sensitive, so don't plant it out too early.

Plant your celery where it will get six hours of sun. In slightly warmer areas, however, it may also need to be shaded during the hottest hours of the day.

Celery should be planted in rich, well-draining soil. This plant also needs a lot of water; make sure to keep the soil consistently moist by watering deeply and frequently. Celery can't tolerate drought of any kind. If the ground isn't kept consistently moist, it will negatively affect its taste. Water the soil only at the base of the plant, however, to avoid risking mildew or fungal infections. You will also need to regularly fertilize the plant.

Harvesting celery

Picking celery should begin when the lower stalks are at least 6 inches (15 cm) long from ground level to the first node. This will usually be three to five months after planting. The stalks should still be close together, forming a compact bunch or cone; the upper stalks should reach 18 to 24 inches (45 to 60 cm) in height and 3 inches (7.5 cm) in diameter when they are ready for harvest.

SIMILAR PLANTS
Celeriac

A variant of celery, celeriac (*Apium graveolens* var. *rapaceum*), also called celery root, knob celery, and turnip-rooted celery, is cultivated for its edible stem and shoots. In cooking, it is treated as a root vegetable and can be roasted, stewed, blanched, and mashed. Sliced, it appears in soups, casseroles, and other savory dishes, adding a slightly nutty, green taste. The flavorful leaves are often used as a garnish. Growing celeriac is basically the same as growing celery.

CORN

Scientific name: Zea mays

A row of maturing corn plants stand tall in a kitchen garden, with their soil protected with plastic sheeting.

The Essentials

planting time early spring to summer

light full sun

soil light, well-draining sandy or loamy soil (early crop); silty or clay soil (later crop)

pH level 5.8 to 6.2

water thoroughly once every 7 to 10 days

size 6 to 8 feet (1.8 to 2.4 m) tall; 1 to 2 feet (30 to 60 cm) wide

harvest in 60 to 100 days

Corn (*Zea mays*), also called maize, was first domesticated by indigenous peoples in southern Mexico about 10,000 years ago. Since then, it has become a staple food in many parts of the world, and these days this annual is one of the most popular vegetables in home gardens. Who doesn't love corn on the cob drizzled with butter on a hot summer day? Furthermore, it can be blanched and frozen, so you can enjoy corn from your garden even in winter.

The two types are traditional and sweet corn. Traditional, or field, corn has a starchier flavor and a slightly harder cob than sweet corn, which is softer and has a pleasantly sweet taste. Sweet corn is a warm-season crop and easy to grow. You can choose either sweet corn or supersweet corn plants, but don't grow them together; different varieties can cross-pollinate, resulting in starchy corn.

Corn can be ready for harvest at 60 days, 70 days, or 90 days. One method for corn planting is to have a continuous growing season by planting several types with varying maturation intervals: for example, plant an early variety near the beginning of the season, wait a couple weeks to plant another early variety, and then plant a third, later variety. You can also plant the same kind staggered by 10 to 14 days so that you have a continuous crop of fresh sweet corn to eat all summer long.

Growing and caring for the plants

Corn thrives growing in full sunshine. If you want to grow corn from seed, plant them in well-drained soil, which will dramatically increase your yield. Make sure the soil has plenty of organic matter, and fertilize before you plant.

Wait until there have been plenty of frost-free days before putting corn into the soil; otherwise, your crop will be sparse. It is best to plant sweet corn in soil that is warm—at least above 55°F (13°C). For super sweet corn, be sure the soil is at least 65°F (18°C). Plant the seeds ½ inch (1.25 cm) deep in cool, moist soil and at least 1 to 2 inches (2.5 to 5 cm) deep in warm, dry soil. To protect plants from cross-pollination, plant the rows 12 inches (30 cm) apart with at least 30 to 36 inches (75 to 90 cm) between rows.

Mulch will help keep your corn weed-free and will retain moisture during hot, dry weather. Cultivate the rows shallowly, so you do not injure the roots. If there has been no rain, make sure to water the plants so that they get enough moisture.

Harvesting sweet corn

Picking sweet corn is an easy task. Each stalk should produce at least one ear of corn, which will be ready to pick about 20 days after you see signs of the first silk growing. You can then just grab the ear, twist, pull in a downward motion, and quickly snap it off. Some stalks will then grow a second ear.

MORE INFO *Varieties of corn*

There are many sweet corn varieties, from hybrids to heirlooms, which ripen at different times of the season in various colors. Here are just some of the best kinds of corn so you can get cracking on your garden planning.

- **Standard sweet corn.** This classic group is one of the most popular. The flavor and texture simply sing "summer," but the drawback is that they don't store for long. There are early- and late-maturing hybrids. Some of the standard varieties are the white 'Silver Queen', yellow 'Earlivee', and bicolor 'Utopia'.

- **Sugar-enhanced corn.** These varieties may have up to 18 percent higher sugar content than the standard sugar types. They hold better than sweet varieties, but the skin around the kernels is more tender and sensitive to damage. Some of the better varieties are the golden 'Sweet Riser', the yellow 'Legend', and white 'Sweet Ice'.

- **Supersweet corn.** Supersweet is also called shrunken corn due to the appearance of the dried kernels. It contains twice the amount of sugar as traditional sweet corn varieties. Because it converts sugar to starch much more slowly, it can be stored far longer. Common supersweet corn varieties include yellow 'Krispy King', bicolor 'Candy Corner', and yellow 'Sweetie'.

CUCUMBER

Scientific name: Cucumis sativus

A cucumber plant trained on a pole support. The ripe green fruit is ready for harvesting.

Cucumbers (*Cucumis sativus*) are warm-weather annuals believed to have originated on the Indian subcontinent and cultivated for at least 3,000 years. Technically fruit, their savory flavor often has them grouped with vegetables. They are now summer favorites, with a crisp, refreshing taste and texture that is great for pickling, tossing in salads, or eating straight off the vine.

There are two main types: slicing and pickling cucumbers. The slicing types are long and usually grow to about 6 or 8 inches (15 or 20 cm) in length, while the pickling types are shorter, reaching around 3 to 4 inches (8 to 10 cm) once mature. Within these categories, there are hundreds of cultivars with various shapes, sizes, flavors, growing habits, and climate preferences.

Growing and caring for the plants

You can start your cucumbers indoors from seed, either purchased or saved and harvested from previous plants, in peat pots, or small flats. Transplant to the garden a couple weeks thereafter, but only when all danger of frost has passed. Before you move them to the garden, harden off the plants in a protected location to lessen any stress that might occur during transplanting. During cool periods, cucumbers can be covered with plant protectors, as well.

Cucumbers like warm, humid weather and plenty of sunlight. Choose a sunny site that has adequate drainage and fertile soil. Good soil will have plenty of organic matter, such as compost. Adding compost to the soil will help get your cucumbers off to a good start, and applying an organic fertilizer, such as manure, will help give the plants nutrients during growth. When you begin preparing the soil, remove any rocks, sticks, or other debris, and then mix ample amounts of organic matter and fertilizer into the soil.

Cucumbers can be planted in hills or rows about 1 inch (2.5 cm) deep, and then thinned as needed. As a vine crop, they usually require a lot of space. In large gardens, the vines can spread throughout rows; within smaller gardens, you can train them to climb on a fence or trellis. Training cucumbers on a support will reduce space and lift the fruit off the soil, while also giving your garden a neater appearance. The bush or compact varieties are quite suitable for growing in small spaces or even cultivating in containers.

Cucumbers will grow quickly with little care, other than adequate irrigation—they need 1 inch (2.5 cm) of water every week. You can also regularly feed them with a water-soluble plant food that both feeds the plants and supplies them with beneficial microbes. Apply it directly to the soil around plant stems, or work a continuous-release fertilizer into the soil.

Harvesting cucumbers

Once the fruit begins to appear, check your vines daily because cucumbers can enlarge very quickly. If you let them get too big, not only will they have a bitter taste, but the plant will also stop producing. The more you harvest, the more fruit the vines will yield. To harvest, cut the stem above the cucumber, using a knife or clippers.

Dig Deeper

LEARN MORE AT GARDENING KNOW HOW

To find out the best time to harvest your cucumbers, just scan the QR code or follow the link below

 "Cucumber Harvest: Learn When and How to Harvest Cucumbers"
LINK: gkh.us/16215

The Essentials

planting time late winter or early spring; autumn

light full sun

soil loose, well draining soil, well supplied with organic matter and plant nutrients

pH level 6.0 to 6.5

water 1 inch (2.5 cm) per week

size 2 to 8 feet (60 cm to 2.4 m) tall; 1 to 3 feet (30 cm to 1 m) wide

harvest in 50 to 70 days

EGGPLANT

Scientific name: Solanum melongena

A purple eggplant ripens in the bright sunlight. Its self-pollinating flower is typical of the nightshade family, with a star shape in various shades of violet.

The Essentials

planting time spring

light full sun

soil well-draining sandy loam

pH level 5.5 to 7.5

water 1 to 2 inches (2.5 to 5 cm) per week

size 2 to 4 feet (60 cm to 1.2 m) tall; 1 to 3 feet (30 cm to 1 m) wide

harvest in 65 to 120 days

Eggplant (*Solanum melongena*), also known as the aubergine or brinjal, is a member of the nightshade family that is grown worldwide for its edible fruit. There are several varieties to choose from, with a range of sizes, shapes, and colors. The most familiar is the glossy, deep purple variety with its egg-shaped fruit that reveals creamy white flesh that has a spongy and "meaty" texture. White cultivars that are longer in shape are also available. Eggplant is classified botanically as a berry, but it is typically used as a vegetable in cooking.

Growing eggplants, a perennial more commonly grown as an annual, can be so rewarding when the time comes to harvest these tasty, versatile plants. By understanding what they need to thrive, you can ensure a good harvest.

Growing and caring for the plants

Like their close cousins tomatoes, eggplants are hot-weather vegetables. They grow during short, high-temperature seasons. If starting from seeds, make sure the soil is between 75°F and 85°F (24°C and 30°C), and use a heating mat if necessary. The seeds need these warm temperatures and two to three weeks to germinate.

Start seeds in soil ¼ inch (6 mm) deep. Thin seedlings so they are 2 to 3 inches (5 to 7.5 cm) apart. You can move the young plants into the garden once temperatures stay reliably above 50°F (10°C). Knowing where to plant eggplant is important. Find a spot in the garden where they will get full sun. The soil should be fertile and well drained. Amend if necessary to make sure the plants will get enough nutrients and will not sit in standing water. Space the transplants about 18 inches (45 cm) from one another and in rows that are 36 inches (1 m) apart.

Eggplants do best when the soil has a consistent moisture level. Water them regularly, especially when the plants are young so that they develop deep roots. Avoid overhead watering to prevent disease, but consider using mulch to keep the soil moist and warm and to keep weeds down. Generally, the plants should get 1 or 2 inches (2.5 or 5 cm) of rain or watering per week.

Harvesting eggplant

You can wait until each eggplant is a mature size for its variety to harvest, but you can also pick those that are not fully mature. When smaller, the fruits will be tender in texture and flavor. Don't let eggplants stay on the plant past maturity; they will not retain their quality. To harvest eggplants, use shears or scissors. If you pull them off, you will most likely damage the plant, the fruit, or both.

Eggplants are always best eaten fresh, and when cut, oxidation will rapidly turn the flesh brown. They also don't keep well, so use your harvested fruits soon after picking, although you can store them uncut for about a week in the refrigerator. Pickling is possible, but other preservation methods rarely result in good quality. For this reason, it makes sense to start picking the fruits when they are smaller and immature to extend the harvest period.

Link to the Experts

READ MORE AT GARDENING KNOW HOW

Flowers are key to an eggplant harvest. Follow these links to be sure your plants have the best chance of thriving.

- "Can You Hand Pollinate an Eggplant: Tips for Pollinating Eggplants by Hand"
  LINK: gkh.us/69285
- "What to Do for Eggplant Blossoms Drying Out and Falling Off"
  LINK: gkh.us/447

GARLIC

Scientific name: *Allium sativum*

A gardener carefully unearths a garlic bulb with a pitchfork. Garlic plants grow throughout the winter, with heads ready for late-spring to midsummer harvesting.

Garlic (*Allium sativum*), a perennial native of South Asia, Central Asia, and northeastern Iran, has thousands of years of history as a cultivated plant used as a food flavoring and as a traditional medicine.

This member of the genus *Allium* is a close relative of the onion, shallot, scallion, leek, and chive. It is just about essential to a kitchen garden—fresh garlic is a strongly flavored seasoning that crops up in cuisines from all around the world. An added plus is that garlic plants (perennials most often grown as annuals) are easy to grow and require very little care once in the ground.

You can choose to plant either softneck or hardneck varieties, which get their names from their types of stalks. Softneck garlic has pliable stalks (which make attractive displays when braided for storage), and hardneck garlic has woody, stiff stalks.

Growing and caring for the plants

Garlic plants need cool temperatures to thrive. As you would with many spring- or summer-flowering bulbs, you should plant garlic in the autumn. Where there are cold winters, you can plant four to six weeks before the ground freezes. In areas with mild winters, you can plant through winter but before February.

Before planting garlic, properly prepare the soil. Unless your soil is naturally loose, add a lot of organic matter, such as compost or well-aged manure to produce large, healthy heads.

Most gardeners grow garlic using bulbs rather than seeds. Choose large, undamaged bulbs to plant; these will produce the biggest heads. Separate the bulbs into individual cloves (just as you do when cooking, but without peeling them), leaving the "paper" on them.

Plant each clove to a depth of about 1 inch (2.5 cm). The fatter end that was at the bottom of the bulb should be at the bottom of the hole. If your winters are colder, you can plant more deeply. Space the cloves 2 to 4 inches (5 to 10 cm) apart in rows spaced 12 to 18 inches (30 to 45 cm) apart. If you want bigger garlic bulbs, you can try spacing cloves on a 6-by-12-inch (15-x-30 cm) grid.

While the plants are green and growing, fertilize them, but stop fertilizing after they begin to "bulb-up." If you feed your garlic too late, it won't go dormant.

If there isn't much rain in your area, water the plants while they are growing just as you would any other green plant.

The Essentials

planting time autumn, late winter

light full sun

soil loose, well-draining sandy to loamy soil

pH level 6.0 to 7.0

water ½ to 1 inch (1.25 to 2.5 cm) per week

size 12 to 18 inches (30 to 45 cm) tall; 6 to 12 inches (15 to 30 cm) wide

harvest in 90 days

Harvesting garlic

Garlic is ready to harvest once the leaves turn brown. You can start checking when five or six green leaves are left.

The harvested garlic will need to cure before you store it. Make sure to bundle eight to a dozen together by their leaves, and hang them in a place to dry.

Editor's Picks

Garlic varieties are divided into two categories: softneck and hardneck. These lists give you a few ideas of cultivars you can try for either one.

Softneck varieties
- 'Early Italian'
- 'Inchelium Red'
- 'Walla Walla Early'

Hardneck varieties
- 'Amish Rocambole'
- 'California Early'
- 'Chesnok Red'
- 'Purple Stripe'

To learn about the differences between the two, scan the QR code or follow the link.

"Softneck vs Hardneck Garlic – Should I Grow Softneck or Hardneck Garlic"
LINK: *gkh.us/157496*

SPOTLIGHT ON:

GROWING ALLIUMS

Alliums (the general term for this vegetable group) belong to the Amaryllidaceae, or amaryllis family, which are herbaceous, mostly perennial and bulbous flowering plants. Created in 1805, the family currently contains approximately 1,600 species, with onions and chives falling into the subfamily Allioideae, with 18 genera. The leaves of these plants are typically linear with bisexual, symmetrical flowers arranged in umbels. The pungent odor associated with alliums comes from the presence of allyl sulfide compounds. Onions, one of the staple alliums, are used to flavor sauces, gravies, soups, stews, curries, and casseroles, and as raw garnishes. Few ingredients add piquancy to salads, burgers, and sandwiches as raw onions; few add depth to cooked dishes as caramelized onions.

Most onions are sold as seedlings in bare-root bundles; each plant will start growing within days after planting. If you can't plant right away, remove the onions' bindings, and place them in a bucket with 2 inches (5 cm) of moist soil at the bottom. Keep them in a cool, bright place but out of direct sunlight until you are ready to plant.

CONTROLLING ONION DISEASES

A wet growing season is bad news for your onion crop. Many diseases, most of them fungal, invade the garden and ruin onions during warm, moist weather. Most onion diseases have similar symptoms, unfortunately, including spots and lesions on leaves and bulbs, areas that look water soaked, and browning foliage. There is no treating these diseases, so focus on protecting next year's crop.

- Place your onion patch on a three- or four-year rotation. Grow other, non-allium crops there in the intervening years.
- Discard culls and other organic debris promptly. Fungi overwinter in garden debris.
- Avoid fertilizing with nitrogen after midseason: it delays the development of bulbs and gives diseases more time to infest your crop.
- Be careful with cultivating tools: cuts in bulbs and foliage create entry points for disease spores.
- Buy certified disease-free seeds, plants, and sets.
- Pull out and discard diseased bulbs. Disease spores spread by wind and by water splashing soil onto the plant; they are also carried on your hands, clothing, and tools.
- Stop disease spores from invading onions after harvest by spreading them on a table or screen to dry, so the air circulates freely around them.

Alliums are easy-care bulbs with pretty flower heads that rise above the foliage, often attracting pollinators to the garden.

Allium cepa Varieties

Bulb onions (*Allium cepa*) vary slightly in flavor, texture, and color, but most of these kinds of onions can be satisfactorily substituted for one another in recipes.

BERMUDA ONION
Large, flat, and mostly white, these sweet, mild onions were first brought to Bermuda in 1616 and soon became a staple crop. They have a sweet, mild taste and can be eaten raw or stuffed, roasted, or French-fried.

PEARL ONION
Also called button, baby, or silverskin onions and creamers, these are a small, sweet variety of bulb onions. Rounded, their diameter ranges from ¼ to ½ inch (6 to 13 mm). Cocktail onions are pearl onions pickled in brine.

RED ONION
These medium-to-large *A. cepa* cultivars, also called purple onions, have purplish red skin and white flesh tinged with red. They are used in cooking and provide tangy, sharp flavor. They can also be eaten raw or pickled.

SWEET ONION
Their low sulfur and high water content mean these pale-colored onions lack the pungency of other varieties. Sweet onions are ideal for deep frying, for making "blooming onions," and for roasting.

YELLOW ONION
This all-purpose variety, astringent and sweet, is the size of a fist, with tough skin and meaty layers. It has a harsh taste that is softened by cooking. Spanish onions are a type of yellow onion, which is milder and often eaten raw.

WHITE ONION
These thin-skinned, rounded onions are more tender than yellow onions and have a sharper, more pungent flavor. They can be cooked in the same ways as yellow onions, as well as minced and added to raw salsas and chutneys.

Other Members of Genus *Allium*

LEEK
Cultivars of the broadleaf wild leek, leeks (*A. ampeloprasum*) are edible bundles of leaf sheaths. With a sweet oniony flavor, leeks are often used in salads, soups, and as a side dish on their own.

EGYPTIAN WALKING ONION
Also called tree onions (*A. × proliferum*), these have clusters of bulblets instead of flowers. The name comes from the bulblets' habit of bending to the ground and taking root.

SCALLION
Also called green onions, scallions (*A. cepa*) are young onions harvested early, before the bulbs form. The white stalks offer an intense oniony bite, while the leaves taste fresh and are milder.

SHALLOT
Shallots (*A. ascalonium*) are small onions with a distinctive tapered shape and skins of a coppery brown; the skins can also be reddish or gray. Their delicate flavor is unique among alliums.

GLOBE ARTICHOKE

Scientific name: *Cynara cardunculus* var. *scolymus*

An artichoke left unharvested forms a purple-colored thistle-like flower. Lovely to look at and delicious to eat, the globe artichoke is a herbaceous perennial that makes a worthy addition to a vegetable or ornamental garden.

Gardeners tend to grow plants either for their visual appeal in a plot or because they produce tasty fruits and vegetables. The globe artichoke is a rarity that is valued for both: not only is it a highly nutritious food, the plant is also so attractive that it is often grown as an ornamental specimen.

Globe artichokes (*Cynara cardunculus* var. *scolymus*) are an edible variety of thistle. The flower bud, the edible part of the plant, develops on a tall stem from the center of the plant. At the base of the bud is the tender, flavorful center known as the "heart." Green globe artichoke plants produce three to four buds, roughly 2 to 5 inches (5 to 12.5 cm) in diameter. If the artichoke bud is not harvested, it will open into an eye-catching thistle-like purple flower.

Growing and caring for the plants

These plants require a 120-day growing season, so direct sowing of seeds in the spring is not recommended. Instead, you should start plants indoors between late January and early March. Use a planter that is about 3 or 4 inches (7.5 or 10 cm)

and a nutrient-rich starting soil. Artichokes are slow to germinate, so allow three to four weeks for the seeds to sprout. Warm temperatures of 70°F to 75°F (21°C to 24°C) and slightly moist soil will improve germination speed. Once they have sprouted, keep the soil moist but not soggy. Artichokes are heavy feeders, so you should apply a diluted fertilizer solution weekly. Once the seedlings are three to four weeks old, cull the weakest plants, leaving only one per pot.

When the seedlings are ready for transplanting, select a sunny location that has good drainage and rich, fertile soil. Prior to planting, test the soil and amend if necessary. These plants prefer a neutral soil pH between 6.5 and 7.5. When planting, space the plants a minimum of 4 feet (1.2 m) apart.

After transplanting, they need little extra maintenance. They do best with yearly applications of organic compost and a balanced fertilizer during the growing season. To overwinter in areas that receive heavy frost, cut back artichoke plants, and protect the crowns with a thick layer of mulch or straw.

The Essentials

planting time early to mid-spring

light full sun

soil light, fertile, well-draining sandy or loamy soil

pH level 6.5 to 7.0

water deeply, between 1 to 3 times per week

size 3 to 6 feet (1 to 1.8 m) tall; 4 to 5 feet (1.2 to 1.5 m) wide

harvest in 85 to 120 days

Harvesting globe artichokes

Artichokes are ready for harvesting in mid- to late summer and will continue well into the first frost. Harvest the buds once they reach full size, just before the bracts begin to spread open.

To harvest, cut off the bud, along with 3 inches (7.5 cm) of stem. After harvesting, continue to water and feed the plants. After several frosts, cut back the artichoke plant, and mulch heavily.

Editor's Picks

There is a wealth of choices when it comes to varieties of globe artichoke to plant. Here is a small sampling of some that work well in home gardens.

- 'Colorado Star' is a fast-maturing variety with purple-green to deep purple buds.
- 'Emerald' is a thornless variety with bright green buds.
- 'Imperial Star' is an early-harvester variety with a sweet, mild flavor.
- 'Purple Italian Globe' is an heirloom variety from Italy.
- 'Tavor', an early maturer, has purple-tipped green heads.
- 'Violet de Provence' is a gorgeous purple heirloom variety from France.

JERUSALEM ARTICHOKE

Scientific name: *Helianthus tuberosus*

The vegetable part of the Jerusalem artichoke, also known as the sunchoke, is just a lumpy tuber, but the plant makes a pretty garden display with its sunny yellow flowers.

Many gardeners are unfamiliar with Jerusalem artichokes (*Helianthus tuberous*), although they might know them by their common name, sunchoke. Jerusalem artichokes are native to North America and have little in common with the more familiar globe artichokes found in your local supermarket.

These plants are perennial relatives of the sunflower. The edible portions are the fat, misshapen tubers that grow belowground. These tubers are dug in the autumn, and they can be cooked like a potato—either fried, baked, or boiled, or eaten raw—and they have a flavor and crunch similar to water chestnuts.

Jerusalem artichoke plants are tall, attractive garden additions. They can grow 6 to 10 feet (1.8 to 3 m) high and are covered with a profusion of flowers in late August and September. The flowers are a bright and cheerful golden yellow. The leaves are about 3 inches (7.5 cm) wide and 4 to 8 inches (10 to 20 cm) long.

For a veggie that is just hitting its stride in popularity, there are already numerous Jerusalem artichoke cultivars. 'Stampede' is a common—but delicious—yellow-skinned variety. White varieties include 'Clearwater', 'French Mammoth White',

'White Fuseau', and 'Wild White'. For purple varieties, look for 'Beaver Valley Purple' or 'Passamaquoddy', and for red, look for 'Skorospelka' or 'Wild Red'.

Growing and caring for the plants

Growing Jerusalem artichokes begins with the soil. These plants grow and produce flowers in almost any type of soil, but yields are much more abundant when they are planted in loose, well-aerated, well-draining soil. An all-purpose fertilizer should be worked into the soil when planting.

Planting Jerusalem artichokes is much like planting potatoes. Plant small tubers (or pieces of tuber with two or three buds each) 2 to 3 inches (5 to 7.5 cm) deep and 2 feet (60 cm) apart in early spring. Start as soon as the ground has warmed enough that it can be worked. Water the area well after planting, and the tubers will sprout in two to three weeks.

Harvesting Jerusalem artichokes

Wait until the first frost to begin digging mature tubers out of the ground. When the plants begin to brown in late summer or early autumn, this is a sign that they're ready to harvest. Dig

carefully, making sure not to injure the plant's delicate skin, and harvest only what you need.

Cut away the dying plants, but leave the remaining tubers in the ground. They can be harvested all winter until they begin to sprout in the spring. It should be noted, however, that any piece of tuber left to overwinter will almost certainly sprout, and your garden could be easily overrun with Jerusalem artichokes. On the other hand, if you assign a permanent corner of your garden to these plants, growing them can be even easier, because they will replenish themselves. Just give your patch a dose of fertilizer each spring.

The Essentials

planting time early spring; midsummer

light full sun

soil moist, well-draining soil

pH level 5.8 to 6.2

water 1 inch (2.5 cm) per week

size 6 to 10 feet (1.8 to 3 m) tall; 3 to 5 feet (1 to 1.5 m) wide

harvest in 110 to 150 days

Link to the Experts

READ MORE AT GARDENING KNOW HOW

Find out which plants make good companions for Jerusalem artichokes and also how to contain them when they get out of control by following these links.

- "Companions for Jerusalem Artichokes – What to Plant with Jerusalem Artichoke" LINK: gkh.us/95611

- "Jerusalem Artichoke Weeds: How to Control Jerusalem Artichokes" LINK: gkh.us/70779

KALE

Scientific name: *Brassica oleracea* var. *acephala*

As well as being a pretty plant, curly-leafed kale is very rich in iron and other nutrients.

In recent years, nutrient-dense kale, a variety of (*Brassica oleracea*) has gained popularity among mainstream culture, as well as with home gardeners. Noted for its use in the kitchen, kale is an easy-to-grow leafy green that thrives in cooler temperatures. A wide range of open-pollinated kale varieties offers growers delicious and extremely beautiful additions to the vegetable garden. Kale plants, which can be annual, biennial, or perennial, are also extremely robust, adaptable to many different situations, and will grow in winter.

Growing and caring for the plants

Although kale is quite versatile, there is a proper way to plant it so that it attains the healthiest growth. It prefers well-drained soil in sunny locations but will tolerate shade, too. It grows in all types of soil, although it prefers sunny, well-drained areas. For best results, choose your garden area wisely–kale grows best when planted after the soil reaches temperatures of 60°F to 65°F (16°C to 18°C). Hot weather can turn it bitter, so you might want to mulch the ground to protect the plants from too much heat and to keep down weeds. Likewise, you can opt for a somewhat shadier location in regions where extreme heat is an issue or even where sun just isn't that plentiful.

Start the plants indoors to get a jump early in the season. Cover the kale seeds with ½ inch (1.25 cm) of soil, and keep it moist while the seeds germinate. After all chance of frost has passed, transplant the seedlings into the ground. In late summer or early autumn, you can also direct-seed kale plants outdoors. Don't cultivate around the seed area until the seedlings appear, and then do so only when necessary–you don't want to disturb the roots. Keep the ground well watered and, as your kale grows, hoe the soil shallowly around the plants, removing any weeds that might pop up. The plants take only about two months to mature. Because they take so little time, you can start a couple of batches early, a couple more later in the summer, and a couple in the autumn. This succession planting provides you with fresh plants to pick from for about six months or so.

Harvesting kale

Kale is ready to harvest when the leaves are about the size of your hand. When it comes to picking kale, simply harvest the young leaves from the bottom of the plant up, avoiding the terminal bud (at the top center of the plant), which helps to maintain the plant's productivity. Grasp the stem of a mature outer leaf at the base of the main stalk, and then pull down and out, away from the center, until it breaks. Although it is best to just pick what you need for a single meal, you can store any excess in a loose plastic bag in the fridge. It will keep for about a week.

Editor's Tip

Collecting seeds from your existing plants can be a smart idea. Unlike many common garden vegetable crops, kale plants are biennials, which means that they produce leafy green growth in the first growing season and will then overwinter in the garden. The following spring, they will resume growth and begin the process of setting seed. Yet, beginner growers might be quite surprised by the presence of bolted first-year kale plants. To learn more about collecting seeds for future planting, scan the QR code or follow this link.

"Saving Kale Seeds – Learn How to Harvest Kale Seeds"
LINK: gkh.us/128517

LETTUCE

Scientific name: Lactuca sativa

Rows of leafy lettuce plants, both red and green varieties, are ready for picking.

The Essentials

planting time early spring to autumn

light full to partial shade

soil well-draining sandy soil to heavy clay soil

pH level 6.2 to 6.8

water 1 to 2 inches (2.5 to 5 cm) per week

size 12 to 18 inches (30 to 45 cm) tall; 6 to 12 inches (15 to 30 cm) wide

harvest in 30 to 70 days

Growing lettuce (*Lactuca sativa*) is an easy and inexpensive way to put fresh gourmet salad greens on the table. As a cool-season crop, lettuce grows well with the cool, moist weather available in spring and autumn. In cooler climates, the lettuce growing season can also be extended year-round using an indoor hydroponic system.

Growing and caring for the plants

The growing season begins in early spring and extends through autumn for northern climates. In warmer areas, it can also be grown outdoors throughout the winter. Increasing daylight hours and hot temperatures stimulates lettuce to bolt, which makes growing it more challenging during summer months.

As a cool-season crop, lettuce can be direct-seeded into the garden as soon as the soil thaws and can be worked in the spring. Lettuce can also be started or grown indoors. Try succession planting and growing varieties of lettuce with differing maturity times to harvest plants throughout the growing season.

Lettuce prefers moist, cool conditions, and you don't even have to worry about chilly weather because the seedlings can tolerate a light frost. In fact, these plants grow best when temperatures are between 45°F and 65°F (7°C to 18°C).

Lettuce tastes more flavorful and the leaves remain tender when it grows quickly. Prior to planting, work organic compost or high-nitrogen fertilizer into the soil to encourage rapid leaf growth. Lettuce prefers a soil pH between 6.2 and 6.8. Due to its small seed size, it's better to sprinkle the seeds on top of fine soil, and then cover lightly with a thin layer of soil. A small hand-held seeder or seed tape can also be used for proper spacing of plants. Avoid planting too deeply, as the plants require sunlight to germinate.

To avoid dislodging newly planted seeds, gently mist the area with a fine spray until the soil is moist. When direct-seeding into the garden, consider using a plastic row cover, cold frame, or scrap window pane to prevent heavy rains from washing away the seeds. Lettuce requires 1 to 2 inches (2.5 to 5 cm) of rain or supplemental water per week.

Give lettuce plenty of room to mature by spacing plants 8 to 12 inches (20 to 30 cm) apart. Planting in full sun will generate faster leaf production, but it can encourage bolting during hot weather. Still, lettuce will actually thrive in a little bit of shade too, making it great for planting between taller crops, like tomatoes or corn, which will provide shade as the season progresses. This also helps save on space in smaller gardens.

Harvesting lettuce

Harvest lettuce when the heads have reached a suitable size for your salad purposes. If you allow the lettuce to become too mature, you'll end up with bitter-tasting leaves.

Dig Deeper

LEARN MORE AT GARDENING KNOW HOW

To learn how to take care of lettuce growing in water, just scan the QR code or follow the first link. For other lettuce-growing options, just follow the other links listed below.

- "Regrowing Lettuce in Water: Caring for Lettuce Plants Growing in Water"
  Link: gkh.us/95353

- "Growing Lettuce in the Garden – How to Grow Lettuce Plants"
  Link: gkh.us/1613

- "Hanging Container Lettuce: How to Make a Hanging Lettuce Basket"
  Link: gkh.us/136790

A Gallery of
LETTUCES AND SALAD GREENS

Growing fresh greens for salad doesn't mean growing only standard *Lactuca sativa*. Lettuce has numerous varieties, including the three main types, butterhead, Romaine (cos), and loose leaf. Butterhead lettuces get that name from their soft, butter-like consistency, and they form loose, open heads. Romaine, or cos, lettuces, form upward heads with stronger leaves growing out of a crunchy spine. They have a stronger flavor than butterheads. Fast-growing loose-leaf lettuces come in colors beyond the basic green. Along with the *Lactuca sativa* varieties are other salad greens, like peppery arugula, crisp cress, delicate mâche, spicy mustard, and the many variants found in the chicory genus, *Cichorium*.

Whichever types of lettuces and salad greens you choose to grow, you will have lots of planting options. They do great in traditional vegetable garden beds, and most will also thrive in containers. Almost anyone, with any amount of garden space, can create their own "salad garden." Nothing beats the great taste and health benefits of a fresh-picked bowl of greens.

ARUGULA
Also known as rocket, Mediterranean rocket, Italian cress, and roquette, *Eruca vesicaria* has a peppery, spicy, and slightly tart flavor that adds zest to a salad. Another cool-weather crop, plant some arugula with lettuce crops for a varied salad garden.

BUTTERHEAD
Also known as butter, Boston, and bibb lettuce, this delicate lettuce variety has a ruffled appearance, with a blanched heart and sweet, buttery flavor. Boston is a lighter green with softer leaves and big heads. Similar to butterhead, bibb has smaller heads.

CORAL LETTUCE
Also known as Lollo Rosso (red variety) and Lollo Bionda (pale green variety), these are curly-edged lettuces with a mild, slightly bitter flavor. The frilly leaves, produced loosely in a whole head, will add pretty color, texture, and volume to your salads.

Editor's Tip

You will want to harvest your lettuce crops in the best way possible to ensure fresh, flavorful greens for your salads.

- For crisper lettuce, harvest in the morning. Wash leaves in cold water, and dry with a paper towel. Place lettuce in a plastic bag, and then store in the refrigerator.

- Leaf lettuce can be picked once outer leaves reach a usable size. Picking young outer leaves will encourage inner leaves to continue growing.

- Harvest iceberg when the head forms a tight ball, and the outer leaves are pale green. Plants can be pulled or heads can be cut.

- Harvest romaine and leaf lettuces as baby greens by cutting straight across the plant 1 or 2 inches (2.5 or 5 cm) above the soil level. Be sure to leave the basal growing point for further leaf development.

- Romaine (cos) lettuces can be harvested by removing tender outer leaves or waiting until a head is formed. When removing the head, cut the plant above the base to encourage regrowth, or remove the entire plant if regrowth is not desired.

CRESS
Also known as watercress, upland cress, curly cress, and land cress, *Nasturtium officinale* is a highly nutritious plant. The leafy dark aquatic green leaves have a crisp, peppery flavor that stands out in a mixed salad. You can also use it for dainty tea sandwiches.

CRISPHEAD
Also known as iceberg, Reine de Glace, and igloo lettuce, crisphead forms a large, dense head that resembles a cabbage. With a crispy, crunchy texture that holds up to shredding, crisphead lettuce has a sweet, mild flavor that makes it a salad favorite.

ENDIVE, ESCAROLE, AND FRISÉE
The genus *Cichorium* gives us these three salad favorites related to common chicory. Crisp endive has a sweet, nutty flavor with a bitter finish. Escarole is less bitter than endive, while frisée's bitter, frilly outer leaves reveal a creamy yellow center.

KALE
Highly popular kale, often touted as a "superfood" is a dark, leafy crucifer you can eat either raw or cooked. It can be somewhat dry and tough, but the crunchy leaves have an earthy flavor. For more information, see page 116.

LOOSE LEAF
Also known as Batavia lettuce, leaf lettuce, green leaf lettuce, red leaf lettuce, and Redina, loose-leaf lettuce is sweet and crisp. When you feel like having like a salad, you can cut off outer leaves, and the rest of the plant will continue to grow.

MÂCHE
Also known as field salad, lamb's lettuce, corn salad, field lettuce, and fetticus, tender *Valerianella locusta* is best eaten raw. It has a soft, velvety, and crisp texture, with a mild, herbal, and nutty flavor that pairs well with a vinaigrette dressing.

MUSTARD GREENS
Brassica juncea, the plant that gives us the condiment mustard, can be served raw or cooked. This salad green is peppery, pungent, and a bit bitter. For best flavor, always harvest mustard greens while young. For more information, see page 187.

OAK LEAF
Also known as royal oak and green oak lettuce, this easy grower is recognizable by the shape of its deeply lobed leaves that resemble those of the tree. The soft, slightly frilled leaves of young oak leaf have a mild and gentle taste, with crunchy stems.

ROMAINE
Also known as cos lettuce, sweet, crisp Romaine has compact hearts of long, broad leaves. It is the centerpiece of Caesar salads, and the outer leaves can be used as wraps. In the garden, it requires higher fertility than loose-leaf lettuce types.

OKRA

Scientific name: Abelmoschus esculentus

Long pods of okra are ready for picking. This warm-weather crop yields the green vegetable found in many world cuisines.

The Essentials

planting time spring

light full sun

soil well-draining sandy soil

pH level 6.5 to 7.5

water 1 inch (2.5 cm) per week

size 6 to 8 feet (1.8 to 2.4 m) tall; 6 to 8 feet (1.8 to 2.4 m) wide

harvest in 50 to 70 days

Okra (*Abelmoschus esculentus*), also called ladies' fingers or ochro, is a flowering plant in the mallow family. The edible green seed pods have become a signature ingredient in the cuisine of several areas, including the American South (where it is often used in gumbo), Cuba and Puerto Rico (where it is referred to as *quimbombó*), and India (where it is called bhindi), along with the Middle East, Brazil, and Sri Lanka.

Okra can be eaten cooked, pickled, or raw. Often disparaged for its slimy texture, an okra pod is mucilaginous, which results in the characteristic "goo" of cooked okra. A tried-and-true method of de-sliming okra is to cook it with acidic foods, such as tomatoes, which lessens some of the slime.

Growing and caring for the plants

Plant about two to three weeks after the last chance of frost has passed. Okra is a warm-season crop that requires a lot of sunshine, so find a spot that doesn't get much shade, and be sure there is good drainage. To prepare the plot, add 2 to 3 pounds (0.9 to 1.36 kg) of fertilizer for every 100 square feet (9.3 m²) of garden space. Work the fertilizer into the ground about 3 to 5 inches (7.5 to 12.5 cm) deep. After fertilization, rake the soil to remove all rocks and sticks. Work the soil well, about 10 to 15 inches (25 to 38 cm) deep, so the plants can get the most nutrients from the soil around their roots. Then, plant rows spaced about 1 to 2 inches (2.5 to 5 cm) apart. Once your growing plants are out of the ground, thin them to about 1 foot (30 cm) apart. It is helpful to plant it in shifts so that you can get an even flow of ripe crops throughout the summer.

Water the plants every 7 to 10 days. Okra can handle dry conditions, but regular water is definitely beneficial. Carefully remove grass and weeds around your growing plants.

Harvesting okra

Okra matures quickly, especially if you have a summer of hot weather. The pods will be ready for harvest at about two months from planting. Harvesting can be tricky, however, because you have to harvest the pods before they become tough. It takes only about four days from the time of flowering to the time to pick okra, so harvest every other day to keep them producing as long as possible.

Pick okra when the pods reach a length of about 2 to 3 inches (5 to 7.5 cm). Harvesting is a simple task: just test the larger pods by cutting them open with a sharp knife. If they are too difficult to cut, this means that they are too old. You should remove these old pods because they will rob the plant of the nutrients it needs to produce new pods. If the pods are tender, use a sharp knife to cut the stem cleanly just below the okra pod. Store the pods in plastic bags in your refrigerator, where they will last about a week, or blanch and freeze the pods if you have too much to use right away. Once thawed, they are perfect for stews and soups.

Editor's Tip

Because okra plants are self-pollinating, you can save some of the pods for seeds to plant the following year. This will make for a great crop the second time around. Instead of harvesting the young, tender pods, leave some pods on the plants, and then collect them when they become fully mature and almost dry. Leaving the pods on the plant to dry out does slow down the development of new ones, however, so wait until you have harvested all the okra you intend to use for the season before letting a few mature.

OLIVE

Scientific name: Olea europaea

You don't need an orchard to enjoy fresh olives. Many varieties can be grown in a container indoors or outside.

Best suited to areas that are prone to high heat and plenty of sunshine, an olive tree can be planted outside and, once established, is fairly low maintenance. These trees have lovely silver leaves, which will complement many other garden plantings but are also grown for their fruit. The fruit can be pressed for oil or cured (brined) and eaten. There are other plants which bear the name "olive," so make sure to look for a European olive tree. Some cultivars are self-fertilizing, such as 'Arbequina' and 'Mission' (grown for oil) and 'Manzanilla', which is the typical "California" black olive suitable for canning. If you don't have enough space for a full tree, or if your climate is too cold, you can still have olive trees, as long as you grow them in containers.

Growing and caring for the tree

Most olive trees take about three years to come into maturity and begin to set noticeable amounts of fruit. To increase fruit set, plant more than one cultivar close together. Trees are usually purchased in either a 1-gallon (3.78-L) pot with a single trunk and a height of 4 to 5 feet (1 to 1.5 m) or in 4-inch (10-cm) pots with numerous side branches and

a height of 18 to 24 inches (45 to 60 cm). Look for specimens that are actively growing with soft new growth sprouting from the shoot tips.

Plant in well-drained soil in a sunny area. This evergreen flourishes in hot dry areas and, as such, will not do well in wet winter soil. If you are lucky enough to have enough garden acreage for an olive orchard, space the trees about 20 feet (6 m) apart to accommodate their eventual size (which can vary according to the particular cultivar).

Dig a hole the size of the container. Leave the root ball alone, except to remove or cut any circling roots. Do not add soil medium, compost, or fertilizer to the newly planted tree. Avoid adding gravel or drainage tubing. It is best for the young tree to acclimate to its soil.

Once your new tree is planted, it is a good idea to provide drip irrigation, as it will need water every day, especially during the summer months throughout its first year. When you begin to see a quantity of new growth, feed it with nitrogen-rich compost, a conventional fertilizer, or a concentrated organic.

Minimally prune during the first four years, only enough to maintain shape. The young olive tree may need to be staked right up against the trunk to assist with stability.

For those gardeners with limited space, a container-grown olive tree is the answer. The best time to start growing olive trees in containers is in spring, after all threat of frost has passed. Plant in a mix of potting soil and perlite or small rocks. Opt for a clay or wood container—plastic containers retain more water, which can be deadly for an olive tree.

Place the container in a spot that receives at least six hours of full sunlight each day. Make sure not to overwater. Only water when the top layer of soil has dried out completely—when it comes to olive trees, it's better to water too little than too much.

The Essentials

planting time spring

light full sun

soil dry, chalky/clay-rich soil (ground); mix of potting soil and perlite or small rocks (container)

pH level 7.0 to 8.0

water when the top 2 inches (5 cm) of soil becomes dry

size 20 to 30 feet (6 to 9 m) tall (ground); up to 10 feet (3 m) tall (container)

harvest in 1 to 6 years

Olive trees are not very cold-hardy, so bring the container indoors before temperatures fall toward freezing. Place it inside by a sunny window or under lights. Once temperatures warm back up in the spring, you can take your potted olive tree back outside where it can hang out all summer long.

Harvesting olives

Commercial olive tree growers harvest fruit in September or October for canning purposes and small fruit is left until January or February and then pressed for oil.

Link to the Experts

READ MORE AT GARDENING KNOW HOW

To learn more about growing olive trees, harvesting the fruit, and pressing the oil, follow these links.

- "Potted Olive Tree Care: Tips On Growing Olive Trees In Containers"
  LINK: gkh.us/101906

- "Picking Olives – Tips for Harvesting Olive Trees"
  LINK: gkh.us/83725

- "How to Press Olive Oil: Making Olive Oil at Home"
  LINK: gkh.us/155870

A Gallery of
DWARF
FRUIT TREES

Home gardeners can grow fruits in a restricted space by choosing dwarf cultivars. These diminutive versions of full-size orchard trees supply normal-size fruit, but have a smaller footprint in the garden. Some of the fruit trees listed here will even yield edible produce when grown in containers. Dwarf fruit trees also add interest to the landscape and often scent a yard with fragrant blooms.

Many dwarf variety fruits are self-fertile, which means that they don't rely on another tree to cross-pollinate with them in order to produce fruit. Before making a purchase, confirm with your grower or vendor if the tree or shrub is self-fertile. Whether you intend to plant your tree in the ground or in a container, be sure to choose a location with full sun and good drainage. Make sure the fruit tree you buy checks off all these boxes:

- It is a live tree grafted onto dwarf rootstock (never buy fruit trees from seed).
- The tree is self-fertile, unless you have room for two or more trees.
- It comes from a reputable nursery, whether you buy local or purchase online.

BANANA TREE
Height: 9 to 10 feet (2.7 to 3 m)
The dwarf Cavendish banana (*Musa acuminata*) produces small, sweet fruit at just 3 to 6 inches (7.5 to 15 cm) in length. The large tropical leaves lend interest to the landscape and can be grown in pots indoors. Banana plants are self-pollinating.

CHERRY
Height: 10 feet (3 m)
Cherry trees (*Prunus* spp.) are renowned for their spectacular spring blooms and sweet or sour fruit. Sweet cherries are perfect for snacking, while sour cherries are better for baking. Consider semi-dwarf, self-pollinating 'Stella', 'Nanking', 'Lapins', 'Northstar', and 'Sunburst'.

APPLE
Height: 10 to 12 feet (3 to 3.7 m)
Imagine the thrill of picking tasty, full-size apples (*Malus domestica*) in your own garden. Dwarf apple tree varieties include 'Cameron Select', a cultivar of the popular Honeycrisp apple, along with such tasty favorites as 'Gala', 'Jonagold', 'Cox', and 'Pink Lady'.

FIG TREE
Height: 10 feet (3 m)
Fairly easy to grow, fig trees (*Ficus carica*) have attractive foliage and produce small green edible fruits that darken when ripe. They require little upkeep, fruit very quickly, and are much easier to grow in pots than in the ground if you live anywhere with cold winters.

LEMON

Height: 2 feet (60 cm)

For a small lemon tree, try the sweet Meyer lemon (*Citrus × meyeri*), a hybrid cross between a lemon and a mandarin orange. This amazing dwarf tree is able to fruit at just 24 inches (60 cm). Grow one on your patio during the summer, then overwinter it indoors.

PEAR

Height: 4 to 8 feet (1.2 to 2.4 m)

A dwarf pear (*Pyrus* spp.) is a good option for those who want a small fruit tree. 'Conference' is a popular dwarf cultivar, sweet and juicy and self-fertile. Try 'Louise Bonne', a sweet dessert pear, or the ubiquitous 'Bartlett' ('Williams') variety. Dwarf pears grow well in pots.

ORANGE

Height: 6 to 10 feet (1.8 to 3 m)

With jasmine-scented flowers, the dwarf Calamondin orange is one of the best patio fruit trees for beginners. This unique little citrus is widely adaptable, and it will even thrive indoors year-round. Its very tart fruit is delicious when made into faux lemonade or marmalade.

PLUM

Height: 10 feet (3 m)

The hardy 'Johnson' cultivar is a dwarf plum (*Prunus domestica*) with red skin and sweet red flesh. It requires a second plum of a different variety for pollination. Or try an heirloom variety like 'Damson' (*Prunus institia*), which is a self-fertile cultivar.

PEACH/APRICOT

Height: 8 to 10 feet (2.4 to 3 m)

If you live in a cold climate, grow a peach (*Prunus persica*) or apricot (*P. armeniaca*) tree in a pot that can move indoors during the chilly months. Dwarf varieties include heirloom 'Belle of Georgia', 'June Gold', 'Bonfire', 'Contender', 'Pix Zee', and 'Pixie-Cot' apricot.

POMEGRANATE

Height: 3 feet (1 m)

The dwarf pomegranate, *Punica granatum* 'Nana', has a full-sized tree's great attributes but stays a manageable size. Grow your patio pomegranate outdoors during the warm season. If you live in colder climates, bring it indoors to overwinter.

ONION

Scientific name: Allium cepa

A key ingredient in countless recipes, onions are a smart choice for a home garden.

The onion (*Allium cepa*) is a premier member of the *Allium* genus. It is most frequently a biennial or a perennial, but it is usually treated as an annual and harvested in its first growing season.

Growing and caring for the plants

The three ways to grow onions are from seed, seedlings, or by purchased onion sets. Growing them from seeds takes longer than other methods, so if you're in an area with a shorter season, you'll need to sow seeds indoors. Start the seeds indoors about 8 to 10 weeks before the last spring frost date. Water as needed, until it is time to transplant. Harden off the seedlings before moving them into the garden. Once the last frost date has passed, the onion planting season begins. The location should be in full sun and with loose and rich, well-draining soil. Before planting, you can amend the soil with a balanced, mild, slow-release fertilizer. Push the seedlings just far enough into the soil to get them to stand up. Plant them 4 inches (10 cm) apart. In an area with a longer season, direct sow the seeds 8 to 12 weeks before the last frost for your area. Cover the seeds with ½ inch (1.25 cm) of soil.

Onions have shallow root systems, so it is important to keep them well-watered, at least 1 inch (2.5 cm) of water every week until harvested.

MORE INFO *Onion types*

There are three main categories of garden onions, based on when the bulbs begin to form.

- Short-day onions begin to form bulbs when there are 10 to 12 hours of daylight each day. Plant these if you live in southern regions where summer days are comparatively short.

- Long-day onions begin to form bulbs when there are 14 to 16 hours of daylight per day. Plant these in northern climates where the summer days are long.

- Day-neutral onions begin to form bulbs when there are 12 to 14 hours of daylight daily. These produce well in most regions.

The Essentials

planting time spring

light full sun

soil loose and rich, well-draining soil

pH level 6.0 to 7.0

water 1 inch (2.5 cm) per week

size 12 to 18 inches (30 to 45 cm) tall; 6 to 12 inches (15 to 30 cm) wide

harvest in 60 to 175 days

Onion sets are small, dry, immature onion bulbs that were grown from seed the previous year. When you buy sets, they should be about the size of a marble and firm when squeezed gently. If you wish to grow your own onion sets from seeds, start these in your garden in mid- to late July, and dig up after the first hard frost. Allow them to air dry before storing them in a cool, dry place for the winter.

The onion planting season for sets starts when the temperatures get to be around 50°F (10°C). Choose a location that gets at least six to seven hours of sun per day. If you'd like to grow big onions, plant the sets 2 inches (5 cm) in the ground and 4 inches (10 cm) apart. This will give the onions plenty of room to grow. If are looking to grow big onions, then your best bet is to grow onions from transplants, which grow larger and store longer than onions grown from sets.

Harvesting onions

Once bulbs form, you can harvest whenever you need an onion. For winter storage, allow the main stalk to get weak and thin so that it falls over naturally. Leave the bulbs in the ground for one to two weeks to develop thick skins, and then harvest after the majority of leaves are dry, leaving 1 to 2 inches (2.5 to 5 cm) of the neck above the bulb. After you dig up your onions, spread them outdoors in a sunny, dry place and leave them outside (as long as it doesn't rain) for three to seven days. Store your crop indoors in a shady, warm, and dry place.

PARSNIP

Scientific name: *Pastinaca sativa*

Parsnips, which look like white carrots, are making a comeback with many gardeners.

The Essentials

planting time late spring to late summer; autumn to early spring

light full sun

soil moist, well-draining, loamy soil

pH level 6.0 to 7.0

water 1 inch (2.5 cm) per week

size 1 to 3 feet (30 cm to 1 m) tall; 6 to 12 inches (15 to 30 cm) wide

harvest in 100 to 120 days

Parsnip (*Pastinaca sativa*), a cool-season root vegetable, is technically a biennial, but because it is grown for its taproot, we treat it as an annual in a home garden. A parsnip plant will grow to 3 feet (1 m) tall, with a top that resembles broadleaf parsley and a taproot as long as 20 inches (50 cm). A member of the Apiaceae, or carrot family, it can be mistaken for a white carrot because of its similar size and shape. Consider growing this root veggie with your carrot crop. Often used in the same recipes, the spicy bite of the parsnip complements the sweeter taste of the carrot.

Growing parsnips isn't much different from growing other root vegetables. These winter crops like cool weather and are actually exposed to almost freezing temperatures for about a month before harvesting. When planting them, remember that cool weather enhances the flavor of the root, while hot weather leads to poor-quality vegetables.

You can grow parsnips in just about any region, as long as you can give them a long growing season. Because they can take up to 180 days to go from seed to harvest, plant in the middle of the autumn for a late-winter or early-spring harvest (in particularly cold areas, you might have to plant in early spring for a harvest the following autumn).

Growing and caring for the plants

Choose a spot that receives at least six to eight hours of direct sunlight (although the plants will tolerate a bit of shade) and that has loose, well-draining soil free of rocks and weeds. Mix 3 or 4 inches (7.5 to 10 cm) of compost into the soil, and then poke down the seeds about ½ inch (1.25 cm) in rows at least 12 inches (30 cm) apart. This gives the growing plants room to develop good roots. The seeds need about 18 days to germinate. After seedlings appear, wait a couple of weeks, and then thin the plants to about 3 to 4 inches (7.5 to 10 cm) apart. Water them well, or the roots will be flavorless and tough. Fertilization of the soil is also helpful. Side dress with fertilizer around June to keep the soil healthy.

Harvesting parsnips

After about 100 to 120 days, the leafy tops of the plants should about reach about 3 feet (1 m) high, which signals that it is time to harvest the roots. Begin by trimming all of the foliage to within 1 inch (2.5 cm) of the roots. To dig up a root, which should now be about 1½ to 2 inches (3.5 to 7.5 cm) in diameter, loosen the soil with a pitchfork to ensure you unearth the whole root, before gently easing it out of the soil. Harvest plants throughout a row, and leave others to mature. You can also leave some of the parsnips in the ground until spring: just throw about 3 inches (7.5 cm) of soil over your first autumn crop to insulate the roots for the coming winter. Harvest this second batch in spring, right after the thaw. These parsnips will be even sweeter than those of the autumn harvest.

You can store your excess harvest in damp sand or sawdust in a root cellar that maintains a temperature of about 32°F (0°C) and a humidity between 90 and 95 percent. The stored parsnips should last for four to six months.

Dig Deeper

LEARN MORE AT GARDENING KNOW HOW

Parsnips generally do best planted in a garden, but what if you don't have an outdoor plot? Scan the QR code or follow this link to find out how to grow them in a container.

"Container Grown Parsnips – Learn How to Grow Parsnips in a Container"
LINK: *gkh.us/107861*

PEA

Scientific name: *Pisum sativum*

Green pea pods are ready for harvest. Pea plants are easy to cultivate but have a limited growing season. As with other legumes, peas will fix nitrogen in the soil, making it available for other plants. This makes them great companion plants.

Peas are tasty, nutritious legumes that are quite easy to grow. Though there are many varieties of *Pisum sativum* to be found, these annuals can generally be sorted into two categories: garden peas and snow peas. Garden peas, also known as English peas, are the most common type of pea. They have tough, inedible pods, and they are a great source of fiber and protein. Garden peas are also the fastest-growing type of edible pea. They are often served boiled or steamed. Snow peas are part of the edible-pod, or sugar pea, category. These peas have thinner, edible pods, and they are generally sweeter than garden peas. Snow pea pods are delicate and almost completely flat, as are the peas inside. Their most common usage is in Chinese dishes, such as stir-fries, although they are also often eaten raw or steamed.

Growing and caring for the plants

Choose a sunny spot in your garden with rich, well-draining soil; pea plants need full sun, though they will tolerate light shade. They need less fertilizing than many other vegetables, so adding a little compost to the soil before planting is usually adequate. For climbing peas, choose a location where they can grow up a sturdy trellis or other stable support structure.

Peas are cool-weather plants; if you sow them too late in the spring, they may struggle in the hotter months. Instead, as soon as the ground is workable and thawed, start sowing peas directly outdoors. These will likely be one of the first plants you start each year. They tolerate cold well, so there is no need to start them inside. Sow the seeds to a depth of about 1 inch (2.5 cm).

Water your pea plants only when there is not enough rain to provide about 1 inch (2.5 cm) of water each week. Spring is usually wet, so some years you likely won't have to water at all. When you do water them, be sure to water the soil only at the base of the plant to avoid increasing the risk of disease and mildew.

Harvesting peas

Harvesting your peas at the right time is essential. These plants grow very quickly, but they also overmature quickly and can become inedible. Once the pods start to flesh out with peas, check on them daily. Pick peas as soon as the pods have reached their maximum size. If you think the pods are ready, pick one, and try it; the peas inside should be thin-skinned, sweet, and tender.

The Essentials

planting time late winter or early spring; autumn

light full sun to partial shade

soil well-draining, sandy to heavy clay soil

pH level 6.0 to 7.5

water 1 inch (2.5 cm) per week

size 12 to 18 inches (30 to 45 cm) tall; 6 to 12 inches (15 to 30 cm) wide

harvest in 60 to 70 days

SIMILAR PLANTS
Snap Peas

A close cousin of the garden and snow pea is the snap pea (*Pisum macrocarpon*). Like the snow pea, the snap pea, also called the sugar snap pea, is part of the edible-pod, or sugar pea, category. It has rounder pods and a much sweeter flavor than other varieties. It is commonly eaten raw or served in salads.

POLE BEANS

Scientific name: *Phaseolus* spp. or *Vigna* spp.

A crop of 'Kentucky Wonder Wax', a variety of *Phaseolus vulgarus* pole bean, is ready for harvesting. A system of bamboo poles supports the growing plants.

Fresh, crisp beans are summer treats that are easy to grow in most climates. Beans may be pole or bush; pole beans include varieties of common beans (*Phaseolus vulgaris*), runner beans (*P. coccineus*), or yardlong beans (*Vigna unguiculata sesquipedalis*). Pole beans allow you to maximize vertical planting space. They also ensures a longer crop period and may yield up to three times as many beans as bush varieties (see page 101). These mainly annuals do require some training onto a pole or trellis, but the height makes them easier to harvest, and the graceful flowering vines add dimensional interest to the garden.

Growing and caring for the plants

Find a sunny spot to plant pole beans. Weather is an important consideration. Sow the seeds when soil temperatures are around 60°F (16°C), and the ambient air has warmed to at least the same temperature. Most varieties require 60 to 70 days to first harvest and are normally harvested at least five times during the growing season. Beans in general do not transplant well and do best when directly sown into the garden.

Pole beans need well-drained soil and plenty of organic amendment to produce a large crop, but they need little fertilizer. If you do use fertilizer, add it to the soil before planting. Side dress with manure or mulch or use black plastic to conserve moisture, minimize weeds, and keep soil warm for increased yield.

Sow the seeds 4 to 8 inches (10 to 20 cm) apart in rows 24 to 36 inches (60 cm to 1 m) apart. Push down the seeds about 1 inch (2.5 cm), and then lightly brush soil over them. To plant in hills, sow four to six seeds at even intervals. Water after planting until the top 2 to 3 inches (5 to 7.5 cm) of soil are damp. Germination takes 8 to 10 days.

These beans need a support structure at least 6 feet (1.8 m) high—vines can grow 5 to 10 feet (1.5 to 3 m). They need a little help climbing their support structure, especially when young. Get them off the ground early to prevent rot and loss of blooms. They will need at least 1 inch (2.5 cm) of water per week and should not be allowed to dry out, but they also cannot tolerate soggy soils.

Harvesting pole beans

A single plant can yield several pounds of beans. Harvest begins as soon as the pods are full and swollen. Pick them every three to five days to avoid harvesting older beans, which can be woody and bitter. The pods are best used fresh, but they can be lightly blanched and frozen for future use. Consistent harvesting will encourage new flowers and promote longer-living vines.

Editor's Picks

There are several varieties of pole beans that have proven to be kitchen garden winners.

- 'Asparagus Yardlong', a stringless, black-seeded variety, grows well in heat.
- 'Blue Coco', an heirloom variety, produces flat, bluish purple pods covering chocolate-colored seeds.
- 'Blue Lake' is an old-time favorite with large, tasty, disease-resistant beans.
- 'Kentucky Wonder Wax' is a vigorous climber that yields slightly flattened and curved yellow stringless pods.
- 'Kentucky Blue', a cross of 'Kentucky Wonder' and 'Blue Lake', yields enormous pods that are straight, smooth, and plump, with dark green stems and light strings.
- 'Romano', also called the Italian flat bean, produces delicious, broad, flat beans with a stringless seam that reveals tiny, lime green to white-colored peas.

POTATO

Scientific name: *Solanum tuberosum*

A gardener harvesting potatoes. This nutrient-dense veggie is easy to grow at home.

The Essentials

planting time spring

light full sun

soil well-draining sandy loam

pH level 5.0 to 6.0

water 1 to 2 inches (2.5 to 5 cm) per week

size 1 to 3 feet (30 cm to 1 m) tall; 1 to 3 feet (30 cm to 1 m) wide

harvest in 75 to 120 days

Harvesting potatoes

When the flowers die and turn yellow, stop watering the potato plants, and wait a week. Then, carefully dig up the tubers with a trowel or dump them out of their container. Once the potatoes have been dug up from the soil, allow them to air dry in a cool, dry place before storing them.

Potatoes are one of the world's most important staple food crops. These versatile, hardy vegetables are nutrient-dense, can be prepared in countless ways, and are used in everything from fast food to haute cuisine. Thousands of potato cultivars have been developed all over the world. Many of these have been selectively bred for specific qualities of skin, color, flavor, and texture; red, white, yellow, blue, and purple potatoes exist in all shapes and sizes. Some of the most popular varieties include 'Yukon Gold', 'Elba', and 'Kennebec'.

All potato plant varieties can be planted in early spring. Don't plant the seed potatoes too early–the pieces may rot in overly damp soil. Likewise, if planted in March, they stand a chance of being frozen back by a late frost.

Growing and caring for the plants

Potatoes can be started from seed or seed potatoes. Seed potatoes are generally recommended because they have been bred to resist disease and are certified. They will also provide you with the earliest and fullest harvest when compared to seed-started plants. Seed potatoes can be planted whole or cut up so that there are one or two buds, or "eyes," on each piece.

The conditions needed to grow potatoes vary only slightly by variety. As a general rule, they require well-drained soil with plenty of organic matter incorporated into it. They need a lot of water, at least 1 inch (2.5 cm) per week, but the tubers will rot if allowed to soak in saturated, poorly draining soil.

Trenches are the most common way to plant potatoes. Dig trenches 4 inches (10 cm) deep and 2 to 3 feet apart (60 cm to 1 m). Cut apart seed potatoes into sections that have at least two to three eyes, or growing points. Plant the pieces 12 inches (30 cm) apart with the majority of the eyes facing upward, and then lightly cover the pieces with soil. As they sprout, add more soil to cover the green growth until it matches soil level; potatoes will turn green and become toxic if exposed to sunlight.

Potatoes can also be grown in containers, compost heaps, or even piles of straw. A large planter or barrel is a common choice of container, but they will grow in just about anything; other popular choices include tires, garbage cans, and burlap sacks.

A growing potato is an undemanding plant. It needs very little, other than mild temperatures, lots of water, and enough soil to keep it away from the sun.

Editor's Picks

The humble spud doesn't have to be boring. Here is a sampling of tasty potato varieties well suited for home gardens.

- 'Elba' is a yellow, flaky, and moist all-purpose potato.
- 'Kennebec' has smooth, thin skin and a creamy texture.
- 'Magic Molly' is deep purple both inside and out.
- 'Masquerade' has strikingly marbled purple-and-white skin and moist, white flesh.
- 'Princess Laratte" is a French variety with a nutty taste
- 'Red Gold' is a pretty potato that offers a nutty flavor with yellow flesh and raspberry-red eyes.
- 'Swedish Peanut Fingerling' has waxy, firm yellow flesh and a rich heirloom flavor.
- 'Yukon Gold' is an all-time favorite for roasting.

PUMPKIN

Scientific name: Curbita pcpo

Orange pumpkins peek out from under their large, green leaves. Growing pumpkins isn't hard and makes a popular activity for children to learn how to care for plants.

Pumpkins—reminiscent of autumn and county fairs. Who doesn't love those roasted pumpkin seeds or homemade pumpkin pie? And let's not forget those jack-o-lanterns for Halloween.

Although the term "pumpkin" is often used as a catch-all for any type of winter squash, the sweet pumpkin we grow for making pies will be a variety of *Cucurbita pepo.* One of the oldest domesticated vegetables, it mostly likely originated in what is now Mexico. Other pumpkin species include *C. maxima,* *C. argyrosprema,* and *C. moschata.*

Growing and caring for the plants

If you plan on growing pumpkins as a food crop, you can start your plants indoors about two to three weeks before the last frost date for your area.

Loosely pack some potting soil in a cup or a container with holes for drainage. Plant two to four seeds 1 inch (2.5 cm) deep. Water the seeds just enough so that the soil is moist but not swamped. Place the cup on a heating pad (which encourages seeds to grow faster). Once seeds have germinated, thin out all but the strongest seedling, and then place the seedling and cup under a light source. Once all danger of frost has passed, move the seedling to

the garden. Carefully remove it from the cup without disturbing the root. Place in a hole 1 to 2 inches (2.5 to 5 cm) deeper and wider than the rootball, and backfill the hole. Tap down around the pumpkin seedling, and water thoroughly.

When you plant pumpkin seeds outside, plan on a minimum of 20 square feet (2 m²) for each plant. To direct-seed outdoors, wait until the soil is at least 65°F (18°C). Mound the soil up a bit in the center of the chosen location to help the sun heat the seeds—the warmer the soil, the faster the seeds will germinate. In the mound, plant three to five seeds about 1 inch (2.5 cm) deep. Once the seeds germinate, select two of the healthiest, and thin out the rest.

If you decide to plant your pumpkins in a raised bed, miniature or pie varieties are good choices. Here are three suitable varieties.

- 'Cherokee Bush' is a classic orange variety producing fruit weighing 5 to 8 pounds (2 to 4 kg) with a spread of 4 to 5 feet (1.2 to 1.5 m).
- 'Jack of all Trades' has a 7-foot (2.1-m) spread and produces uniform orange carving pumpkins on compact vines.
- 'Small Sugar' is an heirloom pie variety with a manageable 4-foot (1.2-m) spread; it also stores well.

The Essentials

planting time early spring

light full sun

soil rich, moist, well-draining loam

pH level 6.0 to 6.8

water 1 to 2 inches (2.5 to 5 cm) per week

size 9 to 18 inches (23 to 45 cm) tall, 20 to 30 feet (6 to 9 m) long; 10 to 15 feet (3 to 4.5 m) spread

harvest in 90 to 160 days

Harvesting pumpkins

Aside from wanting pumpkins to display or carve, the ideal time to pick them is when they are fully ripe. Pumpkins that have reached the peak of maturity will have the best flavor, color, and the longest shelf life. To test if they are ready, look for a mature color and hard skin (press your fingernail into the surface: if it doesn't leave a dent, the skin has hardened). At this time, the stem will begin to turn brown and woody. To pick, use a pair of sharp pruning loppers to sever the vine 3 to 4 inches (7.5 to 10 cm) from the pumpkin. Freshly harvested pumpkins can be used immediately in recipes or preserved for future use.

Link to the Experts

READ MORE AT GARDENING KNOW HOW

To learn more about growing pumpkins in a raised bed, follow this link:

"Raised Bed Pumpkins – Growing Pumpkins in a Raised Bed"
LINK: gkh.us/140022

To learn more about proper pumpkin harvesting and storage, follow this link:

"How and When to Harvest Pumpkins in the Garden"
LINK: gkh.us/189548

SPOTLIGHT ON:

GROWING SQUASH

The *Cucurbita* genus is often referred to simply as "squash," but it includes almost all types of squash, pumpkin, and zucchini, as well as many gourds. Squashes are divided into two categories: summer (soft-skinned) and winter (hard-shelled). Winter squashes are usually vine growers; summer squashes tend to be bushier and don't cover as much ground.

Squashes prefer heat and require full sun, sufficient moisture, and fertile soil. Start indoors or sow directly into the garden when all danger of frost has passed. Plant in hills about 1 inch (2.5 cm) deep, placing four to five seeds per hill. Thin down to two or three of the healthiest plants per hill once the seedlings have developed their true leaves. Space hills and rows of summer squash 3 to 4 feet (1 to 1.2 m) apart; space winter squash 4 to 5 feet (1.2 to 1.5 m) apart with 5 to 7 feet (1.5 to 2.1 m) between rows.

Check plants daily—these crops grow quickly, especially in hot weather. Harvest frequently to encourage more production, and pick the fruits while still small. Overly ripe squash becomes hard and seedy and loses its flavor. Gather summer varieties before the seeds have fully ripened and while the rinds are still soft. Pick winter varieties when well matured. Store summer squash in cool, moist areas for up to two weeks, or you can freeze them. Winter squash can be stored in a cool, dry location for one to six months.

Editor's Tip

It is not just the fruit of these plants that are edible. Squash blossoms are golden blooms that are not only attractive, but are also good to eat. Follow this link to learn about edible squash blossoms.

"Picking Squash Blossoms –
How and When to Pick Squash Flowers"
LINK: gkh.us/14651

Summer Squash Varieties

CHAYOTE
Also called the vegetable pear or mirliton, this lumpy, wrinkly-skinned squash has a mild taste and crunchy texture. It is a staple of New Orleans cookery, where it is used in dressings, puddings, and casseroles or served stuffed.

PATTYPAN SQUASH
This pretty little squash, with its shallow shape and scalloped edges, comes in dark green, light green, yellow, or a mix. With edible skin and seeds, it is a versatile vegetable that you can sauté, grill, bake, or fry.

ROUND ZUCCHINI
Like its long, thin relative, the round zucchini is a fast grower. Best when picked at 3 to 4 inches (7.5 to 10 cm) in diameter, it has a mild flavor that works in recipes that call for stuffing, roasting, grilling, or baking.

YELLOW SQUASH
Easy-growing and fast-maturing, the yellow squash comes in two forms: straightneck and crookneck. Crookneck is a lemony yellow, 6-inch (15-cm) bulbous fruit with a curving neck and a mild, slightly nutty taste.

ZEPHYR SQUASH
A cross of a crookneck squash with a hybrid of the acorn and delicata, this squash is a stand-out with its slender, curved shape and two-toned coloration. Its tender, creamy yellow flesh has a sweet and nutty flavor.

ZUCCHINI
Also called courgette or baby marrow, this prolific producer is found in many home gardens. Whether yellow or green, the flavor is mild, slightly sweet, and slightly bitter. For more information, see page 149.

Winter Squash Varieties

ACORN SQUASH
This small squash grows to 1 to 2 pounds (450 to 900 g) with edible orange-yellow flesh and thick, dark green-and-orange skin. With a mild, subtly sweet and nutty flavor, it can be baked, roasted, steamed, or sautéed.

BANANA SQUASH
Reaching 2 to 3 feet (60 to 90 cm) in length and 40 pounds (18 kg) in weight, this large, elongated squash has smooth orange, pink, or blue skin. Its firm, brilliant orange flesh has a rich, sweet, earthy taste.

BUTTERCUP SQUASH
Squat and round with a dark green rind marked with green-gray, this squash has firm, bright orange flesh. Steam or bake it to bring out its sweet, creamy flavor. A hybrid of this variety and butternut is called honeynut.

BUTTERNUT SQUASH
This pear-shaped variety has a smooth, cream-colored exterior and bright orange flesh. The sweetest of the winter squashes, it can be roasted or sautéed, as well as pureed or made into delicious soups.

CARNIVAL SQUASH
A hybrid of the dumpling and acorn squashes, the carnival has a cream or peachy color covered with dark green stripes and blotches. Its orange flesh is nutty and sweet. Grill, sauté, or roast it for its full flavor.

DELICATA SQUASH
With green-and-white striated skin that is thin and edible, this squash can be cooked unpeeled. The tender flesh has a sweet flavor that works well as a stand-alone side dish or in roasted veggie medleys.

HUBBARD SQUASH
A large variety, about 1 foot (30 cm) wide and 15 to 20 pounds (7 to 9 kg) in weight, this squash has very bumpy skin. Its bright orange, fine-grained flesh tastes like a cross between sweet potato and pumpkin.

KABOCHA SQUASH
Also called Japanese pumpkin or chestnut squash, this small-to medium-sized squash has hard, dark green skin. With its sweet, earthy, and nutty flavor, is tastes great roasted, steamed, stuffed, or pureed.

RED KURI SQUASH
With its bright red-orange skin, this variety resembles a smooth-skinned sugar pumpkin. It has firm flesh with a delicate and chestnut-like flavor, and the skin is edible when cooked. Use it in both sweet and savory recipes.

SPAGHETTI SQUASH
With skin that comes in ivory, yellow, and orange, this squash is large, with an elongated oval shape. When cooked, the flesh shreds into pieces that resemble spaghetti, making it a perfect replacement for pasta.

SUGAR PUMPKIN
Also called pie or sweet pumpkins, these are the familiar fruits used in pies, soups, and scores of other autumn dishes. They are denser and sweeter than carving pumpkins. For more information, see page 129.

SWEET DUMPLING SQUASH
This variety has a flavor profile that works well in both sweet and savory dishes. It is a small variety—about the size of a grapefruit—and has hard, green-and-cream mottled skin with pale yellow or orange flesh.

RADICCHIO

Scientific name: *Cichorium intybus* var. *foliosum*

Growing radicchio shows its colors of green and red. As its common name implies, this vegetable is popular in Italy. In fact, varieties are named after the Italian regions where they originate, such as radicchio di Chioggia and radicchio rosso di Treviso.

The Essentials

planting time early spring; summer; autumn

light full sun

soil rich, moisture-retentive, loam

pH level 5.0 to 6.8

water 1 to 1½ inches (2.5 to 3.5 cm) per week

size 6 to 12 inches (15 to 30 cm) tall; 6 to 18 inches (15 to 45 cm) wide

harvest in 60 to 110 days

Radicchio, a member of the aster family, is one of the *Cichoriums*, or chicories, commonly found and cultivated in many areas of Europe. Its popularity has more recently crossed the pond, and it is now commonly utilized in the Americas, as well. It is often served in salads, sautéed for a side dish, or used as a garnish due to its attractive ruby hue.

Radicchio resembles a small cabbage head with white-ribbed burgundy-colored leaves. It is not to be confused with radichetta, another chicory with similar red coloration but lacking the heading form. Radicchio's leaf texture is similar to that of the French endive, another popular heading chicory variety.

Growing and caring for the plants

Radicchio can be grown as a spring, summer, or autumn vegetable, but the most common red-leaf heading radicchio does best when grown in cool temperatures. It is frost tolerant for a short period, and growing temperatures can fluctuate between 30°F and 90°F (-1°C and 32°C). Higher temperatures for any length of time, however, will burn the leaves, and it can only tolerate extreme cold for short periods.

This plant prefers plenty of sunlight, but it will tolerate shade in the garden, as well. It will grow in a variety of soil conditions, from sandy to clay-like loam, but it much prefers a neutral to alkaline soil pH of 7.5 to 8.0, excellent drainage, and plenty of water.

Radicchio can be directly sown into the ground or transplanted from seeds sown indoors, depending on the time of year and what climate you live in. If transplanting, start the seeds indoors four to six weeks before you plan to transplant them outdoors. If you're starting from direct-sown seeds outside, wait to plant them until after the danger of frost has passed. Plants should be spaced 8 to 12 inches (20 to 30 cm) apart in rows. They will need a constant supply of water to their shallow roots and to encourage the growth of the tender shoots. Consider using an automated watering system or irrigation.

There are several concerns about caring for these plants. Radicchio is often attacked by the same types of pests that menace members of the cabbage family, such as aphids, many beetle types, thrips, and ants. Most of these radicchio pests can be countered by any number of chemical or biological deterrents. Consult with your local garden supply center or agricultural extension about methods of control related to your specific insect invader, type of plant, and climate.

Radicchio can also be affected by a variety of fungal issues and powdery molds. These usually occur due to inadequate drainage and are most common in areas with extremely wet conditions. Make sure each plant has well-draining soil and good air circulation to minimize the risk of mold, mildew, fungal infection, and rot.

Harvesting radicchio

Growing radicchio heads are green or reddish green until cold weather arrives; they will then take on a rich range of reds, from pink to dark burgundy. You can harvest radicchio almost any time during growth, as early as when leaves are just 2 to 3 inches (5 to 7.5 cm) long or after a head fully forms and feels firm to the touch. If you snip away the older leaves, the younger ones at the center will continue growing for later use.

Place your radicchio harvest in a perforated plastic bag, and store in a cold and moist place, such as your fridge's vegetable crisper. It will keep for about three to four weeks.

RADISH

Scientific name: Raphanus raphanistrum subsp. *sativus*

When radishes near maturity, the tops of their swollen roots might begin to emerge from the soil. To check their progress and determine if they are harvest ready, pull up a sacrificial plant to see if the roots have reached a usable size.

The radish (*Raphanus raphanistrum* subsp. *sativus*), an edible root vegetable, has been cultivated for thousands of years and is now grown and consumed throughout the world. Mostly eaten raw, it imparts a spicy, peppery flavor and crunchy texture to salads and adds a decorative accent to relish trays. When cooked, it maintains its flavor and texture, making it an excellent addition to roasted root vegetable medleys. It is also an excellent source of potassium, vitamin C, and folate.

There are five main varieties, with hybrids branching from these. 'Red Globe' is an early, high-yielding variety producing uniform, bright red globes with crisp, tender, juicy, and mild white flesh. Black radish, a winter variety, is crisp and pungent, with spicy white flesh. 'California Mammoth', a large, round, white radish, has a mild, sweet flavor. Daikon is a crisp and juicy Chinese variety with a mild and tangy taste. 'Crisp White Icicles' is a long, white tapered variety with a rich, spicy flavor.

Growing and caring for the plants

Radishes are generally grown from seed and grow best in cool weather. They require a loose soil for proper root formation. You can add composted manure, grass, and leaves to improve soil fertility. Remove rocks, sticks, and inorganic debris from the planting site. Soil should be consistently moist, but heavy rains can compact soil and form a hard surface crust that inhibits root formation; drought stress toughens radishes and alters their mild flavor.

Sow seeds as soon as the soil can be worked in the spring or in late summer for an autumn crop. Spade or till the soil to a depth of 8 to 12 inches (20 to 30 cm). Using a hoe, make rows about 1 inch (2.5 cm) deep. Plant the seeds by hand, with a seeder, or with radish seed tape. Push the seeds into the soil to a depth of ½ inch (1.25 cm), spacing them 1 inch (2.5 cm) apart. Once a row is filled, cover the seeds with a loose layer of soil. Lightly sprinkle the rows with water, enough to settle the seeds in, but not soaking the soil. Watering too hard can wash the seeds out of the soil. Germination takes 4 to 6 days. For a steady harvest, use succession planting by sowing seeds every 7 to 10 days.

Harvesting radishes

Radishes mature quickly, with most varieties ready for harvest in three to five weeks. They can be harvested at any usable size, but smaller radish roots tend to be zestier. As roots mature, they become tougher. If left in the ground too long, they will turn woody. Watering them well the night before harvesting them makes it far easier to pull them from the ground. To harvest round types, firmly grasp the foliage and base of the plant, and gently pull the root from the soil. For longer varieties, use a shovel or fork to loosen the soil so that the root doesn't break when pulling. Harvested radishes store well for several weeks in the refrigerator.

The Essentials

planting time late winter; early spring; late summer; autumn

light full to partial sun

soil lighter, well-draining sandy soil

pH level 6.5 to 7.0

water soak the soil thoroughly at least once per week

size 6 to 18 inches (15 to 45 cm) tall; 3 to 14 inches (7.5 to 36 cm) wide

harvest in 20 to 75 days

Editor's Tip

The following tips should help you harvest a good radish crop.

- If the soil becomes crusty, lightly sprinkle the surface with water. Gently break up the surface using your hands or a small cultivator.

- As roots reach an edible size, harvest every other one to increase the space between remaining plants.

- Radishes need 1 inch (2.5 cm) of rain or supplemental water a week. Water deeply, as they have large taproots and few horizontal roots.

- Full sun gives the best yields, but radishes can also tolerate light shade.

RAMP

Scientific name: *Allium tricoccum*

Ramps, or wild leeks. Some folks say the name "ramp" is a shortened version of Aries the Ram, the zodiac sign for April and the month that growing ramps usually begin to appear. Others say "ramp" is derived from a similar English plant called ramsons.

The Essentials

planting time late summer to early autumn

light shade to partial shade

soil moist, well-draining, loamy soil

pH level 6.8 to 7.2

water 1½ inches (3.5 cm) per week

size 6 to 8 inches (15 to 20 cm) tall; 4 to 20 inches (10 to 50 cm) wide

harvest in 4 to 10 years

Once the province of foragers who would comb the woodlands in search of these wild leeks, ramps (*Allium tricoccum*) have increasingly entered the rows of many kitchen gardens. Both early North American colonists and Native Americans prized ramps as an important early spring food source after months of no fresh vegetables and were considered a tonic. Today they are found sautéed in butter or olive oil in fine dining establishments.

Ramps are native to the moist woodlands of eastern North America's Appalachians, where they are commonly found in groups in rich, moist, deciduous forests. A member of the onion family, these pungent vegetables can now be found at many farmers' markets grown by local farmers. This is creating a demand for more ramps, which is exciting many a home gardener.

Ramps are easily identified by their foliage; usually two broad, flat leaves are produced from each bulb. The leaves are light, silvery green, 1 to 2½ inches (2.5 to 6 cm) wide and 5 to 10 inches (12.5 to 25 cm) long. As spring bloomers, the leaves wither and die by late spring or early summer, and a small cluster of white flowers is produced.

Ramps are harvested for their bulbs and leaves, which taste like pungent spring onions with a garlicky aroma. Ramps and their relatives have been used medicinally to treat a host of ailments, and one of these traditional remedies has crossed over into the world of modern medicine. One of the most common uses of both garlic and ramps was to expel internal worms, and a concentrated form is now produced commercially called allicin, which comes from the scientific name *Allium,* the genus for all onions, garlic, and ramps.

Growing and caring for the plants

Ramps can be grown from seed or via transplants. Seeds can be sown at any time the soil isn't frozen, with late summer to early autumn the prime time. Seeds need a warm, moist period to break dormancy, followed by a cold period. If there is not sufficient warming after sowing, the seeds will not germinate until the second spring, meaning germination can take anywhere from 6 to 18 months.

Keep in mind that ramps naturally grow in shaded areas with rich, moist, well-draining soil high in organic matter. When preparing your garden soil to plant a crop of ramps, think damp forest floor. Incorporate plenty of the organic matter found in decaying forest soil, such as composted leaves or decaying plants. Remove weeds, loosen the soil, and rake to prepare a fine seed bed. Thinly sow the seeds on top of the ground, and then press them gently into the soil. Water and cover the ramp seeds with about 3 to 4 inches (7.5 to 10 cm) of leaves to retain moisture.

If you are transplanting bulbs, plant them in late winter to early spring. Set the bulbs 3 inches (7.5 cm) deep and 4 to 6 inches (10 to 15 cm) apart. Water and mulch the bed with 2 to 3 inches (5 to 7.5 cm) of composted leaves. With such a short growing time, these ephemeral plants will need little care once they are in the ground.

Harvesting ramps

Harvest your ramps as soon as they leaf out, but be careful not to deplete your patch until it has had a chance to enlarge and fully establish itself. Ideally, you should leave a patch undisturbed for a few years. You can then harvest by thinning out the largest plants, carefully digging out the whole clump, including the bulb. You can then chop them to eat raw in salads, or fry or blanch them to flavor other dishes. Ramps can also be pickled or dried for later use.

RHUBARB

Scientific name: Rheum rhabarbarum

Stalks of rhubarb in the garden. The tart flavor of the ruby red stems of this vegetable makes them suitable for use in recipes for pies, crumbles, jams, and sauces.

The Essentials

planting time spring

light full to partial sun

soil well-draining loamy soil

pH level 6.0 and 6.8

water 1 inch (2.5) per week

size 2 to 3 feet (60 cm to 1 m) tall;
3 to 4 feet (1 to 1.2 m) wide

harvest in 2 years

Rhubarb (*Rheum rhabarbarum*) is a perennial vegetable in the buckwheat family, harvested for its long stalks. The stalks have a sour flavor that works great in pies, sauces, and jellies. Rhubarb pairs especially well with strawberries, so you may want to plant both in your garden.

Growing and caring for the plants

Temperature should be your first consideration. Plant rhubarb where the winter temperatures go below 40°F (4°C), so that dormancy can be broken when it warms up in the spring. Summer temperatures below 75°F (24°C) on average will yield quite a nice crop.

Because rhubarb is a perennial, its care is a little different from that of many other vegetables. Choose a sunny spot with good drainage, and plant it along the edge of your garden, so that it doesn't disturb your other vegetable crops when it comes up each spring. You should purchase either crowns or divisions from your local garden center. Each of these crowns or divisions will require enough space to rise up from the soil and provide you with large,

healthy leaves. This means planting them about 1 to 2 feet (30 to 60 cm) apart in rows that are spaced about 2 to 3 feet (60 cm to 1 m) apart. Each growing rhubarb plant requires about 1 square yard (1 m²) of space.

Rhubarb plants prefer loamy soils, and because they are heavy feeders that take in large amounts of nutrients from the soil, you should amend the soil with either a balanced commercial fertilizer or rich compost, or both.

Once you have prepared the soil, take the crowns, and place them in the ground. Don't plant them deeper than 1 or 2 inches (2.5 to 5 cm) into the soil,

Editor's Tip

Use a sweetener when cooking rhubarb. Extremely tart when raw, it is almost always stewed or baked with a generous serving of sugar or honey. It is most famously paired with strawberries in a pie.

or they won't come up. When flower stalks appear on the growing rhubarb, remove them right away so that they don't rob the plant of nutrients. Make sure you water the plants during dry weather; rhubarb doesn't tolerate drought.

The care of established rhubarb plants doesn't require a whole lot of effort from you. They pretty much just come up each spring and grow well all on their own. Just remove any weeds from the planting area, and carefully cultivate around the stalks so that you don't injure the growing plants.

Harvesting rhubarb

Rhubarb is one of the first crops of the year, but don't harvest the first season after planting—this will inhibit your plant from expanding to its fullest size. Wait until the second year, and then begin picking stalks as soon as they have reached their full length—depending on the variety you've planted, this can be as short as 12 inches (30 cm) or as long as 2 feet (60 cm).

Avoid cutting the stalks with a knife. Instead, firmly grasp the stalk, and then pull and twist. After harvesting the stalks, use a knife to trim the leaves from the stalks, and immediately discard them. The leaves are toxic, and keeping them on can speed up the wilting of the stalks.

You can use your rhubarb fresh or blanch and freeze it for later use in pies and other recipes.

Note: *Rhubarb leaves and roots are toxic to both people and pets.*

RUTABAGA

Scientific name: Brassica napus

The harvest-ready roots of a pair of rutabaga plants have emerged from the soil.

The Essentials

planting time early spring; mid- to late summer; autumn

light full sun

soil well-draining, loamy soil

pH level 6.0 to 6.5

water 1 inch (2.5 cm) per week

size 12 to 24 inches (30 to 60 cm) tall; 9 to 12 inches (23 to 30 cm) wide

harvest in 80 to 100 days

Enjoyed as both a root and a leaf veggie, rutabaga (*Brassica napus*) is a hybrid cross between *B. oleracea* (the cabbage) and *B. rapa* (the turnip). This species is known as a swede in Britain; Swedish turnip or neep in Scotland; or turnip in Scotland, Canada, Ireland, and the Isle of Man, although elsewhere "turnip" refers to the white turnip (see page 146). The difference between the two is that the rutabaga's roots are larger, firmer, and rounder than turnip roots, and rutabaga's leaves are smoother. The firm yellow flesh is sweeter, too, and almost buttery when cooked. Served raw, it is crisp and juicy. In parts of the British Isles the large, slightly elongated bulbs are carved into jack-o'-lanterns for Halloween.

Growing and caring for the plants

Although rutabagas are biennials, they are usually grown as annual crops. They require a long growing season and cool weather in which to mature and sweeten, so when to plant greatly depends on your area's climate. In cooler areas, plant them in either early spring, after the danger of frost, or mid- to late summer so that you can allow them to mature in the cool weather of autumn. In warmer climates, you can plant seeds in autumn to grow them over the winter.

Choose a site with full sun and soil rich in organic matter. Rake the soil, and remove any debris and rocks. Throw the seed down in the prepared soil, at a rate of 3 to 20 seeds per row, and lightly rake them into the soil to about ½ inch (1.25 cm) deep. Space the rows about 1 to 2 feet (30 to 60 cm) apart, which will give the roots room to plump up.

If the soil isn't moist, water the seeds to germinate them, and establish healthy seedlings. Once seedlings appear and are about 2 inches (5 cm) tall, thin them to about 6 inches (15 cm) apart. A bonus of thinning rutabaga plants is that you can actually eat the thinned leaves as greens. Cultivate between the plants that are left to a depth of 2 to 3 inches (5 to 8 cm). This helps aerate the soil and gets rid of weeds. You want the dirt to be firm around the bottom of the leaves but looser underneath to allow for larger root growth. If you have well prepared the soil, the plants won't need any additional fertilizer, but a midseason boost of a side dressing of compost will encourage them to make it through to harvest time.

Harvesting rutabagas

Be sure the rutabagas you harvest have grown without any interruptions in the growing season and when they are tender and mild. The best-quality rutabagas should be ready to harvest when they are medium sized, about 3 to 5 inches (8 to 12.5 cm) in diameter. You can remove all leaves, and then store rutabaga in the refrigerator or any cool, dark place for months.

Link to the Experts

READ MORE AT GARDENING KNOW HOW

It's inevitable that problems pop up in garden vegetables now and then, and rutabagas are no exception. To alleviate the majority of rutabaga plant issues, it helps to become familiar with the most common pests or diseases affecting these plants. To learn more, follow this link.

"Common Rutabaga Problems: Learn About Rutabaga Pests and Disease" LINK: gkh.us/19177

SPINACH

Scientific name: Spinacia oleracea

A row of dark green spinach plants grows alongside a row of lettuce. You can create a "salad garden" by planting several greens with similar growing needs in one plot.

The Essentials

planting time late winter or early spring; late summer to early autumn

light full to partial sun

soil well-draining soil rich in organic matter

pH level 6.5 to 8

water 1 inch (2.5) per week

size 6 to 12 inches (15 to 30 cm) tall; 6 to 12 inches (15 to 30 cm) wide

harvest 40 to 60 days

Spinach (*Spinacia oleracea*) has been cultivated for over 2,000 years, and it remains a great addition to any vegetable garden today. This common plant is easy to grow and extremely healthful; spinach is a great source of iron, calcium, and vitamins A, B, C, and K.

Growing and caring for the plants

Spinach is a cool-weather crop that does best in the spring and autumn. It prefers well-draining, rich soil and a sunny location. In regions with higher temperatures, the crop will benefit from some light shade from taller plants.

The soil should have a pH of at least 6.5 and, ideally, it should be close to neutral—between 6.5 and 7.5. Before planting, amend the seed bed with compost or aged manure. Sow seeds when outdoor temperatures are at least 45°F (7°C). Space the seeds 3 inches (7.5 cm) apart in rows, and cover lightly with soil. For successive plantings, sow another batch of seeds every two to three weeks.

Spinach takes about six weeks to mature. For an autumn crop, sow seeds from late summer to early autumn, or as late as four to six weeks before the first frost date. If needed, provide a row cover or cold frame to protect the plants from chilly weather. Spinach can also be planted in containers. To grow spinach in a pot, use a container that is at least 8 inches (20 cm) deep.

Keep spinach consistently moist, not soggy. Water deeply and regularly, especially during dry periods, and keep the area around the plants weeded. Feed the plant at midseason with compost, blood meal, or kelp to encourage rapid growth of new, tender leaves. Spinach is a heavy feeder, so if you do not incorporate or side dress with compost, incorporate a 10-10-10 fertilizer prior to planting.

Look out for leaf miners, which are common insect pests associated with spinach crops. Frequently check the undersides of the leaves for eggs. When leaf miner tunnels are evident, destroy the leaves. Floating row covers can also help repel these damaging insects.

Harvesting spinach

You can begin harvesting spinach leaves as soon as they are large enough to eat. When picking a batch, just remove the outer leaves; this allows the center leaves to continue growing for another harvest later on.

MORE INFO *Varieties of spinach*

Spinach comes in three main varieties, categorized by the types of leaves that they produce: smooth leaf, savoy, and semi-savoy.

- Smooth-leaf spinach. The leaves of this type are smooth and flat, which makes it easy to rinse off any impurities from their surfaces. Most processed, commercial spinach is smooth leaf.

- Savoy spinach. These leaves are thick and deeply crinkled, which makes it hard to clean them of any sand and dirt. Savoy will keep longer and contains less oxalic acid than flat-leaf spinach.

- Semi-savoy spinach. The leaves are crinkled, but not as much as with savoy. Despite the crinkles, they are quite easy to clean because the leaves are partially straight. This is a popular variety for home gardens.

A Gallery of
BERRIES

Berries can be some of the most rewarding plants to grow. When picked at their peak of ripeness, few fruits can rival them for sweetness and flavor. Technically, berries are small, pulpy, often edible fruit . . . juicy, rounded, brightly colored, with a sweet or tart flavor. They do not usually have a stone like a cherry or plum, but pips or small seeds may be present.

Wild berries were a key food source for humans since before the dawn of agriculture and still remain among the primary food sources of other primates. For thousands of years, berries were a seasonal staple for hunter-gatherers, who soon learned to store them for the winter. They eventually began making them into fruit preserves or pemmican, a Native American mixture of berries with meat and fats. Blackberries and raspberries were first cultivated in Europe around the 17th century. Today the most widely grown commercial example is the strawberry, with a yearly yield of twice the amount of all other berries combined.

There are many berry varieties, and most are simple to grow. Strawberries, blueberries, raspberries, and blackberries are typically the most popular garden choices, but there are also plenty of exotic or lesser-known examples that can be grown in containers as part of your edible landscape. Goji berry, black chokecherry, and honeyberry are some unusual candidates that will add interest to a backyard berry patch.

Whether you are planting the more traditional varieties or growing unusual berries in pots, place your beds or containers in a spot with plenty of direct sunlight. The needs of species vary, but most require at least six hours of sun a day to produce the most fruit. When you are growing berries in containers, irrigation is also important. Depending on the types of berries you select, you may have to water several times a week.

If you want to try growing berries in your garden, start with one or more of the examples shown on these pages, and discover how much flavor you will add to your life.

BLACKBERRY
Easy-care, rambling blackberries (*Rubus* spp.)—whose fruit is described as an aggregate of drupelets—are members of the rose family. These tasty berries are some of these easiest fruits to grow in a home garden.

BLUEBERRY
Homegrown blueberries (*Vaccinium* sect. *cyanococcus*) are more flavorful than store-bought berries. They are great eaten fresh or in pies, muffins, or pancakes. Bilberries are a closely related European species of *Vaccinium*.

BOYSENBERRY
This large maroon "bramble" fruit is a cross between dewberry, loganberry, raspberry, and blackberry. Soft-textured and richly flavored boysenberries (*Rubus ursinus*) are ideal for making jam or juice.

CHILEAN GUAVA
Chilean guava (*Ugni molinae*), also called strawberry myrtle, is an evergreen shrub that reaches 3 to 6 feet (1 to 1.8 m) in height when mature. The fruit looks like a reddish blueberry and has a slightly spicy flavor.

CHOKEBERRY
Healthful chokeberries (*Aronia melanocarpa*) are part of the rose family. They enjoy full sun and their strong roots retain moisture. The dark purple fruit makes great jam, jelly, juice, tea, and wine.

CRANBERRY
Cranberries (*Vaccinium macrocarpon*) grow in bogs, but these woody perennial vines can thrive in your backyard. High in nutrients and antioxidants, these tart berries are made into jellies and are added to baked goods.

CURRANT
Clustering, pea-sized currants (*Ribes* spp.) come in several varieties—black, red, and white. With their sweet, bright, acidic flavor, they are popular berries and are tasty when eaten fresh or made into pies and jams.

GOJI BERRY
Also called wolfberry, Goji berry (*Lycium barbarum*) is a popular "health" berry. The goji berry is the bright orange-red fruit of a shrub native to China. This berry is remarkably tolerant of heat and cold.

GOOSEBERRY
Gooseberry is the common name for many species in the genus *Ribes*. The smooth, rounded berries, which may be green, orange, red, purple, yellow, white, or black, have a grapelike flavor.

GROUND CHERRY
Ground cherries (*Physalis* spp.), also called husk tomatoes or cape gooseberries, are low-lying plants, similar to the tomatillo. They grow inside a papery husk and taste very similar to strawberries.

HONEYBERRY
Also known as blue honeysuckle and fly honeysuckle, honeyberry (*Lonicera caerulea*) is a small, almost rectangular blue berry that grows on attractive, silver-green foliage that turns bright yellow in autumn.

HUCKLEBERRY
Related to blueberries, huckleberries are plants in two closely related genera, *Vaccinium* and *Gaylussacia*. The berries may be red, black, or blue and have a somewhat fruity, red wine flavor.

LINGONBERRY
Lingonberry shrubs (*Vaccinium vitis-idaea*) produce brilliant red berries with a pleasing, tart flavor. They are popular in Scandinavian cooking, especially as a garnish for crepes and in sauces.

LOGANBERRY
A hybrid species, loganberry (*Rubus × loganobaccus*) resembles the blackberry, but this slightly tart fruit is a dark red and tastes similar to a raspberry. Eat them fresh or use them to make jam.

RASPBERRY
Raspberry (*Rubus* spp.), a thorny shrub that produces tart drupelets in red, white, yellow, and black, is used in juices, jellies, and pies. Some raspberry varieties produce in the spring, others in the autumn.

SERVICEBERRY
The serviceberry or shadbush tree (*Amelanchier canadensis*) is often used as an ornamental for its showy white flowers, but its fruit, also called juneberry, makes tasty cobblers, wines, and jams.

STRAWBERRY
These succulent red berries (*Fragaria × ananassa*), famous for their delicious taste and scent, will grow in containers, hanging baskets, in the ground, or in raised beds. For more information, see page 138.

WINEBERRY
These red berries, which grow wild along fields and roads in many places, are still used as the breeding stock for hybrid raspberries. Wineberries (*Rubus phoenicolasius*) make tasty wine, jam, and baked desserts.

STRAWBERRY

Scientific name: Fragaria × ananassa

A bright red, harvest-ready strawberry. Nothing beats the taste of a homegrown berry.

Strawberries (*Fragaria × ananassa*) are a delicious addition to any garden and provide a sweet treat all summer. In fact, one plant started in June can produce up to 120 new plants in one season.

Growing and caring for the plants

The best time to plant June- and spring-bearing strawberries is on a cloudy day in March or April, as soon as the ground is workable. This gives the plants ample time to get established before warm weather arrives. Find a spot where the plants will receive six or more hours of full-sun exposure. Many varieties produce blossoms in early spring that can be killed by a late frost unless there's plenty of sun on them. Also keep in mind that the amount of sun will determine the size of the crop and the size of the berries, as well. Do not plant them where tomatoes, potatoes, peppers, or even strawberries have been grown in the previous two years. This will help to avoid root disease problems.

Rich, well-draining soil with a pH factor of 5.8 to 6.5 works best, so work some organic compost into the soil in your beds or pots. Place the plants just deep enough to cover the roots with about ¼ inch (6 mm) of soil, leaving the crowns exposed. Space them 12 to 18 inches (30 to 45 cm) apart in rows about 3 feet (1 m) apart. This will allow June- and spring-bearing plants enough space to send out "daughters," or runners. (Plant everbearing plants individually in mounded hills in mid-September to mid-October for a spring berry harvest.) As soon as your plants are in the ground, water, and then apply an all-purpose fertilizer to get them off to a good start. Once the plants are established, water regularly with an average of 1 to 2 inches (2.5 to 5 cm) every day. Drip or soaker hoses placed nearby work best.

Remove all the blossoms from your June-bearing plant during its first growth season, and remove blossoms from everbearing plants until early July. After these first rounds of blossoms are taken off, the plants will produce berries. Pinching the first blossoms helps the root systems strengthen and helps the plants make better, bigger berries.

Harvesting strawberries

Once the berries are fully colored with no green tips, you can pick them. Morning, when the berries are still cool, is the best time. Strawberries are delicate fruits and bruise easily, so care must be taken— bruised fruit will degrade faster, while unblemished berries last longer and store better. To harvest, grasp the stem between your forefinger and thumbnail, and then lightly pull and twist at the same time. Let the berry roll into the palm of your hand. Gently place the fruit in a container. Continue harvesting in this manner, taking care not to overfill the container or pack the berries too tightly.

Cool the berries as soon as possible once harvested, but don't wash them until you are ready to use them. They will stay fresh for three days in the refrigerator, but after that, they go downhill fast. If your strawberry harvest yielded more berries than you can eat or give away, don't despair, you can salvage the harvest. Strawberries freeze beautifully and can be used later for desserts, smoothies, chilled strawberry soup, or anything that is cooked or pureed. You can also make the berries into jam; frozen strawberry jam recipes are easy to find and simple to make.

Link to the Experts

READ MORE AT GARDENING KNOW HOW

There are numerous uses of strawberry fruit, as well as ways to preserve it. To learn more, follow this link.

"Fresh Strawberry Uses – What to Do with Strawberries from the Garden"
LINK: gkh.us/160205

SWEET POTATO

Scientific name: Ipomoea batatas

A gardener digs up the soil to reveal a nice harvest of sweet potatoes. This flavorful root vegetable is a favorite in many autumn and winter recipes.

The sweet potato is the large, sweet-tasting tuberous root of the *Ipomoea batatas* plant. A native of the tropical regions of the Americas, it is the only major crop plant of the more than a thousand species of Convolvulaceae, or the morning glory family. Along with the starchy root, the young shoots and leaves of the plant are also edible and are sometimes eaten as greens.

Sweet potatoes are warm-weather vegetables; they do not grow like regular potatoes, and in fact they aren't related to potatoes at all. Sweet potatoes grow on vines, require a long, frost-free growing season, and produce a sweet, bright orange-fleshed tuber that is an especially popular ingredient in autumn and winter dishes. Some varieties can be found that produce white, yellow, or purple sweet potatoes.

Growing and caring for the plants

When growing sweet potatoes, start out with "slips," which are small pieces of tubers. (You can also start them from sweet potatoes you buy from the grocery store, but purchased slips are quality-controlled to be disease-free.) Plant the slips into the ground as soon as all chance of frost has passed, and the ground has warmed. Sweet potatoes require a soil temperature of 70°F to 80°F (21°C to 27°C), so you should start them in early summer to midsummer. Otherwise, the soil won't be warm enough.

Plant the slips 12 to 18 inches (30 to 45 cm) apart on a wide, raised ridge of soil that is about 8 inches (20 cm) high. Leave about 3 to 4 feet (1 to 1.2 m) between rows, so that there will be enough space to work between them when harvesting. Keep the soil moist during the growing season, but make sure it drains well to limit the chances of rot setting in. From the moment you plant the slips, it takes only six weeks for the sweet potatoes to be ready to harvest.

Harvesting sweet potatoes

To harvest the growing sweet potatoes, just stick your shovel into the side of the ridge. You can feel around for the sweet potatoes and pull them out that way, being careful not to injure others still growing. They are generally ready around the first frost of autumn.

A standard crop of sweet potatoes will usually produce more tubers than you can eat right away. When stored in a cool, dry place, they can last for several weeks.

The Essentials

planting time early to midsummer

light full to partial shade

soil well-draining light, sandy loam or silt loam

pH level 5.5 to 6.5

water once per week

size 1 to 12 inches (2.5 to 30 cm) tall; 5 to 20 feet (1.5 to 6 m) wide

harvest in 85 to 150 days

SIMILAR PLANTS
Yams

Although the names "yam" and "sweet potato" are often used interchangeably, these are two different plants. They have many similarities—both are sweet, autumn-harvest tubers, for instance—but they are actually members of entirely separate families: yams are related to lilies and are members of the Dioscoreaceae family, while sweet potatoes are members of the morning glory family (Convolvulaceae). Yams grow best in tropical to subtropical climates, because they need up to a full year of frost-free temperatures to mature. They are commonly grown in Central and South America, the Caribbean, and Africa. They should be planted in early spring.

SWISS CHARD

Scientific name: Beta vulgaris subsp. *vulgaris*

The heavily textured leaf blades of highly nutritious and tasty Swiss chard can be a green or reddish color, and the stalks are usually white, yellow, or bright red.

Value your leafy greens? You may want to grow a crop of colorful and highly nutritious Swiss chard. For those on a vegan or keto eating plan, chard is the perfect companion to spinach and kale. Swiss chard, or simply chard, falls into two groups of *Beta vulgaris* subsp. *vulgaris*. The large leaf stalks of cultivars in the Flavescens Group are often prepared separately from the leaf blade; the Cicla Group gives us the leafy spinach beet.

Technically speaking, chard is a beet, but it doesn't have a bulbous root. It's referred to as a member of the goosefoot family due to the shape of its leaves. Swiss chard has been used in cooking for centuries, which has resulted in a plethora of common names, including silver beet, perpetual spinach, beet spinach, seakale beet, or leaf beet. What makes it Swiss? It was identified and named by a Swiss botanist.

Full of vitamins A and C, Swiss chard counts toward the dark leafy vegetable component of your diet. A bit crunchier than spinach, but more tender than kale, this gorgeous vegetable comes in an array of colors. It makes a great addition to soups, casseroles, stir-fry dishes, and salads. The leaves are ready to eat raw or cooked. Its stiffer ribs can be removed and cooked until tender for any dish that needs an extra nutritional boost.

Growing and caring for the plants

Swiss chard is easy to grow, and the plant thrives when given suitable conditions. It just needs enough room, adequate water, and perhaps a bit of fertilizer. It also likes an area with full sun to partial shade and with soil loose enough to drain well.

As part of a spring garden, you'll want to get seeds into the ground in early to mid-spring, or at least when you're sure there's no longer a chance of frost. A good rule of thumb is to be sure the soil is at least 50°F (10°C), which is warm enough for the seeds to germinate. To ensure a steady supply of chard, you can use succession planting, sowing new seeds every couple of weeks, to lengthen the harvest time. If you prefer growing Swiss chard through the winter, get your seeds into the ground at least a month prior to the first autumn frost. As a winter vegetable, chard grows well with other root crops, like carrots, turnips, and parsnips. It also grows well with the aforementioned spinach and kale. This lovely and highly nutritious vegetable is happiest when the temperatures of spring and autumn are cool and moderate. It will still do well in summer weather, but the warmth will make it grow a little more slowly.

To plant, make a row in the soil and insert the seeds about a ½ inch (1.25 cm) or so deep, with 8 to 10 seeds per 1 foot (30 cm). Keep about 18 inches (20 cm) of space between your rows. When the plants are 2 inches (5 cm) tall, thin them so that they're 4 to 6 inches (10 to 15 cm) apart. Swiss chard plants can grow up to 2 feet (60 cm) in a season if they get enough water.

Harvesting Swiss chard

Begin to harvest your greens when your plants reach around 9 to 12 inches (23 to 30 cm) high. If you wait until they're much taller than that, they'll lose some of their flavor. Cut the outer leaves first to allow the tender inner leaves to grow.

Once you've completely harvested a chard plant, pull it up and toss the root into your compost. This will give your remaining plants more space to grow.

TOMATO

Scientific name: Solanum lycopersicum

A pole system supports the growing vines of tomato plants. Favorites with home gardeners, they can be grown in containers for those with only small spaces to spare.

Nothing compares to the juicy taste of a red, ripe tomato straight out of the garden. These delectable fruits not only taste great but are quite easy to grow and mature quite early. They can grow in a variety of conditions, with the exception of the extreme cold, and they don't require a lot of space. You can start them from seed or transplant from seedlings, and they can thrive when planted straight in the ground or in containers. Some common varieties are cherry, heirloom, roma, main crop, and beefsteak tomatoes, but there are hundreds of types to choose from, depending on individual preferences.

Growing and caring for the plants

Tomatoes should usually be started indoors when growing from seeds, because they need a good deal of heat to germinate. Start about six to eight weeks before you plan on planting them out into your garden. For colder areas, plan to plant two to three weeks after your last frost, so you should start growing tomatoes from seed at four to six weeks before your last frost date.

Tomato seeds can be started in small pots of damp seed-starting soil, damp potting soil, or in moistened peat pellets. Plant two seeds in each container to increase your chances of developing a seedling in each, in case some of the seeds do not germinate. The tomato seeds should be planted about three times deeper than the size of the seed—roughly ¼ inch (6 mm) deep or less, depending on the tomato variety.

After the tomato seeds have been planted, place the seedling containers in a warm place. For fastest germination, temperatures of 70°F to 80°F (21°F to 27°F) are best, especially if heated from below. Many gardeners find that placing the planted containers on top of the refrigerator or another appliance that generates heat while running works very well for germination. A heating pad on low, covered with a towel, will also work.

After planting, the tomato seeds should germinate in one to two weeks. Cooler temperatures will result in a longer germination time, and warmer temperatures will encourage the tomato seeds to germinate faster.

Tomatoes can grow roots along their stems, so plant them deep—right up to the first set of leaves. If a plant is unstable, dig a small trench, and lay it on its side, gently bending it into a right angle. Bury the stem in this position, leaving the first two leaves exposed. Allow for 3 feet (1 m) between plants and 5 feet (1.5 m) between rows. They will need support as they grow, either from stakes or cages. Set the stakes in place when you plant the seedlings, and loosely tie the plants to the stakes as they grow.

Harvesting tomatoes

Watch the bottom of the fruit carefully: this is where tomatoes begin to ripen. Lightly squeeze to test for firmness. Once the first bloom of red appears on the skin, it's harvest time. Grasp the fruit firmly, but gently, and pull by holding the stem with one hand and the fruit with the other, breaking the stalk just above the calyx. Store them indoors to continue to ripen. Store them at 55°F to 70°F (13°C to 21°C)—or cooler to slow the ripening and warmer to hasten it—and routinely check for ripeness. They can last from three to five weeks stored this way.

Dig Deeper

LEARN MORE AT GARDENING KNOW HOW

Scan the QR code or follow the link below to learn about container-grown tomatoes.

"Growing Tomatoes in Containers for Beginners" *LINK:* gkh. us/188007

TURNIP

Scientific name: Brassica rapa subsp. *rapa*

The top of a harvest-ready autumn turnip turns pinkish red when exposed to the sun.

The Essentials

planting time spring; autumn

light full sun to partial shade

soil well-draining soil high in organic matter

pH level 6.0 to 6.5

water 1 inch per week

size 6 to 18 inches (15 to 45 cm) tall; 4 to 8 inches (10 to 20 cm) wide

harvest in 30 to 70 days

The fleshy turnip or white turnip (*Brassica rapa* subsp. *rapa*) has long been served as a root vegetable, and small, tender varieties are commonly grown worldwide in temperate climates for human consumption. Yet, the name "turnip" can be confusing—in northern England, Scotland, Ireland, Cornwall, and parts of Canada, the name usually refers to a rutabaga, a *Brassica* cousin (see page 136). The turnip is also sometimes listed under its Latin synonym *B. campestris*.

The most common type is primarily white-skinned, except for the upper part of the globular root that protrudes aboveground, which turns pink, purple, red, or greenish in sunlight. The interior flesh is entirely white. The root typically measures from 2 to 8 inches (5 to 20 cm) in diameter and lacks side roots. The thin taproot measures about 4 inches (10 cm) in length. The leaves grow aboveground from the root, and these are often eaten as "turnip greens." These have a flavor similar to mustard greens, to which they are closely related, and they are commonly served in the American Southeast as a side dish in late autumn and winter. Turnip greens are best when the leaves are harvested while still small—large leaves can often have a bitter taste.

Growing and caring for the plants

Turnips are easy to care for and can be planted either in spring, so you have turnips all summer long, or in late summer for an autumn crop. Like any root vegetable, they do well alongside carrots and radishes. If you are planting a summer crop, plant the turnips early. If you are

Editor's Picks

Here is a small sampling of turnip varieties that are well suited for home gardens. Most will mature in 30 to 60 days.

- 'Golden Ball' is a sweet, peppery turnip variety with yellow bulbs.
- 'Purple Top White Globe', the most popular turnip variety, is mildly sweet.
- 'Scarlet Queen' is a bright red crunchy hybrid salad turnip with upright green tops.
- 'Shogoin' is a firm and crisp turnip with mild greens.
- 'White Egg' is a fast-growing variety and a great keeper, with a flavor that will intensify after storage.

planting so you can have turnips to store throughout the winter, plant late in the summer to harvest before the first frost.

Turnips generally require a full-sun location but will tolerate partial shade, especially if you plan on harvesting the plant for its greens. Preparing the bed is easy: just rake and hoe it as usual for any planting. Once you're done and the soil isn't too wet, sprinkle the seeds, and gently rake them into the soil about ½ inch (1.25 cm) deep at a rate of 3 to 20 seeds per 1 foot (30 cm). Water immediately after planting to speed germination. Once you find your turnips growing, thin the plants to about 4 inches (10 cm) apart to give them plenty of room to form good roots. A smart idea is to plant turnips at 10-day intervals, which will allow you to harvest a batch every couple of weeks throughout the season.

Harvesting turnips

Come summertime, about 45 to 50 days after planting for most varieties, you can pull up a turnip to see if it's ready for harvest. Start harvesting once you find a mature root. Summer turnips will be more tender than the autumn roots, yet growing turnips to harvest in late autumn produces a hardier root that stores well in your refrigerator's crisper drawer or in a cool, dry place. You can then use them throughout the winter. Autumn turnips can make a great root cellar vegetable for storing along with carrots, rutabagas, and beets.

WATERMELON

Scientific name: Citrullus lanatus

A round, green watermelon sits in the soil as it ripens. These melons have become synonymous with summertime. With their juicy, bright pink flesh and sweetly refreshing flavor, they make a perfect hot-weather snack or dessert.

Watermelons are part of the family Cucurbitaceae, making them a somewhat distant cousin of vegetables such as squash, pumpkin, and zucchini. These iconic summer fruits have been cultivated for thousands of years; they are believed to have originally been native to Africa before later spreading throughout the rest of the world.

Growing and caring for the plants

Watermelon plants need very little special attention, especially in areas with hotter temperatures. They prefer a fertile, sandy loam soil, full sun, and plenty of water. They also require a good amount of space to grow, because their vines tend to take up a lot of room.

Wait until the last frost has passed and soil temperatures reach at least 65°F (18°C). Plant seeds about 1 inch (2.5 cm) deep in hills at least 3 feet (1 m) apart, with 7 to 10 feet (2.1 to 3 m) between rows. Keep the area free of weeds, and thin the plants when two or three leaves emerge from the seedlings. Using hot caps, floating row covers, or mulch with black plastic can help retain soil moisture and heat around the plants.

The Essentials

planting time late spring to midsummer

light full sun

soil fertile, well-draining, sandy loam

pH level 6.0 to 6.8

water 1 to 2 inches (2.5 to 5 cm) per week

size 9 to 18 inches (23 to 45 cm) tall; 10 to 15 feet (3 to 4.5 m) wide (vine spread)

harvest in 80 to 120 days

Harvesting watermelon

Most watermelons will take about 80 to 120 days to mature. When a fruit is harvest ready, you will notice that its little curly tendrils have turned brown and a bit crisp. The skin will appear duller and will be resistant to the penetration of your fingernail when you try to press it into the side. Another way to know if a watermelon is ready to harvest is to simply pick it up and turn it over: if the bottom where it sits in the soil is yellow, it is probably ripe.

MORE INFO *Types of watermelon*

Of the hundreds of varieties of watermelon that have been established, there are four basic categories: seedless, picnic, icebox, and yellow/orange fleshed.

- Seedless watermelons were created in the 1990s. These self-sterile hybrids are as sweet as seeded varieties, and they contain tiny, underdeveloped seeds that are more easily consumed that the larger black seeds found in traditional watermelons. They usually weigh 10 to 20 pounds (4.5 to 9 kg).

- Icebox watermelons, developed for single servings, weigh only 5 to 15 pounds (2.25 to 7 kg). Icebox varieties include the 'Sugar Baby' and the 'Tiger Baby' cultivars.

- Picnic watermelons tend to be larger, from 16 to 45 pounds (7.25 to 20 kg) or more, perfect for a picnic. These are the traditional oblong or round melons with a green rind and sweet, red flesh.

- Yellow/orange-fleshed watermelons are typically spherical and can be either seedless or seeded. The flesh is yellow to orange in color, rather than the typical pink.

 For tips on harvesting watermelon at the right time, scan the QR code or follow the link below to make sure you get the most from this summertime favorite.

"How to Pick a Ripe Watermelon"
Link: gkh.us/1935

SPOTLIGHT ON:
GROWING MELONS

Beloved for their sweet, juicy flesh, melons offer a wealth of growing options. Part of the Curcubitaceae family, most melons grown in gardens are members of the *Cucumis* genus, particularly *Cucumis melo* and its many varieties. Botanically, a melon is a form of berry, or "pepo"—a term used for the fruits of the gourd family with a many-seeded interior and hard exterior.

Melons are known for their fleshy interiors and thick, protective rinds. They are annuals that grow on long, trailing or climbing stems, producing large, coarse leaves, and white or yellowish flowers. A single plant produces flowers of both sexes, with male flowers dominating the early growing season. Most prefer temperate to semitropical settings. They prefer slightly sandy, very rich, well-draining soil. Be careful not to overwater melon vines, especially as fruit is approaching maturity. Shown here are some of the more popular melon varieties.

CANARY
The large, elongated Canary, part of the Inodorus Group of *C. melo,* is a bright yellow melon with a somewhat waxy feel. Its soft, light green or yellowish flesh resembles that of a pear and has a juicy flavor that tends toward a tangy sweetness.

CANTALOUPE
The North American cantaloupe (*C. melo* var. *reticulatus*) is tannish with a rough, netted, or reticulated rind that reveals succulently sweet orange flesh and gives off a floral aroma. The European cantaloupe (*C. melo* var. *cantalupensis*) has a lightly ribbed, gray-green rind.

Editor's Tip

Melons are known for their expansive growth habit—a single vine can eat up to 100 square feet (9.3 m²) of garden space. If you have limited room for planting, mini melons can offer you the chance to grow these succulent fruits in a small garden or even in a container. Look for small, prolific producers, such as 'Golden Jenny', a yellow-fleshed, mini version of the classic 'Jenny Lind' cantaloupe; 'Honey Bun', a tiny variety that produces netted fruit and honey-flavored flesh in the classic cantaloupe orange; 'Alvaro', a tiny Charentais type with smooth, yellow-tan skin with dark green ribbing and sweet salmon-orange flesh; or 'Sprite', a Japanese variety with crisp, apple-like flesh in a soft, creamy color under its smooth white skin.

To learn how to cultivate your favorite melons, follow this link, or scan the QR code.

 "Planting Melons: Information on Growing Melons"
LINK: gkh.us/1832

CASABA
A muskmelon cultivar, the casaba is ovoid in shape, with a point at the stem end. When ripe, it has a tough yellow rind, often with greenish markings etched with furrows. The sweet, creamy white to very pale green flesh offers a very sweet and slightly spicy taste.

CHARENTAIS

A small French Charentais displays a grayish green or yellowish gray netted rind and emits a distinctive aroma. The pink-orange flesh is more delicate than an American cantaloupe, and it is small enough to serve just one half per person for breakfast or a snack.

HONEYDEW

With their flavorful celadon green flesh hidden beneath pale, smooth rinds, these muskmelons emit a noticeably sweet aroma that can prove irresistible on a hot summer day. The honeydew is one of two cultivars of *C. melo* in the Inodorus Group.

CRENSHAW

A cross between a casaba and Persian melon, the Crenshaw is notable for its shape: a somewhat flat-bottomed sphere or oval that tapers towards its stem The ridged rind is yellowish green, and the tender, slightly spicy flesh is a golden peachy pink in color.

GALIA

The Galia is a hybrid cross between the green-fleshed cultivar 'Ha-Ogen' and the netted-rind cultivar 'Krimka'. It resembles a pale cantaloupe on the outside, but the flesh inside is more akin to a honeydew, with a pale green color and a spicy-to-sweet flavor.

SANTA CLAUS

Also called Christmas melon or Piel de Sapo, it takes its name from the fact that it will keep for a long time, sometimes until late December. The rind of this huge oval melon is green and yellow, and the sweet, earthy flesh may be pale orange or light green.

MORE INFO *Muskmelons*

The venerable *Cucumis melo*, a member of the gourd family, is the wellspring of many cultivated melon varieties, including the honeydew, Crenshaw, and casaba, as well as the cantaloupe, Persian, and Santa Claus melons. The flesh of a muskmelon can be either sweet or bland, and the aroma might or might not be musky (the common name refers to the characteristically musky smell that emanates from many of the fruits in the species when cut open). The rind of a muskmelon can be smooth, ribbed, wrinkled, or netted. In North America, the term "muskmelon" is used for all sweet-flesh varieties, whether they are musky netted-rind varieties or the smooth-skinned types. These are healthful fruits; they are nutrient-dense, contain antioxidants, and are especially high in vitamin C.

WHEATGRASS

Scientific name: Triticum aestivum

Harness its health benefits by cultivating wheatgrass. Whether you choose to grow it inside or outside, it is a bundle of nutrients that are best accessed by juicing.

The use of wheatgrass as a food, drink, or dietary supplement can be traced back 5,000 years to the Mesopotamian civilization. These days, juicers tout the many health benefits supposedly associated with wheatgrass, which is the freshly sprouted first leaves of the common wheat plant (*Triticum aestivum*). One serving provides the nutritional advantages of five to seven daily servings of vegetables.

Growing and caring for the plants

Growing wheatgrass indoors is easy and makes it readily accessible for daily juicing. You can grow it outdoors too, but it is easier to protect the quality of the plant in an interior setting. The downside to growing it outdoors is that it will be exposed to browsing animals, including kitties, along with bird waste and other contaminants. It is cleaner and less likely to get damaged when it is grown as an indoor crop.

As a short-tern crop, wheatgrass needs a very shallow growing medium. About 2 teaspoons (5 g) of organic seed will fill a small container the size of a piece of standard paper and give you about two glasses of juices. It is a good idea to start a new batch of seed every couple of days for consistent supply.

The first step is to soak the seeds in enough clean water to just cover them for 8 to 12 hours. Select a shallow tray and clean it thoroughly. Remember, this will be a food crop so, if necessary, sterilize it with a mild bleach solution, and rinse with clean water. Fill it 2 inches (5 cm) deep with compost, potting soil, or vermiculite, and pre-moisten the soil before you plant the seeds. It's a good idea to use a tray, even if growing wheatgrass outdoors, just for the ease of care and in order to monitor your crop and move it if necessary. Wheatgrass prefers temperatures between 60°F and 75°F (15°C and 24°C), and does not like temperatures above 90°F (32°C). Drain the soaked seed, and plant it barely covered with the soil. If you choose to grow wheatgrass in an outdoor garden, consider making a mesh cover, or use a row cover to protect the grass from birds, animals, and insect pests as it germinates and grows. Water seedlings twice per day from the base of the plant to prevent fungal issues.

The Essentials

planting time spring

light spring; autumn (outdoors)

light indirect light initially after planting, full sun later

soil potting soil or soil alternative

pH level 6.0 to 7.0

water twice per day

size 1 to 2 feet (30 to 60 cm) tall (outdoors)

harvest in 7 to 14 days

Keep seedlings in a bright location for the greenest sprouts but avoid the burning-hot midday sun. There is very little to the care of wheatgrass, except watering, as it is harvested and used quickly, and the goal is not a long-term plant. Plant a new batch every few days in fresh trays for a constant supply.

Harvesting wheatgrass

Harvesting starts when the sprouts are 6 to 7 inches (15 to 18 cm) tall. You can also use growing mats for ease of extraction and compost them when finished. If any mold problems begin to appear, mix 1 tablespoon (15 g) of baking soda per 1 gallon (4 L) of water, and spray on the plants daily. Keep good circulation on the plants and enjoy their rich health benefits as you harvest.

Editor's Tip

You can make wheatgrass juice with either a juicer or a blender. Both will produce a healthful drink, but with a juicer you can juice just the grass, extracting as much nutrient-rich liquid as possible and leaving you with less leftover pulp. The blender method requires that you dilute the juice, which also somewhat dilutes its nutritional value. For some, however, the diluted juice is far more palatable.

ZUCCHINI

Scientific name: Cucurbita pepo

A green zucchini. Harvest this veggie often and when the fruits are fairly small.

Rapid growth and prolific production make the zucchini (*Cucurbita pepo*) a popular garden vegetable. Also called courgette or baby marrow, it is a long and slender summer squash and is actually the fruit of the plant. In cookery, however, it is used as a vegetable. The plant also produces female and male flowers; both are edible and are often used to garnish a meal. There are a few varieties; the most popular is the basic green zucchini, which has a very mild, slightly sweet, grassy taste. The golden zucchini is a bush type with brilliant yellow to almost orange fruit. Its flavor is much the same as the green's, although some folks say it is sweeter.

Zucchini has two growth habits: vining and bush. Vining grows along the ground, requiring several feet of space between plants. You can also train this type to grow vertically on a very sturdy support. The compact bush variety is great if you have limited garden space, and it can thrive in containers. Whether you choose vining or bush, resist the urge to grow too many; one plant will produce 6 to 10 pounds (3 to 4.5 kg) of fruit over the growing season.

Growing and caring for the plants

You can sow individual plants or group them on hills in a spot that gets at least six to eight hours of full sun per day. Zucchini likes to start off in the area it will grow, but if you can't wait for soil temps to warm up, start seeds indoors three to six weeks before the last frost date. Harden off the seedlings for a week before transplanting them outdoors.

To start individual plants outside, wait until the chance of frost has passed and that soil temperatures have warmed and the air is close to 70°F (21°C). Prior to planting, work a layer of compost or other organic matter into the soil. Space plants about 3 feet (1 m) apart to allow for space to grow, discourage disease, and allow for air flow. Plant each seed about 1 inch (2.5 cm) deep. Thin to one plant per spot once the seeds have sprouted and have grown their first set of true leaves.

If you are planting on a hill, mound up soil about 6 to 12 inches (15 to 30 cm) high and 12 to 24 inches (30 to 60 cm) wide. On the top of the hill, in a circle, plant three seeds. As the seedlings grow and get their first leaves, snip off the two weakest, leaving one strong seedling per hill. Once seedlings are established, mulch around them to retain moisture and control weeds; as the plants grow, the large leaves will shade the soil and act as living mulch.

Make sure the plants get at least 2 inches (5 cm) of water a week. Use a soaker hose or another method to water the plants below their leaves, as watering with a sprinkler can cause the plants to develop powdery mildew. Zucchini are heavy feeders. If leaves become pale or seem weak, side-dress the plants with well-aged compost or use a foliar spray of kelp or liquid fish fertilizer.

Monitor the plants for pests. If early pests become a problem, cover the plants beneath a floating row cover. Drought-stressed plants are more susceptible to insect injury, as well as some diseases.

Harvesting zucchini

Zucchini will be ready to harvest in 35 to 55 days from planting. A mature zucchini can grow to nearly 2 feet (60 cm) in length, but it is typically harvested at about 6 to 10 inches (15 to 25 cm). Just cut the fruit from the plant, and use within three to five days, or store it in the refrigerator for up to two weeks.

MORE INFO
Row Covers

Row covers are a great way to protect your prized plants from damaging cold or pests. Some of the best include floating garden row covers, made of very lightweight woven material that allows light and water to penetrate, while insulating against the sudden drops in temperature common in many growing regions.

 To learn more about these devices, scan the code or follow the link to "Row Covers for Garden Plants—How to Use Floating Row Covers in the Garden" LINK: gkh.us/16602

CHAPTER THREE

THE HERB GARDEN

Growing herbs along with your vegetables allows you to truly create garden-to-table recipes, adding those essential flavors that make a dish complete. The following pages feature a wide range of common and not-so-common herbs that are suitable for growing outdoors and, in many cases, indoors, as well. Included are instructions for planting, tending, and harvesting these plants, along with an "essentials" guide that gives you the pertinent facts: when to plant, how much sun to provide, what soil to use, how much to water, how much space it needs, and when to harvest it, so that you can make an informed decision about which herbs will work best for your edible garden.

EDIBLE GARDEN HERBS

No vegetable garden would be complete without a few flavorful herb plants that will complement and complete the recipes you cook up from a home-grown harvest.

Herbs are among the most rewarding plants to cultivate, and they certainly stimulate our senses. They fill a garden with the pungent, often-deep scents of both flowers and foliage, and they draw in buzzing bees and allow us glimpses of delicate butterflies and hummingbirds. A number of them are fuzzy, sticky, velvety, or raspy to the touch. And so many are edible, which is no small benefit.

An edible herb garden, or culinary herb garden, is made up of herbs that are used mostly for adding flavor to your cooking and salads or for making teas. There are many varieties of herbs, and some have stronger flavors than others. To be sure you're getting the flavor you desire, pinch off a leaf and taste it before purchasing the plants.

Herbs make great container plants, which means you can move them indoors and out to make sure they get the levels of light and warmth they need to thrive.

Link to the Experts

READ MORE AT GARDENING KNOW HOW

Follow these links to learn more about successfully growing herbs.

- "Growing Herbs at Home: Making an Herb Garden in Your Yard" LINK: gkh.us/3400
- "Try Something New This Spring – Grow Your Own Herbs" LINK: gkh.us/454
- "General Care for Your Herb Garden" LINK: gkh.us/26
- "Making Herbs Bigger Through Pinching and Harvesting" LINK: gkh.us/338

THE LIFE CYCLE OF HERBS

Herbs, as with other garden plants can be annuals, biennials, and perennials. A number of herbs grown in temperate regions are tender perennials that are treated as annuals—plants that complete their life cycle, from germination to the production of seeds, within one growing season, and then die as the cold weather approaches. The bad news is that you will need to replant them again the next year, but the good news is that annual herbs are extremely easy to grow.

Certain herbs can be placed in pots and overwintered indoors, and then restored to the garden the following spring. Others will simply die back. Smart gardeners dry these faded specimens indoors, and then collect the seeds to create starter trays for the next growing season. Simply place the seeds in a marked container or zip-top bag, and store them in a dry, dark space. Biennial herbs will grow for two seasons before dying back. Their seeds can also be harvested. When it comes to harvesting annual herbs, you can safely cut back one-half to three-quarters of the plant at one time.

Growing herbs can get expensive, if the only ones you cultivate are annuals that need replacing every spring. Consider mixing in a number of perennial herbs, specimens that can survive for multiple growing seasons and rarely need replanting. Perennial herbs will give you lasting value—along with attractive garden interest—year after year.

True perennials will last for two years or more in the garden; most of them go dormant during the winter, and then return in spring. Tender perennials will also come back for many years when grown in warmer climates. In temperate areas, however, you will need to bring them indoors in pots during freezing weather. In terms of flavor profile, perennial herbs are a force to be reckoned with—some aromatic plants offer piquant lemon, pine, or anise flavors. Other seasonings, such as oregano, marjoram, thyme rosemary, and tarragon, are noted for their richly pungent and robust Mediterranean notes. When autumn arrives, it's a good idea to cut your perennial herbs back to the base with pruners before applying a thick layer of mulch. You'll be surprised at how much bigger and stronger they will be the following spring. And when harvesting perennial herbs throughout the growing season, never take more than one-third of the plant at a time.

THE OPTIMUM GROWING SITE

Herb gardens are meant to be used and admired—that's why it's important to consider practicality when choosing a site. A location near your kitchen or outdoor food prep area will allow easy access, and if your herb garden is right outside your back door, you can also enjoy the rich, savory scents that emanate from it. Choosing a garden site close to the house will also make it easier to water, prune, and tend to your herbs as needed. You can even keep a few pots on the kitchen windowsill.

When choosing an outdoor location, there are several important factors to consider. A site that receives at least six to eight hours of sunlight per day is crucial. Many herbs need plenty of sunshine in order to reach their full potential. Like most sun-loving plants, herbs that don't receive their minimum daily allowance of sunlight will end up leggy, awkward-looking,

and unproductive, instead of lush, beautiful, and fertile. But before you start digging, spend a day making note of all the sunny spots in your yard. Check on these spots at hourly intervals to see exactly how long the sun remains in any given space. Trees, bushes, building structures, and even tall flowers or vegetables can cast shade at different times during the day. Knowing the sunlight potential of these sites will make your garden planning easier.

If sunlight seems in short supply, think about container gardening. You can easily move pots to follow much-needed light. Of course, there are some shade-loving herbs, such as parsley, mint, and chamomile, but finding them shadier locations should not be a problem. Again, these shade lovers can also be placed in portable containers.

Most herbs should be planted in well-drained soil that is somewhat light and easy to till. You can check the quality of your soil by running a hose at the chosen location for several minutes. If the water puddles, you will need to amend the soil, possibly by adding sand, peat, or compost. Be careful when adding compost, though. If you make the soil too rich, your herbs will become weak and more prone to diseases. The ideal pH level for most herbs is 6.5, but they are frequently forgiving and can grow in soil that is slightly acidic or alkaline. For best results, stick to moderate fertilization.

HOW TO HARVEST HERBS

You can harvest herbs when they are large enough to sustain new growth. Timing is essential for getting herbs at their peak flavor. The aim is to pick them when the aromatic and tasty oils in the plants are at their highest levels. This occurs in the morning, after the dew has dried but before it's hot outside. Another important aspect of timing is to pick leaves before the flowers

Snipping a bit of fresh rosemary in the early morning, before the day gets too hot, means that the herb's aromatic oils will be at their peak of flavor.

develop. If you use them after the flowers appear, they will not taste as good. You can pinch off flowers as they begin to show to keep getting a harvest of leaves.

Picking herbs might seem like an easy task, and it generally is, but there are right and wrong ways to do it. Pick leaves, stems, or flowers in ways that ensure the plant will be able to continue growing and producing. Your herb harvest will vary a bit by type of plant. There are also general guidelines for all herbs grown in the garden. Here are some important tips to maximize your harvest.

- Harvest leafy annual herbs, like basil, by pinching off leaves at the tips of stems.
- Harvest leafy perennials—such as sage, tarragon, thyme, and oregano—by removing longer stems of leaves.
- Harvest stemmed herbs, like lavender, rosemary, and parsley, by cutting off stems at the base.
- When harvesting annual herbs, you can cut back one-half to three-quarters of the plant. For perennial herbs, never take more than one-third at a time.
- If harvesting any kind of herbs for their flowers, be sure to remove the blooms before they are in full flower.

THE SHELF LIFE OF HERBS

Most gardeners will find themselves with a surplus of herb plants at the end of a growing season. Learn the best ways to preserve your herbs, as well as store them for future use.

Herbs are some of the most useful plants you can grow. They grow well outdoors and can be kept compact in containers, even in a sunny window in your kitchen. Anyone who's used them knows that homegrown herbs taste better and are much cheaper than store-bought herbs, and they usually only need to be used in small amounts.

Sometimes your herbs can get away from you, though, and if you're growing them outside, they can get beaten back by an autumn frost. In these cases, the best thing to do is to cut and preserve them. There are several methods that you can use to extend the shelf life of herbs, both fresh and dried.

STORING FRESH HERBS

If you pick a few too many leaves from your plants and can't use them immediately, most will last a few days if wrapped in a damp kitchen or paper towel, placed in a zip-top bag, and stored in the refrigerator crisper drawer. Depending on the particular herbs, you can store them whole or chop them before placing them in the fridge.

There are now also "green" bags and lidded boxes that keep fruits and vegetables from spoiling by absorbing the ethylene gas that they produce to hasten ripening. These containers also work to keep herbs fresh far longer than regular plastic bags or snap-top ware.

Green bags and boxes are sold under several different brand names and can be found in the grocery produce section and on TV home-shopping channels.

FREEZING HERBS

When freezing fresh herbs, you can either blanch them first or not. Blanching can dampen the flavor a little, but it helps better preserve the color. To blanch, simply place your herbs in a colander, and then dump boiling water over them for a second—it doesn't take much. Basil really benefits from blanching and will turn black if frozen without it.

Herbs can be frozen whole or cut into smaller pieces. Whatever you

Freezing herbs in ice cube trays results in perfectly sized portions that you can drop into recipes as needed.

A home dehydrator works especially well for leafy, high-moisture herbs.

decide to do, lay your herbs out in a single layer on a baking sheet, and freeze the whole thing overnight. The next morning, combine it all in a resealable plastic bag and store it in the freezer—this method keeps the herbs from freezing together as a solid, hard-to-use mass.

Freezing fresh herbs can also be done using an ice cube tray. Cut up your herbs, and press them into an ice cube tray, about 1 tablespoon (15 ml) per cube. Freeze the tray overnight. The next morning, fill the tray the rest of the way up with water. This will give you easy-to-use portions of frozen herbs.

DRYING HERBS

Another method for storing garden herbs is drying. You can dry herbs in the oven, the microwave, a home dehydrator, or by air.

Oven-drying

To oven-dry herbs, lay them out in a single layer on a baking sheet, and place them in the oven on the lowest possible setting until they're dry and brittle. Prop the oven door open just a bit so that moisture can escape as they dry. Note that they will lose some flavor this way.

Microwaving

Microwave herbs between paper towels for a few minutes for the same effect as oven-drying.

Using a dehydrator

If you grow a lot of herbs and need to preserve a hardy surplus, consider investing in a dehydrator. Most home models will fit on a kitchen countertop, whether they have stackable trays or are constructed out of a rigid box with removable shelves, but there are larger, free-standing ones. Fans are either base-mounted to move hot air vertically or rear-mounted to move air horizontally. Convection dehydrator are fanless. Dehydrators work for nearly all herbs, but they are especially effective for high-moisture herbs like mints, basil, oregano, lemon balm, and tarragon. To prepare the herbs for dehydration, rinse them in cool water, shake them to dry, and then evenly layer them on the dehydrator tray. Follow your model's instructions to complete the process.

Air-drying

A very popular and decorative way of drying herbs is to hang tied-up bundles upside down and allow them to air-dry. Store them in a warm, dark place to prevent the loss of flavor. Tie them in small bundles to allow for good air circulation. Covering the bundles with a paper bag can help keep them free of dust and other contaminants. Punch holes in the bag, place the herbs upside down in the bag, and then gather the bag's edges together, and seal it with an elastic band. Hang in a warm spot with good circulation. The stems will shrink over time, so occasionally check the band for tightness.

STORING DRIED HERBS

You can store dried herbs either whole or crushed (whole leaves will last longer than crushed ones). If you prefer to use crushed or powdered herbs, once the dried herbs are brittle, use a mallet to crush them in a paper bag, or powder them in a food mill. Place the crushed herbs in airtight containers, label with the date, and store in a cool, dark spot—definitely not above the stove.

Air-drying herbs is the oldest method of preserving them. This simple method requires no more than some twine, a cutting tool, and plenty of patience.

AMARANTH

Scientific name: Amaranthus spp.

***Amaranthus caudatus,* called love-lies-bleeding for its pendulous growth habit, yields plentiful tiny seeds that hang in tassels from the top of the plant after the flowers fade.**

Amaranth is typically grown as a decorative flowering plant in North America and Europe, but it is, in fact, an excellent food crop that is cultivated in many parts of the world for both its seeds and its leaves. There about 75 members of genus *Amaranthus,* some of which are annuals and others that are short-lived perennials that easily cross-breed and hybridize with one another. In general, they all have large, broad leaves with prominent veining. The plant develops long flowers, which can be upright or trailing, depending on the variety. A single flower—usually red, pink, burgundy, or salmon—will appear at the end of a tall, reddish stem. The flowers are used to produce the amaranth grain, while the leaves can be used as greens. The seeds can be sprinkled over salads, stirred into soups, baked into breads, or made into porridge. Once ground into flour, you can use amaranth to prepare baked goods, such as bread.

Growing and caring for the plants

Amaranth plants grow well in average-to-rich, well-draining soil with equal amounts of nitrogen and phosphorus. Like many vegetable crops, they need at least five hours of sunlight a day to do well. They grows best in moist but well-drained soil, but they will tolerate somewhat dry soil, too.

Amaranth seeds are very fine, so generally, they are sprinkled over a prepared area after the risk of frost has passed. The seeds can be started indoors, as well, about three to four weeks before the last frost date.

When the amaranth seeds have sprouted, thin them to about 18 inches (45 cm) apart. Once established, the plants needs little care. Amaranth is more tolerant of drought than most other leafy vegetables and will tolerate a wider range of soils than other grain crops.

Harvesting amaranth

The leaves on an amaranth plant can be used at any time. Just like other greens, the smaller the leaf, the more tender it is, but larger leaves have a more developed flavor.

If you would like to harvest the amaranth grain, allow the plant to go to flower. Flowering amaranth plants can still have their leaves harvested to eat, but you might find that the flavor changes after the plant flowers.

When you see that the flowers have begun to appear, let them bloom fully, and then watch carefully for the first few flowers to start dying back or browning a bit. At this time, cut all of the flowers off the plant, and place them in paper bags to dry out completely.

Once the flowers are dry, they must be threshed (basically beaten) either over a cloth or inside a bag to release the grains. Use water or wind to separate the amaranth grains from their chaff.

Editor's Picks

When growing *Amaranthus* species in an edible herb garden, select varieties that work well as a food crops. Choose between those that are grown as grain crops or those that yield leafy greens.

Grain varieties
- *A. caudatus*
- *A. cruentus*
- *A. hypochondriacus*
- *A. retroflexus*

Leafy green varieties
- *A. cruentus*
- *A. blitum*
- *A. dubius*
- *A. tricolor*
- *A. viridis*

ANISE

Scientific name: Pimpinella anisum

The anise plant's feathery leaves and umbels of tiny white flowers, which resemble wild Queen Anne's lace, add a delicate touch to the look of an herb garden.

With a taste reminiscent of licorice, anise (*Pimpinella anisum*) furnishes one of the strongest flavors available in nature. This Southern European and Mediterranean herb is a member of the Apiaceae, a family of mostly aromatic flowering plants commonly known as the celery, carrot, or parsley family, or simply as umbellifers. Anise is an annual plant, which is cultivated as an ornamental bush and grows wild in northern regions of North America, sprawling across open prairie land and creating vast stretches of snowy-colored blossoms all summer long. Anise blooms with delicate flowers, borne in umbels like those of the wildflower Queen Anne's lace. The feathery leaves grow on slightly purple, erect, square stems that rise from thick rhizomes. The plants have a bushy, clumping growth habit and grows to just under 2 feet (60 cm) tall. It requires a warm growing season of at least 120 days.

Anise seeds, which resemble caraway or carrot seeds, are used for baking, seasoning savory dishes, and flavoring liqueurs in many world cuisines, such as the Mediterranean anisette, French pastis, Italian sambuca, or Greek ouzo.

Anise is widely cultivated in many European and Asian countries, and its delightful appearance and fragrance has inspired home gardeners all over to add it to their own kitchen gardens.

Growing and caring for the plants

Anise requires a fairly alkaline, well-draining soil, and although it will tolerate full sun with consistently moist soil, most varieties will prefer shade or partial shade. Directly sow the seed into a prepared bed that is free of weeds, roots, and other debris. These seeds are tiny, but they can be sown with a seed syringe for indoor starting or mixed in sand for outdoor planting.

A soil temperature of 60°F (15°C) is best for germination. Space the seeds in rows 2 to 3 feet (60 cm to 1 m) apart at a rate of 12 seeds per 1 foot (30 cm). Plant the seed ½ inch (1.25 cm) deep in well-cultivated soils. Water the plants after emergence twice a week until they are 6 to 8 inches (15 to 20 cm) high, and then gradually reduce irrigation. Maturing seedlings need regular water until the plants are established, and then can tolerate periods of drought. Apply a nitrogen-rich fertilizer prior to flowering in June to July.

The Essentials

planting time early spring

light full sun to full shade

soil rich, loose, well-draining, sandy or loamy soil

pH level 6.3 to 7.0

water 1 inch (2.5 cm) per week

size 1 to 2 feet (30 to 60 cm) tall; 1 to 2 feet (30 to 60 cm) wide

harvest in 120 to 130 days

Harvesting anise

Anise may be harvested in late summer to early autumn, when the flowers go to seed. Save the seed heads in a paper bag until they are dry enough for the seeds to fall out of the withered blooms, and then store them in a glass container with a tightly sealed lid. Keep the container in a cool, dark location until spring sowing or until you need them for a recipe.

SIMILAR PLANTS
Licorice Plant

Not to be confused with the anise plant, which gives off a similar scent, is the licorice plant (*Helichrysum petiolare*). Despite its common name, this species of flowering plant is not used to make licorice and is only named thus because many of its varieties have a licorice scent. With round, velvety silver leaves growing from trailing stems, licorice plants are more commonly used as foliage accents in a flower bed.

BASIL

Scientific name: Ocimum basilicum

Basil comes in a wide range of varieties, such as the green 'Genovese'. This cultivar is a standard for Italian cookery, with its sweet-flavored leaves and soft texture.

Sweet basil (*Ocimum basilicum*) is one of the most popular herbs in kitchens worldwide and, happily, one of the easiest to grow. Often called the "king of herbs," it has been used in food preparation and for its medicinal properties for more than 5,000 years. A member of the mint family, it is closely identified with Italian cooking, although its origins range from Central Africa to Southeast Asia. The highly aromatic leaves offer a delightful variety of flavors, from the slightly lemony-mint of sweet basil to cinnamon and licorice.

A perennial in areas with mild winters and hot summers, basil is most often grown as an annual. It is a tall herb, with large, glossy green leaves with smooth or crinkled surfaces in colors that range from rich green to deep purple. The flowers are insignificant but are very popular with bees. The flower buds are also edible. Bush basil (*O. minimum*) is a dwarf variety that only grows to 6 inches (15 cm) tall. Compact and sturdy, it may overwinter in milder climates.

Growing and caring for the plants

To grow basil from seeds, start them indoors about six weeks before your last spring frost. Choose a location with great drainage and plenty of sun exposure. Scatter the seeds over the bed, lightly cover them with dirt, and water thoroughly. Thin seedlings to 6 inches (15 cm) apart.

If you choose to grow nursery transplants, dig a small hole and tease out the root ball a bit before placing the basil in the ground. Water thoroughly. It is key to remember that basil is very sensitive to cold—even a light frost will kill it. Do not plant basil until all danger of frost has passed.

Basil's powerful fragrance makes it a popular pest-repelling plant for companion planting. Plus, this fast-growing herb thrives equally well in outdoor gardens and containers.

Harvesting basil

Basil is ready for harvesting 60 to 90 days from seeding. Once your plants mature, harvest often. The more you harvest basil, the more the plant will grow. When you pinch off a stem above a pair of leaves, two more stems will grow back. And keep pinching off the flowers—once a basil plant flowers, the leaves will start to lose their flavor.

The Essentials

planting time spring; summer

light full sun

soil moist, nutrient rich, well-draining soil

pH level 5.1 to 8.5

water 1 inch (2.5 cm) per week

size 18 to 24 inches (45 to 60 cm) tall; 18 to 24 inches (45 to 60 cm) wide

harvest in 60 to 70 days

Editor's Picks

Most of us are familiar with the sweet basil varieties used in Italian cuisine, but many other types have culinary uses. Here is a small sampling.

- 'Amethyst' (*O. basilicum* var. *purpurescens*). With striking purple leaves, this stunner has a sweet, musky taste that goes great in salads.

- 'Cinnamon' (*O. basilicum*). Its spicy aroma is great for teas and baked goods.

- 'Dark Opal' (*O. basilicum*). With its pretty purple leaves, this basil cultivar is often grown as an ornamental.

- 'Mrs. Burns' Lemon' (*O. basilicum*). This large basil is a proven favorite, with a strong lemon aroma.

- 'Lesbos' (*O. × citriodorum*). This tasty lemon basil is great in baked goods and teas.

- 'Napoletano' (*O. basilicum*). This Italian variety has the typical aroma of licorice or anise with a spicy overtone of cinnamon and clove.

- Thai basil (*O. basilicum* var. *thyrsiflora*). This species has purple or green leaves with a delicate taste of cloves.

BAY LAUREL

Scientific name: Laurus nobilis

The leaves of the bay laurel tree are used in many Mediterranean cuisines. A tree can reach an imposing height, but pruned container plants can be more manageable.

Bay laurel, or sweet bay, is a medium-sized evergreen shrub or tree that is native to the Mediterranean region. It is a member of the laurel family, which is made up of roughly 2,850 species. It is used primarily as a culinary herb, known as bay leaf. The dried leaves are added to sauces, soups, stews, and hearty meat and game dishes, and they are one of the components of *bouquet garni,* the noted French seasoning blend. Fresh bay leaves have a much stronger flavor than dried leaves, and they are used mainly in marinades and for preserving fish. For centuries, the herb has also been used medicinally to treat diseases and disorders such as rheumatism, sprains, indigestion, and earaches, and to enhance perspiration.

Bay laurel is hardy in warmer regions, but in cooler climates it may need to move indoors when temperatures dip. Fortunately, it makes an excellent container plant. If you can grow it outdoors all year, it will mature into a tree that can grow dozens of feet in height, but its size can be controlled by frequent pruning. A bay laurel tree is quite tolerant of clipping, and it can be trained into topiary shapes that look gorgeous with its glossy green foliage.

Growing and caring for the plants

Gardeners typically purchase bay laurel seedlings from a nursery, but growing the plant from seeds is also possible, provided the grower has some patience—bay laurel seed germination is a very slow process. To improve your chances, never plant seeds that are dried out, and order your seeds from a reputable purveyor. When they arrive, soak them in warm water for 24 hours, and then immediately plant them.

If you plan to harvest seeds from an existing plant, look for a female tree. Bay laurels are dioecious, meaning male and female flowers are borne on separate plants. In the spring, inconspicuous pale yellow-green flowers bloom on mature female trees, followed by small, purplish black oval berries. Each berry carries a single seed.

To start seeds indoors, fill a tray with a layer of moist, soil-less seed mix. Spread the seeds over the surface, about 2 inches (5 cm) apart, and gently press them down. Cover the seeds with a bit more moist soil mix. Lightly dampen the medium with a spray bottle; do not saturate it or the seeds will rot. Place the seed tray in a warm spot with a temperature of about 70°F (21°C) so that

it gets up to eight hours of sun per day. Keep the seeds moist to slightly on the dry side as they germinate. Be aware that it can take from 10 days to 6 months for bay laurel seeds to germinate.

When leaves begin to appear, transplant the seedlings into pots or into the garden bed once the last chance of frost has passed. Bay laurel roots are very shallow, so frequent watering might be necessary during dry periods, but be careful to avoid overwatering. Apply fertilizer twice annually, in early spring and in early summer.

Harvesting bay laurel

Pick bay leaves year-round by simply snipping them off a tree that is at least two-years-old. Use them immediately, or store them in the refrigerator in zip-top bags for up to a week or so. Fresh leaves have a deeper flavor, but if you want to store bay leaves long-term, harvest them in midsummer, and then dry them out. To air dry them, clean and pat dry the fresh leaves, and then lay them out on drying racks or mesh screening. You can also lay them out on a baking tray lined with paper towels. Leave them in a warm but well-ventilated spot, out of direct sunlight for about 10 to 14 days. Place the dried leaves in a sealed container, and then store it in a cool, dry, and dark spot. Dried leaves can last up to two years before losing their aroma.

Note: *Bay laurel is toxic to dogs, cats, and horses.*

The Essentials

planting time spring

light full sun to partial shade

soil well-draining soil

pH level 5.5 to 7.5

water only when needed; do not overwater

size 10 to 60 feet (3 to 18 m) tall; 5 to 20 feet (1.5 to 6 m) wide

harvest year-round

SPOTLIGHT ON:

CREATING SEASONING MIXTURES

One of the many joys of an herb garden is the bountiful harvest of fresh leaves, flowers, and seeds that can be used immediately in a recipe or preserved for future use. You can store each herb individually, but why not blend up some flavorful mixtures that can serve as pantry staples to liven up your meals no matter the season? You can follow the recipes shown here for several classic seasoning blends that use common herb garden favorites or come up with your own combinations, according to taste.

BOUQUET GARNI

French for "garnished bouquet," a *bouquet garni* is a bundle of herbs tied together with string or wrapped with peppercorns in a porous fabric like cheesecloth. The bundle is dropped into sauces and soups to impart the herbs' flavors, and then is disposed of before serving. Bay leaves, parsley, and thyme are standard ingredients, but other herbs can be added, depending on the recipe.

- 4 to 6 parsley stalks
- 2 to 3 sprigs of thyme
- 1 bay leaf

Place a short length of food-grade twine on a work surface. Stack the herbs on top, and then wind the twine around the herbs to bundle them together. Knot the twine securely. You can also bundle the herbs in cheesecloth tied at the top to make a sachet.

Editor's Tip

Potpourri, a mixture of dried flowers, herbs, and spices, has been used for centuries to perfume clothing or a room. Whether set out in a dish or poured into sachets, it can add wonderful fragrance wherever you place it. Aromatic herbs like lavender and chamomile, as well as lemon verbena and thyme, are perfect for these mixes.

To learn how you can grow a selection of aromatic herbs and other plants to create your own signature blends, scan the QR code or follow the link to "Potpourri Garden Plants: Creating a Potpourri Herb Garden."
LINK: gkh.us/58830

FINES HERBES

This delicate blend of fresh herbs has long been part of classic French cookery. The four herbs listed below make up the "canonical" recipe, but cooks today often add other herbs, such as thyme, marjoram, or savory. This mild blend works well in egg and poultry dishes, as well as in salads.

- 1 tablespoon (15 g) fresh tarragon, chopped
- 1 tablespoon (15 g) fresh chervil, chopped
- 1 tablespoon (15 g) fresh chives, chopped
- 1 tablespoon (15 g) fresh parsley, chopped

Mix all ingredients together in a small bowl, and then add at the end of a recipe. You can also blend these herbs in dried form. Just mix them in a glass jar, and then seal tightly. Store in a dark place for up to four months.

HERBES DE PROVENCE

A fragrant, complex mix of dried herbs that grow in the South of France, herbes de Provence can be added to poultry or fish recipes, tomato sauces, stews, vinaigrettes, marinades, and a host of other foods. As with many herb blends, there are multiple recipes and variations. Here is just one of the classic variations. Please note that all ingredients should be in dried form.

- 3 tablespoons (45 g) thyme
- 3 tablespoons (45 g) marjoram
- 3 tablespoons (45 g) savory
- 2 tablespoons (30 g) rosemary
- 1 tablespoon (15 g) fennel seed
- 1 tablespoon (15 g) lavender
- 1 teaspoon (5 g) basil
- 1 teaspoon (5 g) mint
- 1 teaspoon (5 g) oregano
- 1 teaspoon (5 g) tarragon

Mix together all ingredients. Store the blend in a glass jar with a tight-fitting lid. It will keep in a dark, dry spot for six months to a year.

ITALIAN SEASONING

This versatile blend combines the mainstays of Italian cooking, such as basil, oregano, and rosemary. Use it to season pasta sauce, pizza, and poultry and meat dishes or to add zest to sandwiches or bruschetta. For more of a kick, you can also add red pepper flakes.

- 2 tablespoons (30 g) dried basil
- 2 tablespoons (30 g) dried oregano
- 2 tablespoons (30 g) dried rosemary
- 2 tablespoons (30 g) dried marjoram
- 2 tablespoons (30 g) dried thyme
- 2 tablespoons (30 g) dried savory

Place all ingredients in a food processor, and blend for about a minute. Transfer to a glass jar, and then seal tightly. Store in a dark place for up to six months.

POULTRY SEASONING

With an earthy fragrance associated with autumn recipes, such as roast turkey, gravy, and stuffing, this blend combines herbs that complement the flavor of poultry. Despite its name, it is, of course, vegan, and can add holiday warmth to plant-based recipes. Grind your dried herbs to make this version.

- 4 teaspoons (20 g) ground sage
- 3 teaspoons (15 g) ground thyme
- 2 teaspoon (10 g) ground rosemary
- 1 teaspoon (5 g) ground marjoram
- 1 teaspoon (5 g) white pepper

Mix all ingredients together in a small bowl, or place them in a small food processor, and pulse until the desired consistency is reached. Store in an air-tight container for up to 6 months.

ZA'ATAR

This Middle Eastern herb and spice blend has numerous uses, such as a rub for chicken, beef, lamb, or fish or a coating for a log of soft cheese like a goat cheese. Mixed with a bit of olive oil, you can drizzle it over hummus, labneh, or baba ganoush. There are many variations of this blend; here is just one:

- 2 tablespoons (30 g) dried oregano
- 2 tablespoons (30 g) sumac
- 2 tablespoons (30 g) sesame seeds
- 1 tablespoon (15 g) dried marjoram
- 1 tablespoon (15 g) dried thyme
- 1 teaspoon (5 g) fine sea salt

Mix all ingredients together in a small bowl. You can store za'atar in an air-tight container at room temperature for up to a month.

BORAGE

Scientific name: **Borago officinalis**

The shape of its brilliant blue blossoms gives this plant its alternate name, starflower. Bees love these blooms, which makes them a great choice for a pollinator garden.

The Essentials

planting time spring

light full sun to partial shade

soil well-draining and moderately moist and soil

pH level 4.5 to 8.5

water 1 inch (2.5 cm) per week

size 30 inches (30 cm to 1 m) tall; 9 to 24 inches (23 to 60 cm) wide

harvest in 50 to 60 days

Borage (*Borago officinalis*) is an old-fashioned herb native to the Middle East. In ancient times it was said to foster bravery and courage. The Romans introduced it to Britain, where it is still found growing wild. In the modern garden, it is easily cultivated as an annual herb with vivid blue flowers and the scent of cucumber. It can be somewhat gangly in habit, but its pretty, dangling, star-shaped blooms are its main attraction. The oval leaves are hairy and rough with the lower foliage pushing 6 inches (15 cm) in length. The stems are a greenish gray and covered with a prickly fuzz, which can act to deter insects.

For many centuries, all parts of the plant, except the roots, were considered edible and used in hot dishes, salads, and to make tea. Recent research has shown, however, that borage contains pyrrolizidine alkaloids (PAs), compounds that can be toxic to the liver. Take that into consideration if you consume borage in any form.

Borage still has a lot to offer. It is often grown to lure pollinators like butterflies and honeybees into the vegetable garden. It is also considered a good companion plant for tomatoes, squash, and strawberries and may help increase your yield of fruit.

Growing and caring for the plants

Borage is quite useful if you have a space that needs a reliable plant. It grows quickly and colonizes a corner of the garden by self-seeding and reappearing every year. Look for a spot that gets at least four hours of direct sunlight on most days, and avoid taller plants that might shade it as it matures. Borage also grows quite well in containers.

You can start seeds indoors in the early spring, or you can direct-seed into the ground after the last predicted frost. Prepare a bed with well-tilled, well-draining soil containing an average amount of organic matter. The plant is not fussy about pH levels. If you opt for starting inside, make sure to harden off the seedlings before you transplant them by gradually acclimating them to outdoor conditions. Plant seeds ¼ to ½ inch (6 to 13 mm) under the soil in rows 12 inches (30 cm) apart. Thin the seedlings to at least 12 inches (30 cm) apart when the plants measure 4 to 6 inches (10 to 15 cm) tall. The appealing, small blue blooms will appear in June and July. The borage plant itself may expand to 12 inches (30 cm) or more in width, with a tall bushy habit.

Borage can be perpetuated by allowing the flowers to go to seed and self-sow. Pinching the terminal growth will result in a bushier plant but might sacrifice some of the flowers. If you are supporting your local honeybees, leave the flowers alone. Borage is known for producing an excellent honey.

Harvesting borage

Snip young leaves in spring and summer before they develop bristly hairs, and pick the flowers before they have fully bloomed, using either your fingers or a scissors. Both leaves and flowers can be dried or frozen for future use.

MORE INFO
Honey Plants

Beekeeping at home has become increasingly popular, a crucially important endeavor as honeybee populations shrink. There are some plants well suited to plant near hives that will help produce delicious honeys. Borage produces a light, almost clear honey with a delicate flavor. Other herbs, such as mints, sage, thyme, bee balm, basil, salvia, lavender, and lemon balm, are also known as "honey plants."

CALENDULA

Scientific name: *Calendula officinalis*

Calendulas, also known as pot marigolds, burst into bright summertime bloom. These cheerful flowers can be grown as an herb or as an ornamental in a flower garden.

The Essentials

planting time early spring to early summer

light full sun to partial shade

soil well-draining soil high in organic material

pH level 6.0 to 7.0

water 1 to 1½ inches (2.5 to 3.5 cm) per week

size 12 to 24 inches (30 to 60 cm) tall; 12 to 24 inches (30 to 60 cm) wide

harvest in 45 to 60 days

Calendula (*Calendula officinalis*), also known as pot marigold, common marigold, or Scotch marigold, is a short-lived perennial that is typically grown as an annual in temperate climates. An old-fashioned favorite that is still popular for herb gardens and containers, calendula differs from the common marigold. Yet it is also part of the Asteraceae family, along with daisies and chrysanthemums, and even has a daisy-like appearance.

The common name "pot marigold" originated in Renaissance times from the golden flowers that bloomed during festivals of the Virgin Mary: *Mary + gold = marigold*. Ancient cultures in Greece, Rome, the Middle East, and India employed this plant as a treatment for wounds, as well as a dye for fabrics, cosmetics, and foods like butter and cheese. When added to stews, soups, and salads, the petals have a spicy flavor said to resemble saffron. In the vegetable garden, these versatile plants will draw aphids away from your valuable produce.

The most common varieties produce flowers in sunny yellows, oranges, and reds, but there are also cultivars in subtle shades of pink and cream.

Growing and caring for the plants

Pot marigolds can be grown in beds or containers in full sun to light shade. They prefer cool temperatures, so flowers will last longer in filtered sun areas. If you sow the seeds in spring after the last frost, the plants should flower in six to eight weeks. Like most herbs, calendulas are adaptable and do not require a lot of maintenance—poor-to-average, well-draining soil and only occasional watering after plants are established will suffice. Roots will often confine themselves to the space provided. These plants are also frost tolerant and somewhat cold hardy. Best of all, calendula flowers readily reseed, so with luck you will have a new crop the following spring.

Harvesting calendula

Simply pick or cut off the fully opened flower where it meets the stem, taking the whole head. Harvest the flowers in the morning after the dew has dried.

MORE INFO *Pot marigold versus marigold*

These two plants are a bit like cousins—they share the same family, Asteraceae, but marigolds belong to the *Tagetes* genus of at least 50 species; calendula are members of the smaller *Calendula* genus that contains only 15 to 20 species.

- Pot marigolds are edible; only some marigolds are edible.
- Pot marigolds are native to northern Africa and south-central Europe; marigolds are native to South America, southwestern North America, and the tropical Americas.
- Pot marigold petals are long and straight; marigold petals are rectangular with rounded corners.

- Pot marigold seeds are brown, curved, and bumpy; marigold seeds are straight and black, with white paintbrush tips.
- Pot marigolds rarely exceed 2 feet (60 cm); marigolds range from 6 inches to 4 feet (15 cm to 1.2 m).
- Pot marigolds smell slightly sweet; marigolds have a strong, pungent odor (unpleasant to some).

CARAWAY

Scientific name: Carum carvi

A patch of caraway in full bloom. All parts of this delicate plant are edible.

Caraway (*Carum carvi*), an underused and infrequently grown plant in most herb gardens, is native to Europe and western Asia. This plant has so many uses, however, with all parts of the plant edible. A member of the Apiaceae, or Umbelliferae family (which includes celery, carrot, parsnip, fennel, and parsley), it is an aromatic biennial with wispy foliage and a long taproot. It will grow to about 8 inches (20 cm) tall in its first season. By the second year, it will triple in size, and its foliage will become even more feathery with stouter stems. Tiny white flowers appear on the umbels, which begin to bloom in early spring and last until the end of summer. The spent flowers yield small, hard brown fruit—the caraway "seed" that is an important part of many regional cuisines.

The most-used parts of the plant are these crescent-shaped seeds, which have a strong anise-like flavor. They can be used in baking or preparing soups, stews, and other foods. Havarti and Gouda cheeses, rye bread, sauerkraut, and British caraway seed cake are all made using caraway seeds. The roots of the plant can be cooked as a vegetable, as you would parsnips or carrots, and the leaves can be used as you would any herb—raw, dried, or cooked.

Growing and caring for the plants

Growing caraway requires some patience, because, as a biennial, it doesn't do more than grow vegetatively in the first season. It thrives in full sun and well-drained soil. It isn't a suitable plant for hot, humid climates and prefers cool temperate zones.

Sow the seeds ½-inch (1.25 cm) deep in autumn or in spring, as soon as the soil can be worked, about the time of the last frost. Germination is slow and sporadic, and the herb may be intercropped to help prevent weeds and manage soil conditions. Once the seeds have germinated, thin the plants to 8 to 12 inches (20 to 30 cm) apart. In colder climates, heavily mulch the roots of the plant with straw or organic mulch, which will add nutrients to the soil.

Very little cultivation is required in caraway growing, but adequate moisture is an important component of care during the first year. The foliage needs to be kept dry during irrigation, so a drip hose is an excellent way to keep the soil moisture level up.

The Essentials

planting time spring; autumn

light full sun

soil rich, well-draining sandy soil

pH level 6.5 to 7.0

water 1 inches (2.5) per week

size 2 to 3 feet (60 cm to 1 m) tall; 12 inches (30 cm) wide

harvest in 70 days

Cut the plant back in the autumn—it will die back and re-sprout in spring. Plant a second crop a year after the first for consistent production.

Harvesting caraway

You can harvest the leaves in both the first and second years to add flavor to green salads—although first-year leaves can have a fresh but slightly bitter taste.

When the plant is finished flowering and has gone to seed, dig up the taproot, and use it as you would any root vegetable. The seeds are harvested when they turn a rich, deep brown color. Cut the umbels off the plant, and put them in a paper bag. Let them dry in the open bag for a few days, and then shake the bag to remove the seeds. Store them in an airtight container away from light. They will stay fresh anywhere between six months and a year.

Dig Deeper

LEARN MORE AT GARDENING KNOW HOW

To determine the right caraway variety for your needs, scan the QR code or follow this link.

"Varieties of Caraway – Are There Different Caraway Plant Species You Can Grow" *Link: gkh.us/129694*

CHERVIL

Scientific name: Anthriscus corofolium

Frilly chervil flourishes in a terracotta pot as part of a container herb garden.

Sometimes called French parsley or garden chervil, this herb was once known as myrhis due to its volatile oil, which has an aroma similar to the resinous substance myrrh. The common name is Anglo Saxon and comes from the Latin *chaerephylla* or *choerephyllum*, for "leaves of joy." Native to the regions of the Black Sea, the Caspian Sea, and western Asia, chervil (*Anthriscus cerefolium*) has been cultivated since the days of the Roman Empire.

Chervil looks like a slightly paler, more delicate, and more finely shaped flat-leaf parsley, but with frillier, daintier leaves that somewhat resemble carrot greens. It is one of the plants (along with parsley, tarragon, and chives) used to make *fines herbes,* a delicate herb blend used extensively in French cuisine. It is particularly delicious with eggs—either added to an omelet or sprinkled on scrambled eggs. It also brings a fresh kick to lightly dressed salads.

Growing and caring for the plants

Chervil is a cool-season crop, like lettuce, and should be planted in early spring, late autumn, or in a winter greenhouse. You can also grow it in a small pot on your windowsill. Transplanting chervil can be difficult, due to the long taproot, so it is best to direct-sow seeds in a plot that gets a mixture of sun and shade (about four hours of full sun a day) when soil temperatures are between 55°F to 65°F (13°C to 18°C). The ideal soil is humus-rich and loamy, so amend with well-rotted manure or compost, if necessary. These plants prefer a cool, moist location, or they will rapidly go to seed. Once summer heats up, they will naturally bolt, just like their parsley cousins.

To direct-sow, mix the small seeds with three parts dry sand to more evenly distribute them. Sprinkle the seed-and-sand mix over damp soil, aiming for a few seeds per 1 square inch (6.5 cm²). Once distributed, lightly press the seeds into the soil surface. Keep the soil evenly moist. In about two weeks, the seedlings will emerge, and you can thin them to about 6 to 8 inches (15 to 20 cm) apart. To keep crops coming, sow seeds through the season every three to four weeks, as long as soil temperatures remain above freezing and below 65°F (18°C).

When the plants are established, water their bases, and add a layer of organic mulch around them to retain moisture. For regular watering, check for when the top ½ inch (1.25 cm) of soil is dry. Chervil plants like to stay evenly moist, but avoid overwatering them.

Flowers appear in late spring to early summer, but you can snip any buds as they emerge to extend the leaf harvest.

Harvesting chervil

The leaves of these biennials actually taste best in the first year of growth and are ready to harvest when the leaves are fully open and tender. Avoid harvesting bunches that have blossoms because the herb itself will have turned bitter. Once picked, you can keep the leaves for about a week in a sealed plastic bag in the refrigerator or freeze them in an airtight container. You can also air-dry the leaves, and store them for up to three years.

Editor's Tip

Because chervil is often used to deter veggie enemies like slugs and snails, it is a good companion for radishes, lettuces, and broccoli (as well as other cabbage family plants), protecting them from damage, while also improving the vegetables' growth and flavor. Chervil will tolerate shady conditions, so plant it thickly among the plants you want to protect. You can also cultivate it with parsley, chives, and tarragon so that you can create your own homegrown *fines herbes* mixture.

CHICORY

Scientific name: *Cichorium intybus*

Common chicory, familiar to many as a roadside wildflower, makes a pleasing addition to an herb garden, with daisy-like flowers in soft periwinkle blues. These lovely flowers, along with the plant's roots and leaves, have varied culinary uses.

The Essentials

planting time spring; late summer to early autumn

light full sun

soil fertile, well-draining soil

pH level 5.5 to 7.0

water 1 to 2 inches (2.5 to 5 cm) per week

size 3 to 5 feet (1 to 1.5 m) tall; 1 to 2 feet (30 to 60 cm) wide

harvest in 75 to 90 days

Chicory (*Cichorium intybus*), also known as common chicory, is a rather woody perennial herb that likes dry, stony soil and, as a result, is often seen growing wild on roadsides and in empty lots and scrublands. Common chicory still grows wild in its native Europe and is now also common in North America, China, and Australia, where it has become widely naturalized. It is easy to cultivate in the garden as a cool-season crop that is grown for its leaves. The leaves are tasty braised in butter and served over vegetables, while both the leaves and flowers can be used as an attractive garnish.

There are two types of chicory plant: root chicory (*C. intybus* var. *sativum*) is grown for the leaves and the large root, which can be baked, ground, and used as a coffee substitute and a food additive. In the 21st century, inulin, an extract from chicory root, has been used in food processing as a sweetener and source of dietary fiber. This variant can also be force-grown to create the tender white leaves known as Belgian endive, *witloof,* or *chicon.* Popular varieties to grow include 'Daliva', 'Flash', and 'Zoom'.

Radicchio (*C. intybus*) is the second type of chicory plant. It is a leafy vegetable grown for its tasty leaves (for more information, see page 117). Catalogna chicory (*C. intybus* var. *foliosum*), a type popular in Italy, includes a whole subfamily. Another related species, *C. endivia,* produces curly endive and escarole. (Yes, even botanists find the classification of chicory to be confusing.) Chicory is also commonly grown as a forage crop for livestock.

In structure, common chicory resembles a dandelion plant, with a rosette of lobed or toothed, lance-shaped leaves 3 to 10 inches (7.5 to 25 cm) in length, which form around the base. The leaves are dark green with some red tones and bear fine hairs on both leaf surfaces. As a perennial, chicory produces only leaves during its first season. Tall stalks typically bear bright blue daisy-like flowers, rarely in white or pink, after that.

Growing and caring for the plants

Chicory seeds can be started indoors five to six weeks before they are moved outdoors. Plant the seeds ¼ inch (13 mm) deep in a prepared bed, 6 to 10 inches (15 to 25 cm) apart in rows 2 to 3 feet (60 cm to 1 m) apart. If the plants grow too closely together, thin them when the plants have three to four true leaves.

Cultivating chicory is similar to growing most lettuces or greens. The plants require well-drained soil with plenty of organic matter. They perform best when temperatures are below 75°F (24°C). Extended care requires vigilant weeding and mulching to prevent moisture loss and further weed growth.

Chicory plants require 1 to 2 inches (2.5 to 5 cm) of water per week, or enough to keep the soil evenly moist. They can be fertilized with ¼ cup (60 ml) of nitrogen-based fertilizer (such as a 21-0-0) per 10 feet (3 m) of row. Apply this four weeks after transplanting or once the plants have been thinned.

Harvesting chicory

Chicory plants are ready to harvest when they reach about 12 to 18 inches (30 to 45 cm) high. It is easiest to harvest them when the soil is somewhat moist. Gently pull the plant, roots included, from the soil. You might need to get a shovel relatively deep underneath the root to avoid breaking it. Carefully separate the roots from the greens and stalks, and use a hose to clean off the dirt.

The leaves can be used as greens. After washing the roots, they can be finely cut, ground, dried, and roasted to be brewed into a beverage.

CHIVES
Scientific name: Allium schoenoprasum

The purple globes of chive flowers make this herb garden plant attractive to pollinating bees and butterflies. The narrow foliage can add flavor to a host of foods.

Cooks are always happy to have fresh chives on hand, and you should consider them an essential part of any culinary garden. Chives (*Allium schoenoprasum*), native to Europe, Asia, and North America, are cool-season, cold-tolerant perennials that grow in grass-like tufts that dry wonderfully for year-round use. The edible leaves, with their bright, mild flavor, are a favorite topping for omelets, deviled eggs, and baked potatoes and can adorn meats and cheeses, season breads and soups, and enhance a salad. Members of the onion family, they can substitute for other kinds of onions if you run out. The attractive, edible purple flowers can be added to salads or pickled in vinegar.

Growing and caring for the plants
If there were an award for "easiest herb to grow," chives would win it. Learning to grow chives is so easy that even a child can do it, which makes this an excellent plant to introduce kids to gardening.

Divisions are the most common way to cultivate these plants. Find an established clump of chives in early spring or mid-autumn. Gently dig up the clump, and pull away a smaller clump with at least 5 to 10 bulbs. Transplant this to a bright, sunny spot in your garden.

To start your chives crop indoors, plant the seeds about ¼ inch (6 mm) deep in the soil. Water well, and then place the seeded tray in a dark spot with temperatures ranging from 60°F to 70°F (15°C to 21°C) until the seeds sprout. Once you see the sprouts, move the trays into the light. When the plants reach 6 inches (15 cm) in height, transplant them to the garden. Once seedlings emerge, thin so that plants are spaced between 4 to 6 inches (10 to 15 cm) apart in all directions. If you're sowing seeds directly outdoors, wait until after the last frost in early to mid-spring for an early summer harvest.

Once your plants are established, they will require minimal care. Chives prefer strong light, but they will tolerate some shade and like a rich soil. If your soil isn't nutrient rich, amend it by top-dressing with a nitrogen-heavy fertilizer in late spring or early summer. Keep the soil neither too wet nor too dry. Chives are drought tolerant, but consistent watering throughout the growing season will maximize yields. Be sure to thoroughly moisten the soil when watering. Mulch around the plants to conserve moisture and to suppress any weed growth.

To avoid spreading seeds all over your vegetable garden, remove any flowers after they have bloomed. These perennials will also be more productive if you divide the plants every three to four years in the spring.

Harvesting chives
When the plants reach about 1 foot (30 cm) tall, take a sharp scissors, and simply snip off what you need for a recipe, up to half the plant. Chives are best used fresh or frozen (freeze the leaves in an airtight bag)—dried chives lose their flavor. In late spring or early summer, harvest the fullest and brightest flowers for the best flavor.

Note: *Chives are toxic to dogs and cats.*

Editor's Tip
Mix chives and water in a blender with a little dish soap for a solution that acts like a pest repellent on most plants. It will also deter powdery mildew on many vegetables.

CILANTRO/CORIANDER

Scientific name: Coriandrum sativum

A *Coriandrum sativum* plant in full bloom before it goes to seed. You can grow this herb for both its leaves (the herb cilantro) or for its seeds (the spice coriander).

This delicate herb (*Coriandrum sativum*), with its fresh, piquant flavor, has long been used in Mexican and Thai cuisine but now has fans around the world. It is also an herb that many people dislike—the plant contains saponins, bitter-tasting plant-derived organic chemicals that can give the leaves a soapy or even a "dirty feet" flavor.

This species provides two separate culinary ingredients—the thin, green stems and flat, lacy leaves, which are best eaten fresh, are called cilantro. Under the name "coriander," the seeds of this plant are used as a spice, especially in dishes of Indian, Middle Eastern, and Asian origin. The "seeds" are actually two cilantro seeds encased in a husk, which is hard, round, and light brown or gray in color. Before you plant, gently crush the husk while holding the two cilantro seeds together to increase the chances that they will germinate. Soak the seeds in water for 24 to 48 hours, remove from the water, and then dry.

This plant, which originated in Europe, Asia, and Africa, is not enamored of hot weather. If temperatures get too warm, the plant will bolt—meaning it will flower, and then go to seed. The ideal conditions for cilantro are sunny but somewhat cool weather. It grows best where it gets early-morning or late-afternoon sun, but is protected during the hottest part of the day.

Growing and caring for the plants

Once you have prepared the cilantro seeds, you can start plants indoors or outdoors. Place the seeds in the bed or starter tray about 2 inches (5 cm) apart, and then cover them with a ¼-inch (6-mm) layer of soil. Once the plants reach 2 inches (5 cm) in height, thin them to about 3 to 4 inches (7.5 to 10 cm) apart. It's best to grow cilantro in slightly crowded conditions because the leaves will shade the roots and help to keep the plant from stressing in hot weather.

When transplanting into the garden, dig holes 3 to 4 inches (7.5 to 10 cm) apart, and then gently set the plants in them. Water thoroughly after transplanting. Cilantro can be started in spring or in autumn once temps start to cool. It grows quickly the following spring, often yielding leaves within just 30 days.

Cilantro also does well in containers, which can be moved if the midday sun becomes too intense.

Harvesting cilantro

A cilantro plant that goes to seed will likely grow again the following year, or you can collect the seeds and use them as coriander spice in your cooking. Cilantro leaves will be ready for harvesting when the plant is about 6 inches (15 cm) tall. Pinch a few leaves as needed, or cut full stems. You can pick the leaves all season until the plants bloom. Fresh-picked leaves will keep their flavor for up to 14 days if stored in a zip-top bag in the fridge.

MORE INFO
Herb Combos

Try planting a mix of herbs with similar requirements in a large container. Or consider growing the ingredients for Italian or Mexican dishes in a single pot. Try the combinations below, or experiment with your own mix.

- Mexican: cilantro/coriander, oregano, and epazote (*Dysphania ambrosioides*, a pungent leafy herb)
- Italian: basil, oregano, parsley, and thyme
- Sun loving: marjoram, lavender, rosemary, sage, and oregano
- Moisture loving: tarragon, cilantro, basil, and parsley
- Aromatic: lemon verbena, lemon thyme, and hyssop

CLARY SAGE

Scientific name: Salvia sclarea

Clary sage can both repel garden pests and attract beneficial pollinators. Deer tend to leave it alone, and its papery mauve-pink flowers lure in bees and butterflies.

The Essentials

planting time spring; autumn

light full sun

soil moist, well-draining sandy soil

pH level 4.8 to 7.5

water 1 inch (2.5 cm) per week

size 3 to 4 feet (1 to 1.2 m) tall; 2 to 3 feet (60 cm to 1 m) wide

harvest in 75 days

Aromatic clary sage (*Salvia sclarea*) has a history of use as a medicinal and culinary herb. Also known as cleareye or eyebright, it is easy to grow and adds an ornamental display of flowers to an herb garden. A native of the Mediterranean region and parts of Europe, it yields leaves and flowers that are used in flavorings and teas. The plant also yields an essential oil called clary oil or muscatel sage, which is used for topical afflictions and in aromatherapy applications. Growing clary sage for home use provides all these benefits and is safe for human consumption.

Clary sage is a perennial or biennial that begins as a rosette in the first year and will grow a flower stalk the second. It is a short-lived plant that will usually die after the second year, although in some climates it may weakly persist for one or two more seasons. Its strongly scented leaves are gray-green and crinkly, forming in a basal rosette. The plant can grow up to 4 feet (1 m) tall and produces showy pinkish or purplish blue flower spikes from late spring into midsummer. Flowers are held in panicles that contain four to six blooms. Many cultivators grow clary sage primarily for the flowers, which are dried or pressed for various uses. Clary sage has two common varieties: a variation called *S. sclarea* var. *turkestanica* has longer flower bracts and a more pronounced blue color; the cultivar 'Vatican' is a white-flowering variety.

This herb is deer resistant and attracts honeybees and other pollinators, which makes it ideal for the naturalized or meadow garden. The plant can spread by seed, but volunteer seeding is usually minimal. The herb requires a chilling period of at least three months to produce flowers and, for this reason, is not a good performer in hot climates.

Growing and caring for the plants

Clary sage can be started from seed or cuttings, but is often grown from a nursery specimen, which you can put in the ground in spring, after the last chance of frost has passed (in warm regions you can also plant an autumn crop). To plant, dig a hole twice the size of the root ball, and loosen the soil in the hole, adding compost if needed. Remove the plant form the container, gently loosen its roots, and then place it in the hole so that the top of the root ball is level with the soil surface. Fill in the hole, and press down gently. Space plants about 1 to 3 feet (30 cm to 1 m) apart.

The plant establishes quickly in full sun and well-drained soils. Good drainage is key to its health—wet sites can rot the plant or severely curtail its growth. It will need supplemental irrigation until it is established, but can provide its own moisture thereafter except in very arid zones.

Harvesting clary sage

Harvest leaves for using fresh or dried in the second year, just as the flowers are about to come into bloom. Dry and store them just as you would any other leafy herb. If harvesting for the oil, cut flowering stalks (where most of the oil is) during late bloom when the seeds are in the milky stage.

Dig Deeper

LEARN MORE AT GARDENING KNOW HOW

Hungry deer can be a problem for gardeners. To learn more about which herbs and other plants deer prefer and which they pass over, scan the QR code or follow this link.

"Deer Resistant Plant List – Learn about Plants That Are Deer Resistant"
LINK: gkh.us/16561

DILL

Scientific name: Anethum graveolens

The delicate yellow flowers of the dill plant have begun to bloom above feathery foliage. This herb allows you to waste no portion of it: its flowers, leaves, stems, and seeds are all edible. You can also dry the plant for later use in many recipes.

This popular culinary herb, with a distinctive flavor that's a cross between celery and fennel, is native to Europe and Asia. An annual or biennial herb in the celery family Apiaceae, dill (*Anethum graveolens*) is a popular herb crop that has multiple culinary uses. Its attractive feathery foliage makes it a nice addition to flower or vegetable beds, where it will attract pollinating bees and butterflies, especially the Eastern black swallowtail. It has a habit of self-seeding, however, so make sure to keep it in check by deadheading spent flowers before they go to seed.

Cooks appreciate that both the leaves and seeds of dill are edible. These are used to season a variety of foods, such as breads, salads, soups, and dips, and are sprinkled on potatoes and fish dishes, as well as lamb and vegetables like peas, beets, and asparagus. Dill also plays a big role in seasoning pickled foods that will be jarred or canned and stored for the winter.

Mature plants are multi-branched and upright with finely dissected leaves. Be aware that the wide, flat flowers can make the plant top-heavy, so some specimens might require staking. The entire plant is extremely fragrant—and although the foliage and seeds are most commonly thought of as seasonings, the flowers are also edible.

Growing and caring for the plants

You can buy potted nursery specimens, but it's usually best to sow dill seeds directly in the ground—these plants develop a long taproot that doesn't like to be disturbed. Planting dill seed is easy—simply scatter the seeds in your desired location after the last frost, and then lightly cover the seeds with soil. Water the area thoroughly. Dill will germinate best at soil temperatures between 60°F and 70°F (15°C to 21°C).

Once a plant is established, water it when the top 1 inch (2.5 cm) of the soil feels dry. Dill does best in full sun, but

other than that proviso, this is not a fussy plant. It will happily grow in both poor and rich soil or in damp or dry conditions. In spite of its delicate appearance, it is actually a fairly cold-hardy plant. When started outdoors in spring, after the last chance of frost has passed, it will grow quickly, with seedlings appearing in about 10 to 14 days.

Harvesting dill

You can harvest the leaves at any time until dill blooms, which occurs about eight weeks after sowing. To harvest the leaves, trim off the amount you desire for cooking—up to two-thirds of the plant is the rule of thumb for annuals, which should quickly grow back. Once the flowers develop, however, the plants focus on seed development rather than growing more leaves. Collect the seed pods as they begin to turn brown, and place them in a paper bag. Gently shake the bag, and the seeds will fall out. Use them fresh for cooking, or store them in the fridge for two to three weeks. Dill can also be frozen or dried for later use.

Editor's Tip

Top chefs know that you can't beat fresh dill for its flavor. The best way to ensure the freshest dill possible is to provide a continuing harvest by sowing new seeds every two weeks.

FENNEL

Scientific name: *Foeniculum vulgare*

The fat white root of the fennel plant yields a tasty vegetable known in Italy as *finocchio*. This Italian staple is one of the signature flavors of Italian sausage.

Native to southern Europe, fennel (*Foeniculum vulgare*) is now naturalized throughout Europe, North America, and Australia and is found in gardens all over the world. This herb has a long and varied history. The ancient Egyptians and the Chinese used it strictly for medicinal purposes, and this lore was brought back to Europe by early traders. During the Middle Ages, the herb was believed to hold magical or protective qualities—people hung fennel over their doors to drive away evil spirits. Eventually, the crisp anise flavor established it as a culinary herb for seasoning eggs and fish. Today, every part of the plant is used in the kitchen—fennel seeds add a delicious anise-like taste to sauces, fish dishes, and baked goods. The leaves are lovely in salads, soups, and stuffing. You can even eat the bulbs as a cooked or raw vegetable. Fennel, also known as Florence fennel, belongs to the carrot and parsley family and is a cousin to other umbellifer herbs, such as caraway, dill, and cumin.

This aromatic plant's feathery, branching, yellow-green foliage and tall stature make it attractive in border plantings and cottage gardens. In butterfly gardens, swallowtail caterpillars use it as a food source and pupal site. The plant sports small yellow flowers in summer, followed by aromatic fruits that are commonly, though incorrectly, referred to as seeds. As a short-lived perennial, it blooms best in the second year.

Growing and caring for the plants

Plant your fennel in the spring, in a sunny location in slightly acidic soil at the back of a well-drained bed. There are two methods of propagation—division or seeds. Propagation isn't as easy as with other garden plants because fennel has a long taproot that doesn't like to be divided or moved. Planting fennel seeds is the much easier option.

Seeds can be sown as soon as the soil warms in the spring. Soaking the seeds for a day or two before sowing will ensure better germination. Keep the area moist until the seeds sprout, and then thin the seedlings to 12 to 18 inches (30 to 45 cm) apart when they reach 4 to 6 inches (10 to 15 cm) tall. Plants will begin flowering about 90 days after planting.

The fine-textured foliage has a fast growth rate and can reach up to 6 feet (1.8 m) tall, making it an excellent backdrop for flowers. It readily re-seeds and, while not considered invasive, it has certainly earned its reputation for an aggressive habit. Once established,

fennel doesn't need much care. It appreciates the occasional dose of mild fertilizer and some additional water if the weather is hot and dry. In addition to its culinary contributions, fennel will attract beneficial insects to the garden.

Fennel can be cut back early in the season to encourage bushier growth and should be deadheaded for seed harvest and to prevent overseeding of new plants. There's only one restriction on fennel: don't plant it near dill. Cross-pollination results in strangely flavored seeds from both plants.

Harvesting fennel

You can harvest fennel leaves as soon as the plant is well established, taking only a few leaves at a time to avoid harming the plant. To harvest the bulb, wait until it reaches the size of a tennis ball, and then cut the fronds from its base. Harvest and dry seeds as the flower heads fade.

Dig Deeper

LEARN MORE AT GARDENING KNOW HOW

If your fennel isn't producing as it should, learn how to solve this problem. Just scan the QR code or follow this link.

"No Bulbs on Fennel: Getting Fennel to Produce Bulbs"
LINK: gkh.us/95653

FENUGREEK
Scientific name: Trigonella foenum-graecum

Like other members of the family Fabaceae (the pea or legume family), fenugreek can be planted as a cover crop to fix nitrogen in the soil, a critical nutrient for plant growth.

Fenugreek (*Trigonella foenum-graecum*) has long been used as a flavoring agent and an herbal supplement. The leaves of this annual plant in the family Fabaceae grow in clusters of three oval leaflets that resemble clover. The flowers are typical of the pea family, blooming in white or purplish colors before turning into interesting yellow pods. Native to southern Europe and Asia, it has been cultivated for centuries as a spice and for its medicinal qualities. Herbal fenugreek is used to treat a variety of conditions, including coughs, sore throat, bronchitis, constipation, and minor skin irritations. India is the main commercial producer worldwide. Not surprisingly, fenugreek seeds are a mainstay of Indian cuisine.

In the kitchen, fresh fenugreek leaves are cooked like spinach and the tangy, mustard-yellow fenugreek seeds are used as a maple-like spice, often in Middle Eastern dishes. Dried or fresh fenugreek leaves are brewed into a flavorful tea. The seeds, whole or powdered, are used in India for pickling and to make vegetable dishes, daals, and spice mixtures. The leaves are sometimes used in curries, and the sprouts are mixed into salads.

Growing and caring for the plants

Fast-growing fenugreek isn't difficult to cultivate, and the plant can thrive in the soil in your yard, a container, or even a soil-filled aluminum tray. The plants thrive in full sunlight, but they can tolerate partial shade or even filtered sunlight. In warm climates, fenugreek is grown in spring after all chance of frost has passed and the soil has started to warm, but it can be grown all summer where the weather is mild.

Sow fenugreek seeds directly in the garden—these plants do not tolerate transplanting. To increase their germination rate, soak the seeds overnight before planting them. Freely sprinkle them over well-drained soil that has been amended with compost or well-rotted manure. There is no need to worry about spacing the seeds. Lightly cover the seeds, and then water them until the soil is evenly moist. Seedlings should appear in three to five days. Regularly remove weeds; otherwise, they compete with fenugreek for moisture and nutrients. Fenugreek isn't prone to many diseases, but keep an eye out for powdery mildew, aphids, or charcoal rot. Use only organic pesticides on this food crop, and avoid overwatering.

The Essentials

planting time late spring to late summer

light full sun

soil average, well draining soil

pH level 6.5 to 8.2

water 1 to 2 inches (2.5 to 5 cm) per week

size 1 to 2 feet (30 to 60 cm) tall; 3 to 6 inches (7.5 to 15 cm) wide

harvest in 20 to 30 days

Harvesting fenugreek
When the plants reach about 6 inches (15 cm) in height, they will be ready for harvesting. Carefully snip off the top third of mature stems, allowing the rest to continue growing. You can pick the leaves as desired throughout the summer. If you have a surplus of fresh leaves, place them in an airtight container, and store them in the freezer. They will retain their quality for up to a month.

If you're growing fenugreek for the seeds, uproot entire plants in early to mid-autumn, and hang them in a cool, dry location until the seeds are dry. Remove the dry seeds from the pods, and store them in an airtight container. The seeds best retain their quality when stored in a cool, dry cupboard. Whole seeds will retain their flavor for up to three years; ground seeds keep only a few months before losing flavor.

Editor's Tip
Fenugreek rarely thrives when transplanted, so it is best to directly sow the seeds in the soil in which it will grow to maturity. If you do need to start seeds earlier, use a biodegradable pot that you plant in the ground when outdoor conditions are right. This trick will work for any herb that resists transplantation.

GARLIC CHIVES

Scientific name: *Allium tuberosum*

Honeybees flock to the nectar- and pollen-rich flowers of garlic chives.

The Essentials

planting time spring

light full sun to light shade

soil light, well-draining, loamy or sandy soil

pH level 6.0

water 1 inch (2.5 cm) per week

size 12 to 18 inches (30 to 45 cm) tall; 12 to 24 inches (30 to 60 cm) wide

harvest in 80 to 90 days

They look like onion chives but taste more like garlic. Garlic chives in the garden are also often referred to as Chinese chives plants and, as such, were first recorded between 4,000 to 5,000 years ago in China. So, what are they, and how do they differ from ordinary garden chives? Their scientific name of *Allium tuberosum* is indicative of their oniony roots, and they fall among the family Amaryllidaceae. Unlike onions or other types of garlic, however, their fibrous bulb is not edible, so they are instead grown for their flowers and stems. It is easy to differentiate between onion chives (*A. schoenoprasum*) and garlic chives. Garlic chives have a flat, grass-like leaf; onion chives have hollow ones.

This plant is a bulb perennial that forms clumps of narrow strappy leaves. A late-season bloomer, it displays its umbels of tiny white, star shaped flowers atop leafless stems rising above the foliage in late summer and early autumn. Their sweet scent will draw bees, butterflies, and other beneficial insects to the nectar- and pollen-rich flowers.

A garlic chives plant reaches between 12 and 18 inches (30 and 45 cm) in height and makes a lovely flower in a border planting or container garden and work well in the herb garden. They can also be planted along a path or as a dense ground cover.

The flowers can be eaten or dried and made into floral arrangements. The seed heads are also often used in everlasting arrangements, or they can be allowed to remain and drop seeds for continual reseeding. In the kitchen, the leaves are used much like garden chives, and they impart a mild garlic flavor to egg, fish, poultry, and vegetable dishes and can be used to flavor sauces and stews, as well as vinegars, salads, soft cheeses, compound butters, and grilled meat. Garlic chives not only have a multitude of culinary uses, but are said to be beneficial to the digestive system, stimulate appetite, promote blood circulation, and have diuretic properties.

Growing and caring for the plants

These little perennials thrive under full sun (though they can tolerate some light shade) and can last as long as a decade in a single spot. To plant, lightly sow seeds in moist soil with good drainage as soon as the seeds are ripe in the autumn or in a cold frame in the spring. When seedlings reach 2 inches (5 cm) in height, thin them to 6 to 12 inches (15 to 30 cm) apart. Plant them among carrots, grapes, roses, and tomatoes. They can help deter pests such as Japanese beetles and black spot on roses, scab on apples, and mildew on cucurbits.

Once established, water as needed. These plants are drought-tolerant, but they do enjoy moist soil. You can also feed them with a slow-release fertilizer at the start of the growing season. After a long-term freeze, they will often die back only to return again come springtime.

Propagate either from seed or division. Divide the bulb heads in the spring every three years. These plants aggressively self-seed, so propagation from seed may result in an invasion of garlic chives. You may want to either eat the flowers before they dry and drop seeds or dead-head and discard them to control spreading. Clip the stems either all the way to the ground or with 2 inches (5 cm) remaining to allow the herb to grow anew.

Harvesting garlic chives

You can harvest young leaves any time during the growing season. Just cut the leaves down to the soil line using clean scissors or kitchen shears. Freshly picked leaves have the most potent flavor, but if you have a surplus, chop them up, and place in a zip-top bag. They will keep in the refrigerator for up to a week. You can also dry them for longer-term storage. Pick the edible flowers shortly after they open. These, too, can be dried to use in flower arrangements.

GERMAN CHAMOMILE

Scientific name: *Matricaria chamomilla*, syn. *M. recutita*

German chamomile growing alongside rosemary. The daisy-like flowers add a light touch to the garden while protecting its garden companions from harmful insect pests.

The Essentials

planting time spring

light partial shade to full sun

soil well-draining sandy soil

pH level 5.6 to 7.5

water 1 inch (2.5 cm) per week

size 18 to 24 inches (45 to 60 cm) tall; 8 to 12 inches (20 to 30 cm) wide

harvest in 60 to 90 days

Native to Europe, North Africa, and Asia, German chamomile (*Matricaria chamomilla*) is also known as barnyard daisy, Hungarian chamomile, and wild chamomile. Unlike its sister plant, Roman chamomile, which is a perennial, German chamomile is an annual, growing for only one season. Gardeners will tell you, however, that the German variety self-seeds so readily, it's practically a perennial, as well. These hardy plants can often be found growing wild in meadows and on cliff edges and coastal paths.

The fragrant flowers form at the top of green, hairy stems and have white petals, surrounding vivid yellow centers. The leaves are very small, finely divided, and downy to the touch. They give off an apple-like aroma when they are crushed.

The herb is also believed to have medicinal properties. Its use goes back to the Middle Ages, when it was classed as a carminative, painkiller, diuretic, digestive aid, treatment for menstrual cramps, and a mild laxative with anti-inflammatory and bactericidal effects. It is still a source for herbal remedies, beverages, and skincare products. The plant is known to contain antispasmodic and anti-inflammatory constituents and is quite effective in treating stomach and intestinal cramps. The flowers contain beneficial polyphenol compounds, including apigenin, quercetin, patuletin, and luteolin. Research indicates the plant may have anti-anxiety properties, as well. To make your own calming herbal tea from fresh or dried flowers, simply steep them in boiling water for five minutes. The plant is also used by a few craft beer brewers as a flavoring.

Growing and caring for the plants

Chamomile is best planted in the spring and can be started either from seeds or young nursery plants. Chamomile grows best in cool conditions and should be planted in partial shade, but will also manage under full sun. The soil should be dry. The plants mature quickly, reaching full bloom within 10 weeks or so. Once your chamomile is established, it needs very little care.

Like most herbs, chamomile prefers to not be fussed over. Too much fertilizer will result in weakly flavored foliage and fewer flowers. Chamomile is drought tolerant and only needs to be watered during extended dry spells. For the most part, chamomile is not affected by many pests. A plant weakened by lack of water or other issues, however, may be attacked by aphids, mealybugs, or thrips. The herb is often recommended as a companion plant to place in the vegetable garden because its strong scent is known to keep pests away.

Although mature plants can become a bit floppy, they work well as underplantings for an herb or vegetable garden, to soften the edges on rock walls, and in containers.

Harvesting German chamomile

For chamomile tea, harvest the flowers once they are fully open. After you dry the flowers and leaves, store them in a cool, dark spot in an airtight container, or freeze them.

Note: *Chamomile is likely unsafe for use during pregnancy. Its topical use for skin disorders may cause contact dermatitis.*

MORE INFO
Spot the Difference

The closely related Roman chamomile *(Chamaemelum nobile)* is quite similar in appearance to German (see page 193). To tell the two apart, cut the flower receptacle—the portion of the flower that connects the bloom to the stalk—in half. If the receptacle has a solid interior, the plant is Roman chamomile. If the receptacle has a hollow interior, it is German chamomile.

GINGER

Scientific name: Zingiber officinale

Harvesting ginger plants. This spicy rhizome is often used in Asian cuisine. You can grow your own plants from grocery store gingerroot.

Native to maritime Southeast Asia, the ginger plant (*Zingiber officinale*) was carried to the Mediterranean by Arab traders. Ginger's knobby rhizomes grow tall pseudostems (false stems made of rolled leaf bases) bearing narrow green leaf blades and clusters of white and pink buds that bloom into yellow flowers. Ginger might seem like a difficult herb to grow—you often see the rhizome in grocery stores, but the plant is rarely found in a garden center. Yet, you can easily grow ginger at home.

The rhizomes of the ginger plant—with their slightly peppery, sweet flavor—are the parts we typically turn to when baking or cooking. The leaves can also be boiled and used in teas and will pair well with rice and pork dishes. This moderately tender perennial can be grown in many temperate regions, although in some locations the leaves will die in the winter. For really cold climates, ginger should be grown in a pot and brought indoors during winter.

Growing and caring for the plants

Ginger dealers are available online, or you can head to your local grocery store and buy a gingerroot in the produce section. Choose a healthy, plump root about 4 to 5 inches (10 to 12.5 cm) long with at least a few "fingers." If possible, choose one upon which the tips of the fingers are greenish.

Ginger grows best in partial to full shade and likes rich, loose, and loamy soil. It's a good idea to add compost or rotted manure to the chosen spot. To grow in containers, use high-quality potting soil. Plant your gingerroot in the early spring, after all chance of frost has passed. Break off a finger that is 1 to 2 inches (2.5 to 5 cm) long and has at least one bud (a knob-like rounded point). To help prevent rot, dry the pieces for a day or two before putting them in the ground.

Plant the ginger sections in a shallow trench no more than 1 inch (2.5 cm) deep. If the growing root pushes back up through the top of the soil, this is okay and not uncommon. Plant one ginger plant per 1 square foot (0.1 m²), and then water thoroughly. When the leaves emerge, water sparingly, but deeply. The leaves can grow up to 4 feet (1.2 m) tall and are susceptible to wind damage, so consider staking them if violent storms are predicted.

Harvesting ginger

Ginger takes 10 months to mature, so it will be ready for harvest the following spring, or you can let it grow through to the next summer for a larger harvest. To harvest, lift the plant gently from the soil. If you'd like it to continue growing, break off a part that has foliage and carefully replant it. Snip off the foliage of the segment you are keeping, and wash the root, which can be broken into smaller pieces for easier use.

SIMILAR PLANTS
Wild Ginger

Though not the same as culinary ginger, most wild gingers (genera *Asarum* and *Hexastylis*) can be eaten in small amounts, and as their common names suggests, have a similar spicy, ginger-like aroma. The fleshy root (rhizome) and leaves of most wild ginger plants can be substituted in many Asian cuisines; however, some forms have an emetic property, so care should be taken when selecting and ingesting.

 To read more about these plants, scan the QR code or follow this link to "Caring for Wild Ginger: How to Grow Wild Ginger Plants." *LINK: gkh.us/42215*

The Essentials

planting time spring

light full sun to partial shade

soil fertile, well-draining, moisture-retaining loamy soil

pH level 5.5 to 6.5

water 1 inch (2.5 cm) per week

size Up to 4 feet (1.2 m) tall; Up to 2 feet (60 cm) wide

harvest in 8 to 10 months

HORSERADISH

Scientific name: Armoracia rusticana

The large green leaves of a horseradish plant sprawl out in a corner of an herb garden.

Horseradish (*Armoracia rusticana*) is a clump-forming perennial that's categorized as both a vegetable and an herb. It is primarily grown for its pungent, yellow-white roots that are used to perk up a variety of savory dishes. It can be grated into salads and sauces or used to create mayonnaise-type dressings and sandwich spreads. The fiery, earthy flavor goes especially well with roast beef and fish.

Originally native to Asia and Europe, this plant is hardy in many colder regions. When mature, it features long, shiny, toothed, dark green leaves, and in summer it bears tiny, white, four-petaled flowers on panicles. Horseradish is normally planted in the spring and will grow quickly enough for the roots to be ready to harvest by autumn, although you can also plant in autumn to early winter. Once horseradish is firmly established, you will be harvesting the roots for many years to come.

Growing and caring for the plants

A horseradish plant is typically grown from a root cutting. These can be ordered from a reputable nursery or you may be able to find someone locally who is raising horseradish and would be willing to share some with you. As soon as you get your root cutting in early spring, plant it in the ground. Dig a hole that is deep enough for the root to stand up in. While holding the root upright in the hole, backfill the hole until all but the crown of the root is covered in soil.

Once the root is planted, water thoroughly, and then leave the plant alone. It actually does best if you plant it, and then ignore it. You don't need to fertilize or fuss over it. Horseradish grows to 18 to 24 inches (30 to 45 cm) tall and, sad to say, it is not the prettiest plant, but worth the effort for the zest the roots will add to dishes.

Harvesting horseradish

Horseradish leaves, which have a sharp, bitter taste, can be picked and dried any time. There are two schools of thought when it comes to harvesting the roots. The first says that you should harvest in the autumn, right after the first frost. The other says that you should harvest horseradish in early spring, when the plants need to be divided anyway. Both methods are acceptable.

Dig down around the horseradish plant as far as you possibly can, and then with your spade, gently lift the root out of the ground. Break off some of the roots, and replant them in the ground. Process the rest into ground horseradish. Perform this task in a well-ventilated room, because this is a very pungent herb. To prepare, wash and peel the roots, and the chop them into chunks. Place the chunks in a food processor, and process until they reach the desired consistency (the finer the texture the hotter the flavor). Add a mix of equal parts water and vinegar to the horseradish to stop the heat-producing enzymes—immediately for a mild horseradish or about three minutes for a hot one. It can be stored in jars for up to a month or in the freezer indefinitely.

Note: *Horseradish roots are technically toxic to both people and pets.*

The Essentials

planting time early spring; autumn to late winter

light full sun

soil rich, moist loamy soil

pH level 6.0 to 7.5

water 1 to 2 inches (2.5 to 5 cm) per week

size 24 to 32 inches (60 to 81 cm) tall; 32 to 36 inches (81 cm to 1 m) wide

harvest in 140 to 160 days

Editor's Tip

Horseradish is known for spreading vigorously if steps are not taken to halt it, so keep in mind that when growing this spicy herb, you need to either give it lots of room or provide firm boundaries. If you do not want it to take over your garden, either grow it in a deep container or place a plastic tub around it in the ground to keep its roots in check.

HYSSOP

Scientific name: Hyssopus officinalis

Hyssop is an herbaceous flowering plant used in cooking and in traditional medicine, as well as by beekeepers for the production of a rich, aromatic honey.

This native of Southern Europe and the Middle East is a perennial, evergreen member of the mint family. Throughout history, hyssop (*Hyssopus officinalis*) has been a valued part of herbal medicine, relied on to relieve colds and sore throats. In modern times, penicillin has been made from the mold that grows on the leaves. The herb was also used for ceremonies of religious purification. Other common names include *herbe de Joseph, herbe sacrée, herbe sainte, hiope, hisopo, hissopo, hysope, jufa, rabo de gato,* and *ysop*. In the kitchen, pungent, aromatic hyssop leaves are combined with game and fish dishes or added to soups, stews, and salads. Hyssop leaves steeped in boiling water also make a soothing tea to treat a cold or sore throat.

Hyssop is also an attractive flowering shrub or sub-shrub. The woody stem supports upright branches with green, lance-shaped leaves. In summer, the plant produces fragrant pink, blue, purple, or, more rarely, white flowers, which are loved by winged pollinators. It can also be successfully grown in containers big enough to accommodate the large root system.

Growing and caring for the plants

Sow hyssop seeds indoors or directly in the garden about 8 to 10 weeks before the last predicted frost. Plant them about ¼ inch (6 mm) deep and about 6 to 12 inches (15 to 30 cm) apart. Hyssop seeds usually take between 14 and 21 days to germinate; indoor seedlings can be transplanted outside after the last threat of frost. Heavily trim back established plants in early spring and again after flowering to prevent them from becoming too spindly. This also encourages bushier growth.

Once blooming has ceased and the seed capsules have completely dried, they can be collected and stored for producing hyssop the next season. In some areas, hyssop plants will readily self-seed. In addition, the plants can be divided in autumn.

Harvesting hyssop

In the kitchen, hyssop leaves are best used fresh, but it can be dried or frozen and stored for later use. When harvesting hyssop, collect it in the morning once any dew has dried. Suspend the plants upside down in small bunches to dry in a dark, well-ventilated area. Or you can put the leaves in a plastic bag, and place it in the freezer until ready to use.

Note: *The essential oil includes the chemicals thujone and phenol, which give it antiseptic properties, but which can also cause seizures.*

The Essentials

planting time	spring
light	full sun to partial shade
soil	fertile, well-draining loam
pH level	6.6 to 8.5
water	1 to 2 inches (2.5 to 5 cm) per week
size	12 to 24 inches (30 to 60 cm) tall; 12 to 18 inches (30 to 45 cm) wide
harvest	in 75 to 85 days

SIMILAR PLANTS
Other Hyssops

Agastache, another genus in the mint family, is native to North America and includes several species with "hyssop" in their common names. *A. rupestris* goes by the name threadleaf giant hyssop; *A. mexicana* is sometimes called Mexican giant hyssop; and *A. foeniculum* (below) is also known as anise hyssop. The leaves of anise hyssop have a strong anise scent and can be used as a seasoning, as a tea, and in salads.

LAVENDER

Scientific name: *Lavandula* spp.

Mounds of lavender line a staircase in a water-wise xeriscape garden. Place this aromatic herb in a spot you pass often in order to breathe in its calming scent.

The Essentials

planting time spring

light full sun

soil well-draining sandy soil

pH level 6.7 to 7.3

water 1 to 2 inches (2.5 to 5 cm) per week

size 2 to 3 feet (60 cm to 1 m) tall; 2 to 4 feet (60 cm to 1.2 m) wide

harvest in 75 to 100 days

Lavender is a popular Mediterranean herb renowned for its fragrant aroma and spikes of purple flowers. Used to flavor jams and vinegars, the flowers are also combined with savory herbs in soups and stews. When crystallized, they make a tasty dessert garnish. This easy-care member of the mint family enjoys hot, dry conditions, making it suitable for use in a variety of landscape settings and an excellent candidate for xeriscapes and areas prone to drought.

There are 47 species of lavender, with over 450 varieties, but the main types are English and French (or Spanish), Portuguese, and lavandin.

Growing and caring for the plants

Lavender seeds are slow to germinate, so purchasing seedlings makes the most sense. Although lavender is quite tolerant, it thrives best in warm, sunny conditions in well-drained soil. An alkaline soil rich in organic matter can encourage plant oil production, enhancing the fragrance.

As a native of arid regions, the plant will not tolerate overly wet conditions.

Placing lavender in areas with adequate drainage will reduce the chance of root rot. The plants should be watered regularly early on, but established plants need little water—no more than 1 or 2 inches (2.5 to 5 cm) a week. Regular

pruning keeps them neat in appearance and helps to encourage new growth. Low-growing varieties can be cut back to new growth, while larger types can be pruned to about a third of their height.

Harvesting lavender

Lavender may take up to a year or more to be ready for harvesting. When your crop is ready, it's best to harvest the plants early in the day, picking flower spikes not fully opened. Gather the spikes in a bundle, and hang them upside-down in a dry, dark space for one or two weeks. You can then use the dried lavender in cooking or crafts.

MORE INFO *English and French lavender*

The English and French types of lavender have different qualities and smells and even differing appearances, habits, and needs.

- English lavender (*Lavandula angustifolia*) is the most common type, called "English" because it thrives in the climate of the British Isles. Hardier than other species, it provides a gentle, relaxing, and complex scent and the highest-quality oil. 'Hidcote' is one of the most popular English lavenders, with long-lasting dark purple flowers. 'Alba Nana' is a dwarf variety that combines beautiful white blooms with a soothing scent. 'Munstead' has a compact habit and flowers of a light, rosy purple. 'Rosea' has a strong, calming scent and a profusion of pale pink flowers.

- French lavender (*L. stoechas*) is emblematic of the South of France, where its scent fills the summertime air. It is known for its "ears"—long, attractive petals (bracts) at the top of each spike, or inflorescence. It has a more resinous scent than English lavender and is not usually used for oil. In the United States, it is called Spanish lavender. 'Anouk' is a showy magenta variety with very large ears. Stunning 'Ballerina' has short, plump spikes of deep violet flowers and large white ears. Elegant 'With Love' has unusual green foliage, plump, short spikes of cerise, and delicate pink ears with bright magenta veins.

LEMON BALM

Scientific name: Melissa officinalis

The lush leaves of lemon balm spill over the edges of a raised-bed herb garden. Its fragrant, citrus-scented essential oil makes it a versatile herb in the kitchen and out.

Lemon balm (*Melissa officinalis*) was considered a sacred plant by the Greeks, but today it is one of the least commonly cultivated herbs. Although it may be a rare sight in modern herb gardens, it deserves a spot in an edible garden. Growing it will also attract pollinators and help restore our sadly dwindling bee populations.

Native to the eastern Mediterranean and western Asia, this citrus-scented herb has for centuries been grown for its medicinal value. Today, the leaves are used in teas and potpourris. In cooking, they add a lemony taste to salads, fruit dishes, teas, and poultry recipes. They are also used to make essential oils and are a natural insect repellent.

A perennial member of the mint family, the plant grows into a bushy, leafy herb about 2 feet (60 cm) high. In the spring and autumn, it produces clusters of light yellow flowers. A crushed leaf is simultaneously sweet and tart in flavor, with the distinctive aroma of lemons.

Growing and caring for the plants

Lemon balm plants are not picky about their environment. The soil needs to be rich in nutrients and organic matter and have ample drainage. They will thrive in full sunlight but can do well in partial shade. In dry climates, choose a spot for lemon balm that gets partial shade over one that gets full sun.

The herb can be easily propagated from seeds, cuttings, or by plant division. Start seeds indoors six to eight weeks before the last frost in your area. After all threat of frost has passed, move seedlings outside, spacing them 12 to 15 inches (30 to 38 cm) apart. Provide a deep watering to help ease the transition. Germination should occur between 12 to 21 days.

Once established, the plants will require very little care, other than careful irrigation. Watering by hand is especially important in extreme heat or drought conditions—the soil around the plants should remain consistently moist.

These plants are aggressive reseeders, and if not carefully controlled, can quickly become invasive in the garden. Removing the flowers as soon as they appear will reduce this threat. This herb can be susceptible to whitefly, spider mites, thrips, and powdery mildew.

The Essentials

planting time	late spring
light	full sun to partial shade
soil	slightly sandy, well-draining soil
pH level	6.5 to 7.0
water	1 inch (2.5 cm) per week
size	2 to 3 feet (60 cm to 1 m) tall; 18 to 36 inches (45 cm to 1 m) wide
harvest	in 70 to 200 days

Harvesting lemon balm

Harvesting will encourage healthy new growth, but never trim more than one-third of a plant at a time. You can snip leaves off a mature plant to use any time during the growing season. Harvest larger, older leaves first. Lemon balm loses its scent when dried, so it is usually used only when freshly picked.

Editor's Tip

There are lots of uses for herbs outside the kitchen. Make a bug repellent from lemon balm oil, which can repel a variety of biting insects, as does a crushed basil leaf. Place lemon verbena near doorways or in windows to drive mosquitoes and other pests from your home. Lavender will repel flies and mosquitoes, or you can use it fresh or dried in closets or dresser drawers to deter moths; repel fleas by crumbling a bit onto your pet's bedding. Put some of those leftover bay leaves into your canisters of flour, pasta, or rice. The herb's bitter smell discourages many pests and can keep weevils from invading dried goods. The pungent aroma of rosemary will repel flies and will also keep cats from using your garden as a litter box. Mint and catnip repel flies, as well as ants and mice.

LEMONGRASS

Scientific name: Cymbopogon citratus

The thin blades of the lemongrass plant lend a lemony citrus note to recipes.

The Essentials

planting time spring

light full sun

soil fertile, well-draining soil

pH level 6.5 to 7.0

water 1 inch (2.5 to 5 cm) per week

size 2 to 4 feet (60 cm to 1.2 m) tall; 2 to 3 feet (60 cm to 1 m) wide

harvest in 70 to 100 days

For gardeners who ask something extra of their plants, lemongrass (*Cymbopogon citratus*) easily fulfills two roles. This fast-growing ornamental grass increases curb appeal, while offering a tasty herb for soups, stir-fries, and teas. Native to Sri Lanka and India, it is perennial in warm regions, but treated as an annual in temperate zones. It grows in abundance in areas that mimic its warm and humid habitat. Provide lots of heat, light, and moisture, and your lemongrass will grow and multiply quickly.

Lemongrass—also known as barbed wire grass, silky heads, Cochin grass, Malabar grass, oily heads, citronella grass, or fever grass—grows into a tall plant, with long, slender gray-green foliage that turns to gorgeous reds and burgundies to bring color to autumn gardens. The plump stems, and sometimes the leaves, are used for cooking. All parts of the plant have a strong lemon flavor with hints of ginger. Lemongrass's fragrance also acts as a pest repellent—its oil seems to deter unwanted insects, such as mosquitoes.

This herb is used in recipes throughout Southeast Asia, particularly in Thai and Indonesian dishes. It also has a long and varied history in herbal medicine.

Growing and caring for the plants

Lemongrass may not always be available in your local supermarket, so it makes sense to grow it yourself. For indoor cultivation, go to the grocery store, and buy the freshest lemongrass plants you can find. Trim a couple of inches (5 cm) off the top, and peel away anything that looks dead. Place the stalks in a glass of shallow water, and set it near a sunny window. In a few weeks, tiny roots should emerge. After they mature a bit, transfer the plant to a pot of soil with the crown just below the surface. This pot can stay indoors or go out on the deck or patio. Growing the plant indoors gives you easy access to the fresh herb when you need it. If you live in a warm climate, you can plant your lemongrass in the backyard in a bog or pond. Cool climate gardeners need to bring their plants indoors in autumn.

Outdoors, lemongrass is best planted from potted nursery specimens in spring, after all danger of frost has passed. It grows best in full sun, at least six hours daily. Plants grown in the shade will be sparse and could attract pests. Lemongrass prefers moist soil—the standard 1 inch (2.5 cm) per week of water will allow it to thrive—yet once established, the herb has a tolerance for drought. A layer of mulch can help conserve soil moisture and will enrich the soil. You can also supply a slow-release 6-4-0 fertilizer to feed your plants throughout the growing season. Manure tea will add important trace nutrients.

Harvesting lemongrass

Once the plant reaches a height of 1 foot (30 cm), you can cut, twist, or break off a stalk that is at least ¼ inch (6 mm) thick. Freeze or dry any leftovers. Store frozen lemongrass for up to six months; dried lemongrass lasts for up to a year.

Note: *This plant contains cyanogenic glycosides and other oils that are mildly toxic to dogs, cats, and horses.*

Editor's Picks

If you are purchasing a nursery-grown plant, look for these other two edible *Cymbopogons.*

- East Indian (*C. flexuosus*), an edible heirloom variety, contains potent essential oils.

- Citronella (*C. nardus*) is familiar to many as the source of the oils used in outdoor candles and mosquito repellents. Its bulbs can be crushed and used to flavor an assortment of foods. The dried leaves are often used to prepare an herbal tea.

LEMON VERBENA

Scientific name: Aloysia citriodora

The fragrant leaves of lemon verbena reach out over a garden chair. Plant this herb in containers near seating areas or well-used pathways—every time you brush past the plants you will be rewarded with a waft of its fresh, lemony aroma.

The Essentials

planting time spring

light full sun

soil rich, moist, well-draining loam

pH level 6.0 to 7.5

water 1 inch (2.5 cm) per week

size 18 inches to 6 feet (45 cm to 1.8 m) tall; 18 inches to 4 feet (45 cm to 1.2 m) wide

harvest in 40 to 85 days

Lemon verbena (*Aloysia citriodora*) is yet another lemon-scented herb that is used in the kitchen. If you live in a frost-free region with milder winters, the plant behaves as a perennial. It can grow into a valued landscape shrub about 6 feet tall by 8 feet wide (1.8 x 2.4 m), one that will release its refreshing citrus aroma as you brush past it. In cooler climates, it is best to treat it as an annual and bring potted specimens inside in the autumn.

Also known as lemon beebrush and vervain, this native of Chile and Argentina is a small, woody, delicate shrub with narrow glossy leaves and small white flowers. Due to its strong aroma, it is often used to scent oils. It is often presented as a garnish, because the leaves tend to be quite sharp in flavor. You can also add chopped leaves to sweet drinks and tea and use them to flavor desserts, jams, and alcoholic beverages. It can even be used as a substitute for fresh lemons or lemon zest. Lemon verbena is sometimes used in making perfumes and toilet waters.

The leaves can be used fresh, or you can dry them for future use. When dried, the sprigs hold their scent for many years.

Growing and caring for the plants

Growing it isn't too difficult, but this herb can be sensitive, having a high water requirement. It can be propagated from either seeds or cuttings. The cuttings can be placed in a jar of water while you wait for new roots to form. Once they form, wait a few weeks for a good root structure to develop before planting them into soil. Set them out at the same time you plant tomatoes, coleus, and other heat lovers. Lemon verbena yields the most intense flavor in full sun.

To grow from seeds, scatter them in starter trays, and cover with a light layer of soil. Moisten well, and give them plenty of sun. Once the seedlings have grown several leaves, transplant them into the garden after first hardening them off with gradual exposure to outdoor temperatures. Space the plants 12 to 18 (30 to 45 cm) inches apart to give them room to spread out. Once plants are established, water them when the top 2 inches (5 cm) of soil are dry.

To encourage leaf production, feed regularly with a water-soluble plant food. In periods of bad weather, your plants might get a bit beat up. Revive a battered plant by trimming it back to one-third. It will come back even fuller and healthier.

Harvesting lemon verbena

When the plant reaches about 10 inches (25 cm) in height, begin to harvest the leaves. Unlike many flowering herbs, the oils are at their strongest while the plant is in bloom, meaning the flavor will be at its most intense. Harvest in the morning hours, and avoid plucking the leaves off a stem; instead, cut off branch tips with a garden pruner or scissors. Remove no more than a quarter of the stem so that the plant can continue growing.

For most recipes you will need to finely mince these tough leaves, but you can use whole leaves to infuse flavored oil, sugar, or tea. Fresh leaves will keep in the refrigerator for up to two days in a sealed plastic bag, or you can freeze them. You can also harvest the tiny heavily scented blossoms to use much in the same way you would the leaves. Air-dry any surplus leaves. After drying, strip the leaves from the stem, and store in an airtight container in a cool, dark place for up to two or three years.

Note: This herb is edible by humans, but it is toxic to horses, dogs, and cats.

LOVAGE

Scientific name: *Levisticum officinale*

A gardener harvests the leaves from a lovage plant. This plant is an all-around star when it comes to harvesting—the leaves, stalk, stems, and roots are all edible.

The Essentials

planting time spring; autumn

light full sun to partial shade

soil rich, moist, well-draining, sandy or loamy soil

pH level 6.0 to 7.0

water 1 to 2 inches (2.5 to 5 cm) per week

size up to 5 feet (1.5 m) tall; 2 to 3 feet (60 cm to 1 m) wide

harvest in 85 to 95 days

Lovage (*Levisticum officinale*) is a tall, perennial, culinary herb often grown for the celery-like flavor of its leaves, stems, roots, and seeds. This member of the carrot family is also known by the name "love parsley." Originally found in western Asia, parts of the Middle East, and the Mediterranean region, lovage is cold hardy in most temperate regions but may need some protection where winters regularly reach temperatures below 0°F (-18°C). These plants shoot up like weeds and can reach more than 5 feet (1.5 m) tall. They bear thick, lacy green foliage and yellow flowers that form umbrella-shaped umbels and produce seeds of ½ inch (1 cm) in length. The base of the plant is composed of thick, celery-like stems with glossy green leaves that decrease in number as you move up the stalk.

All parts of lovage are edible and delicious, plus the plant can be included in any recipe that calls for parsley or celery. It has a high salt content, however, so a little will go a long way. The stalks and stems are best used in carbohydrate-based dishes, such as pasta and potato recipes. The young leaves are typically added to salads, and the root is dug up at the end of the season and used as a vegetable. Interestingly, the herb's seeds and stems provide a commonly used flavoring for confections. The seeds are also steeped to flavor oils and vinegars. Lovage is quite popular in Europe, where it is found in German and Italian cuisines. The flower yields an aromatic essential oil used in perfumery, while the root and rhizome are said to have medicinal properties.

Growing and caring for the plants

Start seed indoors five to six weeks before the date of your last frost. Scatter them on the surface of the soil, and then dust with sand. You can also sow seeds outdoors in late spring when soil temperatures have warmed to at least 60°F (16°C). The keys to growing lovage are plenty of sunlight and well-draining sandy and loamy soil.

Seedlings require consistent moisture until they are 1½ to 2½ inches (3.5 to 6 cm) tall, and then irrigation may diminish. Transplant lovage plants so that they are spaced 8 inches (20 cm) apart in rows 18 inches (45 cm) away from one another. Expect flowers on transplants in early summer that will last until late summer. Seeds will arrive late in summer or early spring. Lovage will bloom earlier when planted indoors.

Lovage has a reputation for being a good companion plant for potatoes and other tubers and root crops, such as asparagus and rhubarb. They also do well sharing space with other herbs like parsley, hyssop, and fennel. Leaf miners that feed on the leaves seem to be the primary pest of the plant.

Harvesting lovage

You can harvest lovage leaves at any time, but they are best when young. To harvest the tasty leaves, snip or pinch off as needed to use fresh. Harvesting when they are young and tender is optimal, but you can take the leaves and stalks any time during the growing season. Gathering them in the morning, just after any dew has dried, is best.

If you intend to dry your harvest, be sure to gather the leaves before the plant has flowered. Roots should also be harvested just before the plants flower. Gently lift them out of the soil with a garden fork. You can also dry these by first cutting them into small pieces. Use any dried lovage within a year.

In late summer, you can harvest seeds when they have turned brown. To gather them, gently rub them off the plant, or place the seed heads in a paper bag, where they will drop as they ripen.

MARJORAM

Scientific name: Origanum majorana

When tiny flowers cover the plant in summer, marjoram makes a pretty sight. Still, if you are growing it to use as a fresh herb, harvest leaves before the blooms appear.

Also known as sweet marjoram and knotted marjoram, marjoram (*Origanum majorana*) is a perennial herb that is a close relative of oregano. Originally native to Europe, this small, low-growing plant has a mounded, shrubby appearance with aromatic, ovate, gray-green leaves that grow to about 1 inch (2.5 cm) in length. The clusters of tiny white or pink flowers bloom from mid- to late summer and, while pretty, are not especially showy. Best planted in the spring, marjoram grows slowly and eventually becomes a spreading ground cover.

Like its cousin oregano, marjoram has become a popular herb in kitchens around the globe. The leaves have a flavor that is both sweet and spicy; they can be used in making teas and do a great job of adding pizazz to salads. The herb is often used in Italian cooking, as well as in other Mediterranean-style cuisines.

Marjoram is said to be hardy in warmer temperate regions, but many gardeners swear they have overwintered the plants in colder areas. If your winters are particularly severe, grow marjoram as an annual in containers, and bring them inside in the autumn.

Growing and caring for the plants

Marjoram is easy to cultivate, providing you offer it full sun with some midday shade and the usual well-drained soil. There are three varieties that are commonly grown: sweet marjoram, pot marjoram, and wild marjoram (also known as common oregano). All three types are popular for use as a kitchen seasoning, and they are also known for their enticing fragrances.

When growing marjoram, it's generally best to start the seeds indoors during late winter or early spring. Push seeds just below the soil surface in your starter tray. Seedlings with at least two sets of leaves can be transplanted outdoors once all threat of frost has passed.

Marjoram can also be grown indoors year round as a windowsill herb, as long as you give it light, provide a loose soil mixture, and don't overwater it. Keep the temperatures between 65°F and 75°F (18°C and 24°C). During mild weather, marjoram containers can be placed outside in a sunny area. They should, however, always be moved back indoors once frost is imminent.

Plants established in the garden require little care, other than occasional watering. Because marjoram is tolerant of drought, it makes an exceptional plant for novice herb gardeners. If you forget to water it every now and then, that's okay. In warm weather, you can mulch around the plants to protect roots from too much heat, but there's no need for fertilizer with marjoram. It's hardy enough to basically care for itself.

Harvesting marjoram

To harvest marjoram for immediate use, cut fresh leaves as needed once plants reach 4 to 6 inches (10 to 15 cm) tall. The cut-and-come-method is great for this herb, because frequent harvesting will renew plants. You can also extend the harvest season by removing flower buds as they form—as with most flowering herbs, marjoram's flavor is best before the plants bloom.

When harvesting marjoram for future kitchen use, pick the shoots just after flower buds appear but before they open. This results in the best flavor, as fully opened blooms may produce a bitter taste. Remove no more than a third of a plant's leaves. Bundle the cuttings, covering them with a paper bag, if necessary, to avoid dust and other contaminants settling on the leaves. Hang the bundles upside down in a dark, well-ventilated area. Once they are dried, strip the leaves from the stems, and place them in airtight containers. Keep the containers in a cool, dark spot. They can last from one to three years.

Note: *Marjoram is toxic to dogs and cats.*

The Essentials

planting time spring

light full sun

soil fertile, well-draining loamy soil

pH level 4.9 to 8.7

water 1 inch (2.5 cm) per week

size 12 to 24 inches (30 to 60 cm) tall; 12 to 24 inches (30 to 60 cm) wide

harvest in 70 to 90 days

A Gallery of MINTS

Members of the genus *Mentha* in the family Lamiaceae (mint family) are valued additions to an herb garden. Numerous mint species and hybrids exist, and just about all of them are worth cultivating. Mints are most often used for flavoring dishes or as garnishes, but many types are also grown for their unique aromas. Their biggest downside is their aggressive growth habit. These fast growers can quickly extend through a patch of ground through a network of runners, taking over the landscape. Although some species are more invasive than others, it is best to control their environment by planting them in deep, bottomless containers sunk in the ground or in aboveground pots, tubs, and barrels.

AMERICAN WILD MINT (*Mentha canadensis*)
Pinched or crushed, the leaves emit a peppermint smell. This native North American mint can be used to make jelly, tea, and candy.

APPLE MINT (*Mentha suaveolens*)
Its fruity-minty flavor and scent gives it its common name. Lighter in color than most other *Menthas,* it can be used to make jelly or tea.

Whichever of the many mints you choose, planting them in a container is a smart way to control their aggressive spreading.

Dig Deeper

LEARN MORE AT GARDENING KNOW HOW

For more about mints and their many varieties, scan the QR code or follow this link.

 "Mint Plant Varieties: Types of Mint for the Garden" LINK: gkh.us/35575

CHOCOLATE MINT (*Mentha × piperita* f. *citrata* 'Chocolate')
Despite its name, this mint has an orangey taste. It is the leaf that has the scent of chocolate. Use it to flavor drinks and desserts.

CORSICAN MINT (*Mentha requienii*)
The flavoring of crème de menthe liqueur, this is a shorter mint with tiny leaves that makes a good companion for brassica plants.

CUBAN MINT (*Mentha × villosa*)
The preferred variety to make the Cuban rum cocktail mojito, this strongly scented and flavorful species can be used in many recipes.

PEPPERMINT (*Mentha × piperita*)
A cross between watermint and spearmint, its fresh or dried leaves are used to flavor teas, ice cream, candy, preserves, and cocktails.

PINEAPPLE MINT (*Mentha suaveolens* 'Variegata')
An apple mint cultivar, it stands out in an ornamental garden with its variegated leaves. It can be used to flavor fruit salads, jellies, and teas.

SPEARMINT (*Mentha spicata*)
The shape of its leaves gives it its common name. This refreshing mint is a favorite in iced beverages and also works beautifully in salads.

WATERMINT (*Mentha aquatica*)
Unusual for its habit of growing in shallow water, it makes a great choice for a water feature. Its leaves can be harvested to make herbal teas.

MINT

Scientific name: Mentha spp.

A young mint plant shares space with other culinary herbs on a kitchen windowsill.

The Essentials

planting time spring

light full sun to partial shade

soil rich, moist, well-draining soil

pH level 6.0 to 7.0

water 1 to 2 inches (2.5 to 5 cm) per week

size 12 to 18 inches (30 to 45 cm) tall; 18 to 24 inches (20 to 60 cm) wide

harvest in 90 days

Widely distributed and found in many environments around the world, especially in temperate and subtemperate regions, members of the genus *Mentha* originated in the eastern Mediterranean area. The numerous species that make up the genus are aromatic, almost exclusively perennial herbs. Within the numerous species, there are also many recognized hybrids.

Members of the genus will vary in appearance. Their leaves can be lanceolate to oblong in shape, in colors from pale yellow to dark green or gray-green to purple and blue. The flowers are white to purple.

The scent of these plants can also vary, but the distinctive smell of mint is easily recognizable. Their taste ranges from mildly cool to icy hot. The leaves produce an essential oil that flavors many of the foods we commonly consume, from stomach-soothing teas to refreshing ice creams and candies.

Growing and caring for the plants

All mint varieties, except peppermint, can be grown from seed. Peppermint does not produce seeds; therefore, this type must be propagated only by taking root cuttings from established plants. All types of mint, however, can be grown by this method. Taking a cutting is, in fact, one of the easiest methods. Simply pull or snip off a rooted piece of mint growing from the parent plant. Pot it up, and water. Large clumps can also be dug up and divided into smaller plants.

One of the best ways to grow mint in the garden without the threat of rampant spreading is by using containers. Merely sink the plant into the soil, leaving the top sticking out about 1 inch (2.5 cm) or so. You might also want to keep containers spaced at least 1 or 2 feet (30 to 60 cm) apart to prevent various types from cross-pollinating.

Although most varieties of mint are easy to grow in various settings, these plants thrive best when located in organically rich, moist, and well-drained soil. A spot that receives full sun to partial shade is also acceptable.

Growing mint usually presents few problems other than aggressive spreading on the part of the plant itself, but pests can occasionally affect the plants. Some of the most common include aphids, spider mites, cutworms, and mint root borers. Mint can also be susceptible to diseases such as mint rust, verticillium wilt, and anthracnose.

Harvesting mint

As with most herbs, it is best to harvest leaves just before the plant begins to flower. You can simply pluck a leaf or two directly off the stems, if you need a small amount. If you wish to harvest for bulk storage or your recipe calls for a large quantity, cut whole stems with leaves using garden shears or a pair of sharp scissors. Whichever method, to ensure peak flavor, pick your mint in the morning, after dew has dried, when the essential oils are percolating.

Editor's Tip

Mint's reputation as an aggressive plant that will take over the garden is well deserved, yet growing it can be a rewarding experience if it is kept under control.

MUSTARD

Scientific name: Brassica juncea

The leafy greens of the mustard plant have a peppery taste and are highly nutritious.

The Essentials

planting time spring, autumn

light full sun to partial shade

soil fertile, well-draining soil

pH level 5.5 to 7.5

water 2 inches (5 cm) per week

size 1 to 2 feet (30 to 60 cm) tall; 12 to 18 inches (30 to 45 cm) wide

harvest in 40 to 50 days

A versatile member of the *Brassica* genus, mustard (*Brassica juncea*), can be grown as a cover crop or green manure, as well as for its culinary value—the leaves, seeds, and stems are all edible. Originally from the foothills of the Himalayas, it has been cultivated for food in Europe and Asia for hundreds of years and is now commercially grown in various parts of the world for its seeds, the source of spicy brown mustard.

Garden plants typically grow to about 1 or 2 feet (30 to 60 cm) in height, with short basal leaves and upper stem leaves that are much smaller and toothed, scalloped, or frilled. They bloom with masses of bright yellow, four-petaled flowers that are colorful but not particularly ornamental. Mustard is hardier than many of its cole crop cousins, but it can become invasive, so care needs to be taken when including it in a home herb or vegetable garden.

Growing and caring for the plants

You can grow mustard for its tasty greens, or you can allow the plants to flower in order to harvest the seeds, which are used as a spice in cooking or ground into the popular condiment. Mustard plants are typically grown from seed but can be grown from purchased seedlings, as well. Sow seeds about three weeks before your last frost date. If you are growing them primarily for their greens and would like a steadier harvest, plant mustard seeds about every three weeks to give you a successive harvest. Mustard greens will not grow well in the summer, so you should stop planting seeds a bit before the end of spring and start planting the seeds again in midsummer for an autumn harvest.

For mustard greens, press each seed about a ½ inch (1.25 cm) apart. After the seeds sprout, thin the seedlings to 3 inches (7.5 cm) apart. For seed plants, space them about 1 inch (2.5 cm) apart, and thin the seedlings to 6 inches (15 cm) apart. Plants grown for seed are spaced farther apart to account for the larger size they will attain before flowering. If you're planting seedlings, plant them 3 to 5 inches (7.5 to 12.5 cm) apart for the greens and 6 inches (15 cm) apart for the seeds beginning three weeks before your last frost date.

Once mustard plants start growing, they need little care. Give them plenty of sun or partial shade, and keep in mind that mustard likes cool weather and grows rapidly. They require about 2 inches (5 cm) of water a week. During cool weather, you should get enough rainfall to supply this; if not, you'll need to do additional watering. Keep your mustard bed weed free; the less competition the plants have from weeds, the better they will grow. You can fertilize with a balanced fertilizer, but these plants rarely need it when grown in a well-amended vegetable garden soil.

Watch for bolting (flowering) in warmer weather. This may seem like a great thing if you are growing mustard for their seeds, but mustard plants that bolt due to warm weather will produce poor-quality flowers and seeds.

Harvesting mustard

Harvest mustard greens while they're still young and tender; older leaves will get tough and increasingly bitter. Discard any yellow leaves. You can either pick individual leaves and leave the plant to grow more, or cut down the entire plant to harvest all the leaves at once.

As mustard flowers grow and mature, they will form pods. Watch for these pods to start to turn brown. Yellowing leaves are another sign that you are nearing harvest time. Don't leave the pods on the plant for too long—they will burst open when fully ripe. Remove the seeds from the pods with your hands, or place the flower heads in a paper bag, and allow them to finish maturing. The pods will open on their own in one to two weeks, and a gentle shake of the bag will loosen most of the seeds. Mustard seeds can be used fresh, but like other herbs and spices, if you plan on storing them long term, they will need to be dried.

NASTURTIUM

Scientific name: Tropaeolum majus

Nasturtiums spill over the sides of a wooden planter. The colorful flowers, in vivid red-oranges and yellows, rise over the distinctive oval leaves of this herbaceous plant.

Flowers can be eaten as buds or when in full bloom, but the leaves have the best flavor when young and tender, so pick off newer growth for culinary uses. The flavor gets spicier as the day wears on, so pick early for milder tastes and later in the day for a greater kick.

Nasturtiums have a lot going for them: lovely, jewel-toned flowers that peek out from dense foliage and large, beautifully shaped leaves that resemble those of a lotus; plus both the blossoms and leaves make tasty additions to salads and sandwiches. These plants are also quick to germinate and easy to grow. The humorous advice, "Be nasty to nasturtiums," is not far off the mark—they really do best with a little neglect.

The flowers of this South American native are funnel-shaped and trend toward the hot end of the color spectrum, with varying shades of yellow, orange, pink, and red. There are growing habits for almost every garden need: bushy plants for borders and edges; trailing specimens for walls and containers; and climbers that add dramatic height to the garden. They also do well in hanging baskets, window boxes, and ground planters. Because nasturtium leaves and flowers are edible, with a peppery tang, the plants are often found in vegetable gardens. When planted alongside broccoli, cabbage, and cauliflower, they keep pests like aphids away.

Growing and caring for the plants

You can start nasturtiums from seeds or from seedling pots purchased from a nursery. Plant seedlings immediately in a container or sunny part of the garden that allows plenty of room for growth. These plants should be placed directly into their permanent location; nasturtiums do not transplant well.

If you start from seed, you might need to manipulate the seed coat for faster germination: either nick the seeds with a knife or soak them overnight in lukewarm water. Use peat pots that can be placed in the ground without disturbing the seedling's roots. For climbing varieties, you may want to set up a trellis near the planting site.

The seeds germinate quickly, and the plants will start blooming soon after. Once established, they generally take care of themselves. Their watering needs are average, but if the soil is too rich or you've added too much fertilizer, you will get lush foliage but few flowers.

Harvesting nasturtiums

Picking nasturtiums to eat is as simple as plucking off flowers and leaves as needed throughout the growing season.

OREGANO

Scientific name: Origanum vulgare

Blooming oregano winds along a slope in a rock garden. The essential oils peak just before the plants flower, but these blooms supply high-energy nectar for butterflies.

The Essentials

planting time spring

light full sun

soil fertile, well-draining soil

pH level 6.5 to 7.0

water 1 inch (2.5 cm) per week

size 18 to 24 inches (45 to 60 cm) tall; 18 inches (45 cm) wide

harvest in 80 to 90 days

No list of perennial herbs is complete without oregano (*Origanum vulgare*), which continues to be one of the top kitchen seasonings. The genus *Origanum,* part of the mint family, includes numerous perennial herbs and sub-shrubs that are native to western Asia and the Mediterranean. Some have even naturalized in North America. The most common species are popular culinary herbs, which include oregano and marjoram (*O. majorana*). There are many varieties of oregano, including both Italian and Greek versions, and it is part of the traditional French *bouquet garni* mixture that flavors soups and stews. It is used in tomato sauce recipes, especially those for pizza, hence its nickname "the pizza herb."

This herb's leaves are generally oval, dark green, and positioned in opposite pairs along the stems. Some varieties have fuzzy leaves. Oregano starts as a ground-hugging rosette of leaves, but it can easily reach 2 feet (60 cm) in height. The clusters of flowers are usually white or a pinkish rose-purple.

Oregano is such an easy-care herb, it can be grown indoors or in regions prone to drought. As a companion in vegetable gardens, it repels the insects that plague beans and broccoli.

Growing and caring for the plants

Oregano can be grown from seeds, cuttings, or purchased container plants. Seeds should be started indoors prior to your region's last predicted frost. There's no need to cover oregano seeds with soil—simply mist them with water, and then cover the seed tray or container with plastic wrap. Place them in a sunny window to germinate, which usually happens within a week or so. Once the seedlings have reached approximately 6 inches (15 cm) in height, the plants can be thinned to 1 foot (30 cm) apart.

Plants can be transplanted into the garden once the risk of frost has passed. Be sure to place oregano in areas with full sun for at least six hours a day and in well-drained soil.

Established plants do not require much attention and need supplemental watering only during excessively dry periods. Oregano doesn't need to be fertilized either. For overwintering outdoors, plants should be cut back to the ground and covered with a layer of mulch. Container plants can also be grown indoors all year round or brought inside from the garden in the autumn.

For optimal flavor if you are growing oregano for kitchen use—or if you desire more compact plant growth—pinch back the flower buds before they bloom. Flavorwise, after the plant blooms, the leaves will either become milder or more bitter, depending on the variety.

Harvesting oregano

Oregano grows quickly, providing leaves suitable for harvesting almost immediately. The leaves and stems can be harvested anytime, as long as the plants have reached 4 to 6 inches (10 to 15 cm) in height. It's best to pick the leaves in the morning hours once the dew has dried. The leaves can be stored whole, placed in freezer bags, and then frozen. Stems of oregano leaves can also be bundled, hung up, and dried in a dark, well-ventilated area. Strip the dried leaves to store in airtight containers until you are ready to use them.

Note: *Oregano is toxic to pets, so be mindful of where you plant it.*

Editor's Tip

To encourage healthy oregano plants, when harvesting from a dense specimen, instead of snipping off just the leaf ends, reach down and snip off the entire woody stem at the base. Trimming the lower, outer branches in sections all around the plant allows air to circulate in the interior. This promotes better growth.

PARSLEY

Scientific name: Petroselinum crispum

A potted flat-leaf parsley plant is ready for harvesting. The taste of this variety's leaves is less robust than the slightly bitter and stronger flavor of the curly-leaf varieties

Parsley (*Petroselinum crispum*) is popular in both the garden and the kitchen. It occurs in a flat-leaf variety, also called Italian, and a curly-leaf variety. Both are European in origin but have now spread around the globe. This hardy herb, with its bright, herbaceous flavor, is added to many savory dishes or used as a decorative garnish; its fern-like foliage is also high in vitamins. In the garden, parsley is rarely affected by disease, though insect pests, such as aphids, can occasionally present a problem. Parsley is considered a biennial but is treated as an annual in colder climates. It can be grown in containers or in a bed and is generally established through seeds.

This plant grows in clumps with its lacy foliage reaching about 1 foot (30 cm) in height. It is the triangular, dark green leaves that make a good garnish or an aromatic addition to recipes. In summer, butterflies love the petite whitish yellow blossoms that form lacy, flat-topped clusters in the classic umbel shape typical of the family Apiaceae.

Different varieties of parsley yield different flavors, so consider how you'd like to use the herb before choosing which to plant. For example, curly parsley can be a little bitter for some palates, while the less-robust taste of flat-leaf parsley is more in favor with today's cooks. The latter is available throughout the year.

Growing and caring for the plants

Parsley seeds can be started outdoors— sown directly in the garden as soon as the soil is manageable in spring—but the proven method is to sow them indoors in peat pots about six weeks before planting time. This step is helpful because parsley germinates very slowly, taking three weeks or more to sprout. Most varieties of parsley also grow fairly slowly, establishing maturity between 70 to 90 days after planting. Parsley seeds are quite small, so there is no need to cover them with soil. Simply sprinkle seeds on top of the soil, and mist well with water. Once the seeds have sprouted, thin the seedlings down to only one or two plants per pot.

Although this herb tolerates poor soil and drainage, it's always preferable to situate plants in organic-rich, well-drained soil. A planting bed with full sun to partial shade is also recommended. Once established, this easy-care herb requires little maintenance, other than an occasional watering or weeding. A decent layer of mulch around the bases, however, will reduce the need for both watering or weeding.

Harvesting parsley

Parsley can be harvested throughout the year, even indoors during winter. You can start harvesting parsley once the leaves start to curl. For optimal flavor, pick parsley early in the morning when the plant's oil is strongest. Parsley is best used while fresh; however, it can be frozen until you need it. Freezing parsley is actually better than drying, which can cause the herb to lose some of its flavor.

Note: *The chemical compounds called furanocoumarins are toxic to pets.*

The Essentials

planting time spring

light full sun to partial shade

soil rich, well-draining soil

pH level 6.0 to 7.0

water 1 to 2 inches (2.5 to 5 cm) per week

size 9 to 12 inches (23 to 30 cm) tall; 9 to 12 inches (23 to 30 cm) wide

harvest in 60 to 70 days

Dig Deeper

LEARN MORE AT GARDENING KNOW HOW

Scan the QR code or follow this link to learn how this plant can bring important pollinators to your culinary herb garden.

"Using Parsley for Butterflies: How to Attract Black Swallowtail Butterflies"
LINK: gkh.us/82393

PINEAPPLE SAGE

Scientific name: Salvia elegans

An Anna's hummingbird sips nectar from a vibrant red flower of a pineapple sage plant. This attractive herb will draw beneficial pollinators to the garden.

The Essentials

planting time spring

light full sun to partial shade

soil moist, rich, well-draining soil

pH level 6.0 to 8.0

water about 1 inch (2.5 cm) every 7 to 10 days

size up to 5 feet (1.5 m) tall; up to 3 feet (1 m) wide

harvest in 75 to 80 days

The smaller leaves will have a more intense and fresh taste than the larger ones. You can also dry the leaves to use later. For the flowers, pick only what you will use within a day or two; older flowers will develop a bitter taste.

Most gardeners are familiar with culinary sage (*Salvia officinalis*), but there are many different types of sage plants available. Some have medicinal or aromatic properties and others are grown purely for ornamental purposes. Of the varieties grown in an edible garden, pineapple sage, with its delightfully fruity fragrance, is one of the most popular.

Pineapple sage (*Salvia elegans*) is a perennial native to Mexico and Guatemala, but in some temperate climates it can be treated as an annual. This semi-woody sub-shrub can reach 3 feet (1 m) in height, with red, tubular flowers that bloom in late summer to early autumn. These flowers are a favorite of desirable pollinators like hummingbirds, butterflies, and bees.

The plant's crushed leaves smell like pineapple, hence the common name, but the strength of the scent differs depending on your region's climate. The leaves can also be dried and used to steep tea. The minty-flavored blossoms make a pretty garnish for salads and desserts and are also used in jellies, jams, potpourris, and flower arrangements. The plant also has a history as a medicinal herb due to its antibacterial and antioxidant properties.

Growing and caring for the plants

Pineapple sage should be grown from seeds started indoors; the seeds will germinate within two weeks. Don't transplant seedlings outdoors until they are at least 8 inches (20 cm) tall and after any danger of frost has passed. Space the seedlings in the bed 18 to 24 inches (45 to 60 cm) apart.

Once transplanted, the seedlings will grow rapidly if located in a plot that receives morning sun and afternoon shade. They like well-drained soil that is consistently moist, but established plants will tolerate drought conditions. If your winter temperatures go below freezing, locating the plants in a protected, sunny spot with a layer of mulch will encourage them to return in spring. This herb is known for its deer resistance and has relatively few insect pests.

Harvesting pineapple sage

Once the plants have been established, you can harvest the leaves at any time.

Editor's Picks

With brightly colored foliage and flowers, pineapple sage can enliven a vegetable garden. Here is a sampling of the most popular cultivars.

- 'Frieda Dixon' has mid-green leaves and flowers in a soft salmon to watermelon pink.
- 'Golden Delicious' features chartreuse leaves and fire engine red flowers.
- 'Honeydew Melon' is a smaller variety that blooms early, making it a great choice for cool-climate gardens. Its red flowers rise above melon-scented foliage.
- 'Scarlet Pineapple', a prolific bloomer, has mid-green leaves and big red flowers that butterflies love.
- 'Scarlet Tangerine', a smaller and earlier-blooming variety, is grown as a tender perennial with dark red flowers on dark purple stems rising amid its citrus-scented leaves.

PURSLANE

Scientific name: *Portulaca oleracea*

Purslane is growing in a planter to contain its spread through the garden. This is a crawling plant with succulent leaves that have a light, lemony taste.

The Essentials

planting time spring

light partial to full sun

soil average, well-draining soil

pH level 5.5 to 7.5

water 1 inch (2.5 cm) per week

size 3 to 8 inches (7.5 to 15 cm) tall; up to 18 inches (45 cm) wide

harvest in 60 days

Purslane (*Portulaca oleracea*) is often considered to be a weed, but if you get to know this fast-growing succulent, you'll discover that it is both edible and delicious. It grows naturally in the wild, but growing it in the garden can be beneficial for your health and taste buds.

Also called common purslane, little hogweed, or pursley, this tropical perennial is treated as an annual in most regions. It is native to Asia but has spread all across the world and is commonly found in cleared areas. It also grows well near the Mediterranean Sea, which indicates that it needs some heat to truly develop well.

The purslane herb, a type of rose moss, has red stems and fleshy, green leaves. The flowers are a bright yellow. The leaves, stems, and flowers are all edible, with a slightly tart, salty taste. Edible purslane is a very healthy plant to add to your diet—it is high in omega-3 fatty acids and contains vitamins A, C, and B, as well as magnesium, calcium, potassium, and iron.

Growing and caring for the plants

You may notice that although you have been pulling purslane out of your flower beds for years, it has suddenly disappeared. Once you do locate a purslane plant, you can either harvest some seeds or trim off a few stems. You can also purchase potted plants online or at garden centers.

All purslane needs to grow is partial to full sun and clear ground. The plants aren't picky about soil type or nutrition, but it does tend to grow better in drier soil. If starting from seed, sow in spring or summer in a full-sun spot after the soil has warmed up. Simply scatter the seeds over the area where you plan on growing it. Don't cover the seeds with soil. Purslane seeds need light to germinate, so they must stay on the soil's surface. If you are using cuttings, lay them on the ground where you plan on growing them. Water the stems, and they should take root in the soil in a few days. If you've purchased your garden purslane in nursery pots, you can transplant them from early spring to early autumn. Space the plants about 8 inches (20 cm) apart.

Water well while plants are young, and then cut back as they establish themselves. Caring for established plants is as simple as it gets—you don't need to do anything. The same traits that make it a weed also make it an easy-to-care-for herb. Just be sure to harvest it regularly, and be aware that it can become invasive. Harvesting before it develops flowers will help cut down on its spread. Also, keep in mind that purslane is an annual. The chances are high that it will reseed itself, but you may want to collect some seeds at the end of the season so that you have some on hand for next year, rather than hunting for a new purslane plant. If you decide to harvest wild purslane instead of growing purslane, make sure that you only harvest purslane that has not been treated with pesticides or herbicides.

Purslane is also a great candidate for container planting. Its succulent leaves are highly resistant to drought, so you don't need to water it every day, as you would with many other potted plants.

Harvesting purslane

Harvest purslane leaves while the plants are still young, because the young leaves are tastier than those on older plants. When the plants are around six to eight weeks old, you'll have plenty to harvest. You can typically get three harvests from one planting by cutting from the main plant, but be careful not to cut too short to enable regrowth.

Purslane is best eaten fresh, but any surplus will keep for two to three days wrapped in a paper towel in the crisper drawer of your refrigerator. You can also pickle purslane in vinegar. Pickled purslane will last for several months.

ROMAN CHAMOMILE

Scientific name: Chamaemelum nobile

Roman chamomile has tiny daisy-like flowers. This low-growing plant can work as a fragrant ground cover that can take the place of high-maintenance turfgrass.

The Essentials

planting time early spring

light partial shade to full sun

soil loose, well-draining soil

pH level 5.6 to 7.5

water 1 inch (2.5 cm) per week

size 3 to 6 inches (7.5 to 15 cm) tall; 9 to 12 inches (23 to 30 cm) wide

harvest in 60 to 65 days

There are two types of chamomile—Roman chamomile, a perennial, and its relative German chamomile (*Matricaria chamomilla*), an annual (see page 174). The Roman variety is the true chamomile, but both are native to Europe and have been adorning herb gardens and lawns—and acting as companion plants for vegetables—for many centuries. The German variety has larger flowers, but the Roman's flowers offer more intense scents. And compared to German chamomile, this plant's morphology, properties, and chemical composition are distinctly different.

The word *chamomile* derives from the Greek *chamaimēlon,* meaning "earth-apple," so-called because of the plant's apple-like scent. Extracts or dried flowers of *Chamaemelum nobile* are used in hair and skin care products and in herbal teas, perfumes, and cosmetics and to flavor foods.

A creeping ground cover that grows like a mat, Roman chamomile has leaves that are feathery, finely dissected, and downy to smooth to the touch. The solitary, daisy-like flower heads, rising little more than 6 inches (15 cm) above the ground, consist of prominent yellow disk flowers and silver-white ray flowers. Their fragrance is described as sweet, crisp, fruity, and herbaceous. It is roughly the same height as normal turfgrass, so it can be used in the yard to create a fragrant chamomile lawn for those who want an easy-care and eco-friendly alternative to grass. This works especially well in spots where foot traffic is light or in places with little or no mower access.

Growing and caring for the plants

Chamomile can be started from seeds or purchased as seedlings from a garden center. It appreciates cool conditions and should be planted in partial shade, but will also tolerate full sun. Once your chamomile is established, it needs very little care. Go easy on fertilizer, if you use it at all. Overfertilizing will result in lots of weak foliage and fewer flowers. And because chamomile is drought-tolerant, it only needs to be watered during extended dry periods. Healthy chamomile plants are not affected by many pests, but ailing specimens may be troubled with aphids, mealybugs, and thrips. Roman chamomile is often recommended as a companion plant in a vegetable garden because its strong scent keeps pests away.

Harvesting Roman chamomile

Roman chamomile is best harvested when the blossoms are open to their fullest, before the petals begin to droop backward. Harvest on a dry day, in the morning just after any dew has dried to gather them when their essential oils are at their peak. Gently pinch the stem just below the flower head. Then, place your forefinger and middle finger under the head, between the head and your other pinched fingers, and pop off the flower head. Remove all of the heads that are in full bloom, and leave behind any that are just budding. Lay the flowers out in a single layer on paper towels or cheese cloth, and allow them to dry for one to two weeks in a dark, warm, dry area. You can also dry them in a dehydrator at the lowest possible setting. When the flowers are dry and cool, store them in a sealed glass jar. You can use the dried flowers for up to six months, but the flavor will be less intense.

MORE INFO
An Herb of Many Names

Known botanically as *Anthemis nobilis*, as well as *Chamaemelum nobile,* it has a number of common names, too. Depending on the region, Roman chamomile is also called English chamomile, garden chamomile, ground apple, low chamomile, sweet chamomile, mother's daisy, and whig plant.

ROSEMARY

Scientific name: Salvia rosmarinus

Rosemary in an herb garden. Plant this evergreen near walkways to take advantage of its rich, pinewood scent. This scent pairs well with other members of the mint family.

The common culinary herb rosemary has long been listed under the scientific name *Rosmarinus officinalis,* but since 2020 it has gone by the new name of *Salvia rosmarinus*. Whichever name you find it under, rosemary is an attractive, fragrant, perennial herb that grows into a rounded evergreen shrub. It features slender, needle-like, gray-green leaves on erect woody stems and produces clusters of small, blue-to-white flowers. They typically bloom in late spring to early summer, filling the garden with their piney fragrance for two seasons.

This herb's astringent taste has come to be associated with the cuisine of the Mediterranean and Middle Eastern regions. The leaves are used to flavor grilled meats, especially lamb, along with fish, chicken, potatoes, and other vegetables. They can even be added to fresh fruit. The edible flowers are sometimes used as a dessert garnish.

Growing and caring for the plants

Rosemary is most often propagated from cuttings because it can be tricky getting evergreen rosemary seeds to germinate. To take cuttings, snip stems that are about 2 inches (5 cm) long, and remove the leaves on the bottom two-thirds of the cutting. Place the cuttings in a mixture of perlite and peat moss, spraying to keep them moist until roots begin to grow. After that, you can plant the cuttings directly into the garden after any threat of frost has passed. The shrub has a moderate growth rate and will reach its mature size and begin flowering in its second season.

In the garden, space rosemary seedlings or nursery plants at least 2 to 3 feet (60 cm to 1 m) apart. Rosemary does best in well-drained soil and in a spot with six to eight hours of sunlight. Make sure no taller trees or shrubs are close enough to shade the bed. Although this herb is not a heavy feeder, mixing compost into the soil at planting time can ensure the shrub gets a healthy start. Providing a balanced liquid fertilizer will continue to encourage quality growth. These perennials don't do well in temperatures below freezing. Fortunately, this versatile herb also grows well in containers—both outdoors and indoors—as long as it receives enough light. Rosemary plants are prone to becoming root-bound, however, and should be repotted at least once a year.

The Essentials

planting time spring

light full sun to partial shade

soil well-draining loamy soil

pH level 6.0 to 7.5

water 1 inch (2.5 cm) per week

size 2 to 6 feet (60 cm to 1.8 m) tall; 2 to 4 feet (60 cm to 1.2 m) wide

harvest in 80 to 100 days

Harvesting rosemary

Pruning the plant above the leaf joints will make it bushier, but don't harvest more than a third of the foliage for seasonings. Cut the stems in the morning just after the dew dries and before the heat of the day is at its height. Use pruners when harvesting from mature plants with woody stems. Fresh rosemary is easiest to use because the leaves are soft and pliable. Wrap any surplus in a damp paper towel, and store it in a freezer bag or airtight container. For longer-term storage, bundles of the herb can be dried in a cool, dry place, and then stored in airtight containers. You can also lay out rosemary stems on a baking sheet to dry, or use a dehydrator. Dried rosemary leaves are hard and woody; grinding them with a mortar and pestle or food processor will leave you with a flavorful powdered seasoning.

Dig Deeper

LEARN MORE AT GARDENING KNOW HOW

To learn more about the various rosemary types available for inclusion in a edible herb garden, scan the QR code or follow this link.

"Rosemary Plant Types: Varieties of Rosemary Plants for the Garden"
LINK: gkh.us/95807

SAGE
Scientific name: Salvia officinalis

Stems of soft, downy sage leaves sit in a mug of water. You can place the stems in water, as you would a bouquet of flowers, to keep them fresh before using them.

I f you enjoy making your own poultry stuffing, you'll be familiar with the savory scent and taste of *Salvia officinalis*, also known as garden sage, common sage, or culinary sage. This flavorful culinary herb is used either fresh or dried, and it especially complements rich meats like pork, game, and turkey. It also goes well with cheese dishes and makes a delicious herb-infused vinegar. Originally native to the Mediterranean region, this pretty shrub is notable for its pale, velvet-soft, gray-green leaves. The small, camphor-scented flowers—in bluish lavender to pinkish lavender—grow in whorls on short, upright spikes. There are at least 900 species of *Salvia*, which is the largest genus of plants in the mint family, but this is the species most people mean when they refer to "sage."

Growing and caring for the plants
This perennial herb loves full sun—but it will tolerate some light shade. It requires well-drained sandy or loamy soil, so avoid wet feet at all costs. Sage originally comes from a hot, dry climate and will grow best in similar conditions.

Start sage in the milder weather of spring or autumn. Sow seeds on the average date of the last spring frost.

Indoors, scatter them over seed-starting soil, and cover with ⅛ inch (3 mm) of soil. Keep the soil damp but not soaked. Sage seeds are slow to germinate, so starting them requires patience—not all the seeds will germinate, and the ones that do may take six weeks to sprout. If using nursery plants, position them at the same depth as in their previous container. Space plants about 2 feet (60 cm) apart.

Sage is often grown from cuttings. In spring, take a softwood cutting from a mature plant, dip the cut tip in rooting hormone, then insert it into a small container of potting soil. Cover the plant with clear plastic, and keep it in indirect sunlight until new growth appears. You can then plant the cutting in your garden. Note that sage is one herb where flowering intensifies the flavor.

Harvesting sage
Harvest leaves just before the plant flowers in the morning, after the dew has dried. Simply pick them individually, or with clean, sharp secateurs, cut off a shoot, avoiding the woody plant parts. To keep sage fresh, wrap the shoots or leaves in a damp kitchen towel. They will keep in the fridge for up to two weeks. Air-dry bundles, or use a dehydrator or oven for longer storage up to three years.

The Essentials

planting time	spring
light	full sun
soil	well-draining, sandy or loamy soil
pH level	6.0 to 7.0
water	1 inch (2.5 cm) every 7 to 10 days
size	2 to 3 feet (60 cm to 1 m) tall; 2 to 3 feet (60 cm to 1 m) wide
harvest	in 75 days

Editor's Picks
Not all *Salvias* are edible, but the following *S. officinalis* cultivars are favored by many chefs and share the same culinary profile.

- 'Aurea'—or golden sage—is a creeping sage with gold-and-green variegated leaves.
- 'Berggarten' is similar to common sage except that it does not bloom. It does have the same lovely soft and fragrant silvery green leaves.
- 'Minimus', or dwarf garden sage, has purple-blue blooms and offers the same robust flavors as its larger cousin.
- 'Purpurascens', or purple garden sage, has purple foliage when young and brims with vitamins A and C.
- 'Tricolor' is a pungent sage with uneven variegations on the grayish green leaves, including white, pink, or purple marbling.
- 'Window Box' is small variety that is great for containers.

 To learn how to bring your sage plants indoors, scan the QR code or follow this link to "Care of Potted Sage Herbs – How to Grow Sage Plant Indoors." *LINK:* gkh.us/15822

SALAD BURNET

Scientific name: Sanguisorba minor

As with many herb garden favorites, salad burnet can be grown as a container plant.

The Essentials

planting time spring; autumn

light full sun to partial shade

soil well-draining sandy loam

pH level 6.0 to 8.0

water 1 inch (2.5 cm) per week

size 9 to 24 inches (23 to 60 cm) tall; 1 to 2 feet (30 to 60 cm m) wide

harvest in 70 to 100 days

Salad burnet (*Sanguisorba minor*) is a hardy Mediterranean native that is naturalized in Europe and North America. A perennial member of the rose family, it is used for erosion control, as a salad green, and as a flavoring for vinegars and sauces. It is an easy-to-grow herb that makes a useful addition to the edible herb garden.

Clumps of the plant spread to about 12 inches (30 cm) across and remain small with consistent harvesting. This herb is a low, leafy plant that begins as a rosette. It has pinnate basal leaves with 4 to 12 pairs of oval leaflets with lightly serrated edges. The leaves taste like cucumber and add a fresh taste to salads and can be mixed into an herb butter or spreading cheese, chopped and sprinkled over vegetables, or used as an ingredient in a potato dish.

Flowers appear in late spring and early summer and grow in a rounded cluster of tiny purple to pink blooms. The flowers are not self-pollinating and must be pollinated by wind. In good conditions, the plants will form seeds in the autumn. They will self-seed easily and form a patch of the herb. Salad burnet flowers can be used as a garnish for fresh drinks or cakes and can take the place of mint leaves in some recipes.

Growing and caring for the plants

Salad burnet thrives in an average, well-draining soil and in a sunny to partially shady location. Plants can be started from seed sown in the spring or autumn or from division. The herb starts easily from seed indoors in the spring four to five weeks before the last frost. Sow seeds in flats or individual pots, lightly covering over the seeds and keeping the seed starting mix just moist. The seeds will germinate in about 7 to 14 days. Transplant indoor seedlings after all danger of frost has passed.

You can also direct-sow outdoors about two weeks after the last frost. Sprinkle the seeds in the garden bed, and cover lightly with a dusting of sand. Thin direct-sown plants to 12 inches (30 cm) apart—you can use the thinned seedlings in a salad.

Once established, these herbs require very little maintenance. Side-dress the plants with aged compost early in the spring, and then feed them with a diluted water-soluble fertilizer or fish emulsion every six weeks. The bed needs to be weeded, and giving the plants at least 1 inch (2.5 cm) of water per week will help keep the plants cool during dry periods. Salad burnet does not tolerate transplanting, so ensure you

like their location before you plant. To force new growth, the old foliage and flowering stems need to be removed as they appear. Older plants should be removed because flavor deteriorates as the plant ages. New plants grow so easily that a constant supply of tender new leaves can be had by saving seeds and successional sowing.

Harvesting salad burnet

Begin to harvest the tender young leaves when the plants are 8 to 10 inches (20 to 25 cm) tall. To store fresh leaves, wrap them in a damp paper towel and place them in a perforated plastic bag. They will keep in your fridge's crisper for two to three days. You can also freeze them in a freezer bag or in ice cube trays.

SIMILAR PLANTS

Great Burnet

Salad burnet's larger cousin, *Sanguisorba officinalis*, known as great burnet, can reach a height of 3 feet (1 m). It blooms with showy dark red to purple-red catkin-like flowers. The leaves of great burnet are sometimes harvested to use in salads and have a flavor profile similar to that of salad burnet.

SCENTED GERANIUM

Scientific name: Pelargonium graveolens

The deeply divided leaves of scented geranium give off a sharp citrus scent when crushed or bruised. The 'Citronella' cultivar has a heady citronella-like fragrance.

Scented geraniums, with their varied and textured leaves, the bright hues of their flowers, the scented oils they produce, and the flavor they add to food and beverages, appeal greatly to our senses. The leaves can be used to flavor teas, jellies, jams, or baked goods, and the aromatherapy is free for the taking.

Scented geraniums are not true geraniums, but rather members of the *Pelargonium* genus. They are categorized as tender perennials but are treated as annuals throughout most of Europe and North America. It's an added bonus that they are so easy to grow.

Scented geraniums, which are native to Africa, come in more than a hundred varieties, with differently shaped and textured leaves and numerous flower colors and aromas. The varieties are first categorized by their scent, which includes mint, rose, citrus, and spice. The leaves run the gamut from smoothly rounded to finely cut and lacy and from gray-green to dark viridian to lime. Furthermore, they have glands at the base of their leaf hairs where the scent is formed. The tiny flowers range from white to shades of lilac and pink to red, often combining colors on one bloom.

Growing and caring for the plants

Scented geranium care is fairly basic. You can grow them in pots, indoors or out, or in the ground. They prefer lots of sun, but might need some protection at midday. They aren't fussy about soil type, although they don't like wet feet. Fertilize them lightly and sparingly while they're actively growing. Before the first frost, dig up your plants to bring them inside, or take cuttings for winter growing. Keep them in a sunny window, water regularly, and fertilize very little.

Their biggest downside is that they tend to get leggy and need to be trimmed back to encourage bushiness. Over-fertilization will only increase this problem. Don't throw those trimmings away! You can easily propagate scented geranium from cuttings to replace older plants or to give as gifts.

Harvesting scented geranium

Whether they are in containers or in the ground, locate scented geraniums where they will be touched or brushed against, because the leaves need to be bruised or crushed to release their aromatic oils. To harvest the leaves, snip them in early morning when the oils are at their strongest. When they come into bloom, pick the flowers as needed.

Note: *All plants in the* Pelargonium *genus are toxic to dogs and cats.*

The Essentials

planting time spring

light full sun to partial shade

soil well-draining loamy soil

pH level 5.8 to 6.5

water water deeply whenever the soil starts to feel dry

size 1 to 3 feet (30 cm to 1 m) tall; 1 to 2 feet (30 to 60 cm) wide

harvest in 100 days

Editor's Picks

It's worth exploring some of the delightfully fragrant cultivars of scented geranium.

- 'Apricot' has deeply lobed pink flowers and fruity-scented leaves.
- 'Attar of Roses', with pale pink flowers, emits a heady rose fragrance.
- 'Chocolate Mint' has minty-scented leaves in a rich chocolate color.
- 'Cinnamon' smells like the spice and has pink flowers.
- 'Fringed Apple' has creamy white flowers and a sour apple aroma.
- 'Ginger' is softly scented of spice, with lavender blooms.
- 'Mrs. Taylor' is scented of musky woods and has deep red flowers.
- 'Nutmeg', with pink-accented white flowers, has a spicy nutmeg scent.
- 'Prince Rupert', in variegated pink, has a lemony aroma.

A Gallery of
EDIBLE FLOWERS

Flowering plants, such as violets, nasturtiums, and pot marigolds, add a pop of color to a vegetable garden and also yield pretty, edible blossoms. Even a weed like dandelion supplies tasty blooms—just be sure to harvest only those that have grown in a pesticide-free lawn. Your other vegetable garden plants, such as arugula and cilantro, might flower before you can harvest the leaves, but you can use them in salads and other recipes.

BORAGE
Garnish a soup, quiche, salad, or side dish with the stunning star-shaped blooms of borage. For more information, see page 158.

CALENDULA
Add a bit of zesty bitterness to a salad with the bright orange or golden blooms of calendula. For more information, see page 159.

DANDELION
Every part of these plants (*Taraxacum officinale*) is edible: the flower, roots, stems, and leaves. The blooms and leaves are great in salads.

HIBISCUS
The tart flavor of the deep crimson–colored calyces (sepals) of the flowers of *Hibiscus sabdariffa* is perfect for tea, jam, or sweets.

LAVENDER
Use the lovely flowers of lavender in baked goods and beverages, or candy them for a pretty garnish. For more information, see page 175.

NASTURTIUM
These showy little flowers impart a peppery note while dressings up a salad with bright color. For more information, see page 185.

PANSY
Use these adorable little blossoms (*Viola × wittrockiana*) as cake and cupcake decorations, or add them to a salad for a fresh, grassy note.

ROSE
These elegant flowers (*Rosa* spp.) can flavor beverages and desserts. The taste can be sweet or spicy, with darker colors usually more intense.

SCENTED GERANIUM
Use the scented leaves to flavor beverages like iced tea and cocktails or the delicate flowers as a garnish. For more information, see page 197.

SQUASH
The blossoms of squash plants can be battered and fried, stuffed, or made into donuts. For more information, see pages 129 and 149.

VIOLET
Edible violets, such as *Viola odorata,* can be candied for decoration or picked fresh to sprinkle on salads or make into tea.

SORREL

Scientific name: Rumex spp.

The large leaves of garden sorrel (*Rumex acetosa*) make tasty additions to salads or vegetable dishes. Its cousin, French sorrel (*R. scutatus*), is also widely used in cookery.

Sorrel is a culinary herb that adds a tangy, lemon flavor to dishes. It is also known as sourwood, sorrel dock, sour dock, sour leek, and spinach dock. The two cultivated species are garden sorrel, *Rumex acetosa,* and French sorrel, *R. scutatus*. The main difference between the two is that French sorrel has smaller leaves and a subtler flavor than garden sorrel. These perennial herbs also grow wild in many parts of the world.

Sorrel is an upright plant with leaves that look a lot like those of Swiss chard or spinach. The leaves grow 3 to 6 inches (7.5 to 15 cm) in length and can be plain green or veined in red with either smooth or crinkled surfaces. If allowed to bloom, sorrel produces attractive whorled purple flowers.

This delicate herb is widely included in French cookery, as well as in the Middle Eastern herb mixture za'atar. Chefs often use sorrel leaves as the base of creamy sauces for eggs and fish dishes. It adds an interesting element to salads and cooked vegetables and is delicious when made into sorrel soup. Young leaves tend to have a more acidic taste and do well in salads; mature leaves are tasty sautéed as you would spinach or broccoli rabe.

Growing and caring for the plants

Sow sorrel seeds in the autumn or in spring after the soil has warmed up. (Sorrel can also be started by dividing the roots of a mature plant.) Prepare a bed in well-drained soil and full sun, and sow the seeds 6 inches (15 cm) apart, just barely under the surface of the soil. Keep the plants moderately moist until germination occurs, and then thin the seedlings once they are 2 inches (5 cm) in height. At this stage, the needs of the two species will differ slightly. Garden sorrel needs damp soils and temperate conditions and at least 1 inch (2.5 cm) of water every week. French sorrel performs best when it is grown in dry, open areas with inhospitable soils. These plants have very deep and persistent taproots and grow well with little care.

Sorrel will often bolt (flower) when temperatures begin to soar in summer. When this happens, you can enjoy the plant's lovely appearance, but flowering will slow the production of leaves. If you want to encourage larger leaves and more abundant production, cut the flower stalk off, and the plant will give you a few more harvests. You can even cut it to the ground, and it will produce a full new crop of foliage.

The Essentials

planting time spring

light full sun to partial shade

soil rich, well-draining soil

pH level 5.5 to 6.8

water 1 inch (2.5 cm) per week

size 12 to 18 inches (30 to 45 cm) tall; 18 to 24 inches (45 to 60 cm) wide

harvest in 40 to 60 days

Harvesting sorrel

Sorrel can keep producing from late spring until autumn with proper management and providing you harvest only what you need from the plant. This herb is much like lettuce and greens, in that you can cut the outer leaves away, and the plant will continue to produce foliage. You can usually begin to harvest sorrel when the plants are 4 to 6 inches (10 to 15 cm) tall.

SIMILAR PLANTS
Blood Dock

Another edible member of the *Rumex* species is blood dock (*R. sanguineus*), which also goes by the common names red-veined dock and red-veined sorrel. This European native has beautiful leaves intricately veined in blood red or dark purple that offer both ornamental and edible value. It can bloom with tall stalks of flowers, but these can be trimmed back to encourage bushier leaf growth and prevent rampant self-seeding.

STEVIA

Scientific name: Stevia rebaudiana

Stevia does well in containers, as well as in garden plots. It is a natural sweetener, which accounts for its common names of candyleaf, sweetleaf, and sugarleaf.

Stevia (*Stevia rebaudiana*)—an herbal sweetener with essentially no calories—is welcomed by people interested in both weight loss and those hoping to maintain a healthier diet. Its recent heyday arrived at a time when the safety of synthetic sweeteners was being called into question, and many people were looking for sources of more natural types of foods.

Stevia itself is a nondescript-looking plant with small, moderately broad green leaves; at maturity it reaches approximately 2 to 3 feet (60 cm to 1 m) in height. It is native to Paraguay, where the indigenous people have used it as a sweetener for centuries, possibly millennia. Stevia is now used as a food additive in many countries; for example, it accounts for 40 percent of Japan's sweetening agents. It was banned as an additive in the United States for over a decade due to possible health risks; however, in 2008 it was again approved.

Stevia leaves are estimated to be anywhere between 10 to 300 times sweeter than traditional white refined cane sugar, yet they contain neither calories nor carbohydrates. This is because there are molecules in stevia called glycosides, essentially molecules with sugar attached to them, that give the leaves their sweet taste. Our bodies, however, cannot break apart the glycosides, meaning that the leaves have no calories when consumed by humans. Use the leaves fresh, dried, or ground as a sugar substitute to sweeten desserts, fruit, and drinks.

Growing and caring for the plants

Stevia care is not too labor intensive. You can direct-sow seed outdoors two or more weeks after the last frost in spring when the soil has warmed up and nighttime temperatures stay above 60°F (16°C), or start the plants indoors six to eight weeks before the last frost in spring. The seed will germinate in 7 to 21 days at 70°F (21°C). When the last chance of frost has passed, choose a site with full sun (or dappled sunlight in hotter regions), and place the starter plants in loose, well-draining, loamy soil about 10 to 18 inches (25 to 45 cm) apart. If necessary, you can amend the soil with aged compost before planting. Water frequently, but shallowly, to keep the soil evenly moist. Beginning in early summer, you can side-dress the plant about every two weeks with compost tea or a dilute solution of fish emulsion. Be careful when weeding around the branches of a mature plant, because they can be quite brittle.

The Essentials

planting time spring

light full sun

soil rich, well-draining soil

pH level 6.7 to 7.2

water 1 to 2 inches (2.5 to 5 cm) per week

size 2 to 3 feet (60 cm to 1 m) tall; 12 to 18 inches (30 to 45 cm) wide

harvest in 65 to 120 days

Harvesting stevia

You can harvest the leaves of the stevia plant to use as your own natural sweetener throughout the summer, but they're at their sweetest in autumn, just as they're getting ready to flower. Pick the leaves—all of them if you're treating the plant as an annual—and dry them by placing them on a clean cloth in full sun for an entire afternoon. Save the leaves whole, or crush them into a powder in the food processor, and then store them in an airtight container.

MORE INFO
Nature's Other Sweetener

Stevia is just one of nature's sweeteners. For millennia, bees have furnished humans with another form of natural sweetener. These small wonders of the insect world are capable of converting the nectar they harvest from flowers into liquid gold—the sweet, viscous, amber back-up food of the hive, otherwise known as honey. After they collect nectar with their long tongues, enzymes in their stomachs make it stable for long-term storage. A honey's flavor is determined by the nectar source—typically flowers, herbs, and trees.

SUMMER SAVORY

Scientific name: *Satureja hortensis*

The diminutive leaves of summer savory add zesty, peppery notes to a recipe.

The Essentials

planting time spring

light full sun

soil rich, well-draining soil

pH level 6.7 to 7.3

water 1 inch (2.5 cm) per week

size 12 to 24 inches (30 to 60 cm) tall; 12 to 20 inches (30 to 50 cm) wide

harvest in 60 to 65 days

Native to the eastern Mediterranean and the Caucasus region, summer savory (*Satureja hortensis*) is an annual herb and part of the large mint family. It is sometimes used as a substitute—or in conjunction with—rosemary, thyme, or sage. It is considered less bitter than its winter savory cousin (see page 205), and, with its peppery notes, summer savory is thought to have the more superior flavor. It adds a piquant boost to meat recipes, as well as oil, butter, and vinegar infusions. Its flavor really comes to the fore in bean dishes, however, earning it the title, "the bean herb."

Cultivated for at least 2,000 years, both summer and winter savory have a range of uses after harvesting and are worthy additions to any herb garden. Savory is a key addition to *herbes de Provence,* a famous blend of dried herbs intrinsic to southern French cuisine, alongside marjoram, rosemary, thyme, and oregano. Though both species are edible, summer savory is much more common than its winter counterpart. Their names reflect the fact that summer savory is an annual plant (that only lives for one season), and winter savory is a perennial plant that returns year after year. Summer savory peaks between July and September.

This herb matures into a low-growing shrub with a mound-like formation that rarely exceeds 1 or 2 feet (30 or 60 cm) in height. The plant features many thin, branching stems with a purple cast and are covered in fine hairs. The gray-green leaves are 1 inch (2.5 cm) in length and are typically longer than they are wide. The tiny flowers bloom during the late summer in shades of pink, lilac, or white; these are also edible, with a spicy flavor, and are said to have medicinal, aromatic, and decorative value.

Growing and caring for the plants

This tolerant herb likes rich, moist, well-drained soil and full sun. It also grows quickly and easily enough that it's not at all a hassle to start a new crop each spring. Summer savory can be sown as seed directly into the ground after all danger of frost has passed. Drop one to two seeds per 1 inch (2.5 cm), and sow shallowly, because light is required for germination. The seeds will germinate in 7 to 14 days. The seeds can also be started indoors about four weeks before the last frost, and then transplanted out in warmer weather. It can even be grown indoors during the winter. Once they are established, they require very little plant care, other than watering.

Harvesting summer savory

Harvest summer savory by cutting off the tops when flower buds are just beginning to form and the stems reach 6 to 8 inches (15 to 20 cm) long. Cut the leaves and shoots from mature stalks only, and don't snip all the way down to the base of each stalk. Leave most of the stalk behind so the plant will continue to grow. Harvesting encourages the plant to grow, but cutting the plant too severely does not. Continue picking savory throughout the growing season. Store the fresh cuttings in a glass of water until ready to use, which should be as soon as possible to take advantage of their fresh, peppery essential oils. The longer any fresh herb sits, the less flavorsome it becomes.

To dry summer savory, bundle the stems with twine, and hang in a well-aerated and dust-free area out of direct sunlight. You can also dry savory in a dehydrator. Set the temperature of the food dehydrator at no higher than 95°F (35°C). Strip the leaves from the stems, and place in an airtight glass jar. The flavor can last for up to three years.

Editor's Tip

In order to guarantee access to summer savory all season long, sow new seeds once every week. This will furnish you with a constant supply of plants that are ready to harvest.

TARRAGON

Scientific name: Artemisia dracunculus

French tarragon in a jute bag planter takes a turn outdoors, adding a feathery feel to an herb garden. This variety will also do well grown as an indoor herb.

The Essentials

planting time spring

light partial sun to partial shade

soil light, well-draining, sandy soil

pH level 6.5 to 7.5

water 1 to 1½ inches (2.5 to 3.5 cm) per week

size 2 to 3 feet (60 cm to 1 m) tall; 12 to 24 inches (30 to 60 cm) wide

harvest in 90 days

Tarragon (*Artemisia dracunculus*), also known as estragon, is a perennial herb that is part of the sunflower or daisy family. There are actually two types of tarragon—the French version is more widely available and has a stronger flavor than the Russian variety. The French variety (subspecies *sativa*) grows erect and bears slender, often branching stems that bear long, needle-like leaves that are a glossy light green and very aromatic. The tiny flowers are yellow or a greenish hue. Just one plant is usually sufficient to supply a generous amount of leaves for a season's harvest.

Native to milder European regions, it is, surprisingly, a very cold-hardy perennial, surviving temperatures as low as -20°F (-28°C). It does not do well in overly hot climates. In the garden it is easy to grow in well-drained soil when placed in a sunny or partially shaded spot that is protected from the wind.

Tarragon is commonly grown for its aromatic leaves with their peppery, anise-like flavor. These are used for flavoring many dishes and are especially popular for flavoring vinegar. It is a valued seasoning in soups and stews and is delightful with chicken, fish, and game dishes. It is also part of the traditional French recipe for sauce béarnaise.

Growing and caring for the plants

French tarragon cannot be grown from seeds. This variety must be propagated by cuttings or by division only. The extra effort involved in these methods is worth it, however, adding a sophisticated culinary herb to your garden.

Space tarragon cuttings approximately 18 to 24 inches (45 to 60 cm) apart to ensure adequate air circulation. Ideally, they should be located in well-draining, fertile soil, but these hardy plants will endure and even thrive in areas with poor, dry, or sandy soil. Tarragon has a vigorous root system, making it quite tolerant of arid conditions. Established plants do not require frequent watering, except during periods of extreme drought. Applying a thick layer of mulch in the autumn will help them through the winter. Garden plants should be divided every three to five years

Tarragon also does well as a container plant. Grow it indoors all year round as a houseplant or greenhouse plant, or grow it outside in warm weather, before moving it inside in the autumn.

Harvesting tarragon

Both the leaves and flowers of tarragon plants can be harvested. Harvesting usually takes place in late summer. Although it will have the brightest flavor when used fresh, you can wrap it in a damp paper towel and store in your crisper drawer for up to two weeks. You can also freeze it, or dry it by hanging the stems and leaves in bundles in a dark, dry spot, and then placing them in an airtight container until ready for use.

MORE INFO

Tarragon from Seeds

Although French tarragon is grown from cuttings or divisions, varieties like Russian tarragon can be propagated from seeds. These should be started indoors around April or before your area's last predicted frost. Sow about four to six seeds per pot using moist, composted potting soil. Cover the seeds lightly, and keep them in low light at room temperature. Thin seedlings when they reach about 3 inches (7.5 cm) in height. You can then transplant the seedlings outdoors once temperatures have significantly warmed.

THYME

Scientific name: *Thymus vulgaris*

A patch of common thyme *(Thymus vulgaris)* thrives in an herb garden. This hardy, drought tolerant plant is great for use in xeriscapes in which water is at a premium.

The Essentials

planting time spring

light full sun

soil fertile, well-draining sandy or loamy soil

pH level 6.0 to 8.0

water 1 inch (2.5) every 2 weeks

size 2 to 4 feet (60 cm to 1.2 m) tall; 1 to 3 feet (30 cm to 1 m) wide

harvest in 75 to 90 days

Members of the mint family, plants of the genus *Thymus* are aromatic evergreen herbs. One of the most popular choices for edible herb gardens, *T. vulgaris* is a low-growing, woody perennial of Mediterranean origin. Not surprisingly it performs quite well in dry, sunny locations. This beloved culinary herb, also known as common thyme, garden thyme, and English thyme, provides a distinctive earthy-minty-citrus taste, similar to a toned-down rosemary. The leaves can easily be stripped of the stems and added to recipes for stuffings, sauces, and soups, and it adds flavor to poultry, fish, seafood, and vegetable dishes. It blends well with other cooking ingredients from its native region, such as garlic, olives and olive oil, and tomatoes.

This versatile herb is also lovely to look at and is often used as a decorative plant in a flower garden. It has a compact habit and stays fairly small, growing best in full sun and well-draining soil. Its tiny gray-green leaves remain evergreen, and the petite, tubular pink, white, or lavender flowers grow at the top of the stems in a sphere shape. They typically bloom from May to September. Thyme flowers are edible and are also a favorite of bees.

Other species include Mediterranean thyme (*T. capitatus*), a very fragrant type from southern Spain used in the preparation of olives. *T. citriodorus* includes various citrus-scented thymes. Caraway thyme (*T. herba-barona*) has a very strong caraway scent and is both a culinary herb and an effective ground cover. Wild thyme (*T. praecox*) is often cultivated as an ornamental. Woolly thyme (*T. pseudolanuginosus*) is a ground cover, and creeping thyme (*T. serpyllum*) provides nectar for bees.

Growing and caring for the plants

Thyme should be planted in spring after the last chance of frost has passed. It will mature enough to allow for harvest within a few months, and then will reliably return year after year. Most thyme varieties are cold tolerant in regions where temperatures dip below freezing. A thick layer of mulch will offer protection during the winter, but be sure to remove it in the spring.

Thyme is typically grown from a division. In the spring or autumn, select a mature plant, and use a spade to gently lift a clump from the ground. Tear or slice a smaller clump from the main plant, making sure there is a root ball intact

on the division. Replant the mother specimen, and plant the division in the new location you have chosen.

Thyme can also be grown from seeds, but the seeds are difficult to germinate and can take a long time to sprout. To use this method, start by scattering seeds in a soil-filled tray, then gently cover the seeds with soil. Water the tray thoroughly with a sprayer, then cover it with plastic wrap, and place it in a warm location. Germination will occur from 1 to 12 weeks. Once the seedlings reach 4 inches (10 cm), they can be transplanted into your garden. Thyme is easy to care for once it's established, and it even tolerates drought conditions.

Harvesting thyme

To harvest, simply snip off the leaves you need for a recipe. Once a thyme plant is established—in about a year—it's very hard to overharvest the leaves. For newer plants, however, cut back no more than one-third of the foliage.

Editor's Tip

Thyme benefits from active neglect. Growing the herb in poor soil with little water will actually cause it to flourish, resulting in more strongly flavored leaves. For this reason, thyme is an excellent choice for low-water landscapes.

WINTER SAVORY

Scientific name: *Satureja montana*

Fragrant winter savory is often planted near beehives to lend its flavor to honey.

The Essentials

planting time spring

light full sun

soil light, well-draining sandy soil

pH level 6.0 to 8.0

water 1 inch (2.5 cm) per week

size 6 to 12 inches (15 to 30 cm) tall; 8 to 12 inches (20 to 30 cm) wide

harvest in 90 days

Unlike its annual cousin, summer savory (see page 202), winter savory (*Satureja montana*) is grown as a perennial in many temperate regions. It also has a more powerful flavor than the summer version, will grow in less-fertile soil, and is often used in dried form, whereas summer savory is typically consumed fresh. Winter savory also has higher nutritional value—the shoots and leaves are a rich source of vitamins A, C, and the B group and in minerals such as zinc, magnesium, calcium, and iron.

The plant is a hardy semi-evergreen with erect, woody, bushy stems that bear glossy, dark green oblong leaves with a pinelike scent. The small lilac or white flowers, arranged in terminal spikes, contain both types of reproductive organs and attract many bees. The fruit matures into four nutlets. This herb can be used as a companion plant for beans, where it is said to keep weevils away, and for roses, where it may reduce mildew and aphid infestations.

Winter savory is a native of the dry hillsides of southern Europe and the Mediterranean; it was Roman writer Pliny who named the genus *Satureja*, derived from "satyr," a creature half goat and half man who reveled in all savory delights.

The ancient Romans introduced the herb to England, and today, it is cultivated in culinary herb gardens worldwide.

Both savories have a strong peppery flavor, although winter savory is more pungent. It helps to enliven a variety of foods without the use of salt and pepper. In fact, winter savory is often paired with beans during cooking to prevent the addition of salt from toughening the beans. It combines well with the taste of beef, pork, beans, and cheese and is frequently used to prepare potato salads, mushrooms, pasta, broths, seafood, and mayonnaise. It is also used to make infused vinegar, herb butter, and steeped tea, while the dried leaves are added to potpourri. Its flavor is at its best just before flowering, yet even when dried, it retains its strong flavor.

Growing and caring for the plants

Once it is established, care of winter savory is nominal. It can survive soil of poor quality, but like most herbs, it requires at least six hours of full sun and well-draining soil. Sow seeds in the spring in starter flats, and transfer the seedlings outdoors once the soil warms; be sure to space seedlings 10 to 12 inches (25 to 30 cm) apart. Winter savory can also be propagated via cuttings. Collect cuttings—the tips of new shoots—in late spring and place them in pots of wet sand. When the cuttings root, transplant them to the garden.

Harvesting winter savory

Harvest winter savory in the morning when the essential oils are at their most potent. It can then be used fresh or dried. In temperate climates, winter savory will go dormant in the winter and put out new leaves in the spring. Older plants tend to get woody, so keep them pruned to encourage new green growth.

MORE INFO
Herb-Infused Vinegars

A smart way to make the most of a surplus of fresh herbs like winter savory is to use them in infused vinegars. These make tangy additions to the kitchen condiment shelf, and they also make great gifts for a home cook, especially if presented in a pretty bottle.

 To find out how to create these delicious herbal vinegars, scan the QR code or follow the link to "Herbal Vinegar Recipes – How to Infuse Vinegar with Herbs." *Link: gkh.us/146545*

PART THREE
Appendices

SOURCE YOUR SEEDS

A vegetable garden begins with seeds, so finding reliable sources for your selections is crucial. With a little research, you can find the right plants for your wants and your area.

A century ago, dedicated vegetable gardeners hunted for fresh sources of new plants and seeds beside the local farm shop or garden club swap meet. These days, in early spring, commercial nurseries, local garden centers, and big box home improvement stores are simply brimming with tempting varieties of fruits, vegetables, and herbs. Meanwhile, online sites offer everything from old-fashioned favorites to trendy new cultivars.

MAIL-ORDER CATALOGS

In spite of all the brick-and-mortar retailers and the countless online garden shops, one of the oldest outlets for plants and seeds, the mail-order catalog, still continues to enthrall gardeners.

One of the ways gardeners survive the "deprivations" of winter is by poring over seed and plant catalogs and jotting down wish lists of the items they plan to order.

Vegetable gardeners now have multiple options for sourcing their seeds.

Usually around the New Year these publications appear in the mailbox, harbingers of spring and finer weather to come, which means getting some seeds started indoors and preparing the outdoor plots for the new growing season.

Plant catalogs have a history that goes back to *Florilegium amplissimum et selectissimum* by Dutch grower Emanuel Sweerts, It was the first-known garden catalog/bulb catalog, which appeared at the 1612 Frankfurt Fair. It doubtless inspired a similar sense of excitement and expectation in those early horticulturists.

Modern catalogs that sell vegetable seeds and plants typically feature popular varieties, along with information on their eventual height, spread, and harvest time. Many showcase new cultivars and may offer heirloom species that hark back to the gardens of earlier decades. Some companies feature native plants or seeds from the national seed bank. Some give back to the community or address global concerns. You can look for companies that match your gardening philosophy; for example, there are online shops for organic gardeners to order organic, non-GMO heirloom seeds or shops that list great plants to cultivate hydroponically. If price is an issue, a number pride themselves on keeping costs relatively low. Catalogs can also tell you which plants do best in your growing region and advise you on species considered invasives in your specific county, state, province or region; those that are disease resistant;

and which ones attract pollinators. Not surprisingly, most mail-order companies now also sell online and offer catalogs online. Still, the printed catalogs remain a cherished winter distraction.

In North America, among the oldest and arguably the most popular catalogs are Burpee, which was founded in Philadelphia in 1876 and Gurneys Seed & Nursery, which went into business in 1866, the same year as Canada's Halifax Seed Company. In the UK, Dobies is an international supplier of flower and vegetable seeds, selling direct to gardeners since 1894. Mr Fothergill's, a more recent UK company, has catalogs and websites geared toward plants in the British Isles, Canada, and Australia.

ONLINE PLANT STORES

You now have the convenience of ordering seeds and plants from various online sources. All the catalog favorites have websites, and there is a host of purveyors. An online retailer like Gardening Express sells thousands of plants and seeds every week throughout the UK and Europe. Others, such as Franchi Seeds, Italy's oldest family-owned seed company, was founded in 1783 and is now known worldwide for the quality of its seeds, which yield vigorous plants and delicious food. Seeds From Italy is its U.S. distributor. For each region of the globe, there are sources that offer varieties suitable for cultivation in that particular place. No matter where you live, there will be an online source for your choice of produce seeds and plants.

A GLOSSARY OF VEGETABLE GARDENING TERMS

A

acidic soil A soil with a pH lower than 7.0. *See also* pH.

aeration Loosening soil to introduce air and improve drainage. May refer to the act of tilling, turning, or physically aerating soil (including compost piles), or used in reference to the condition of existing soil. Perlite, pumice, sand, and earthworm activity also increase aeration in soil.

alkaline soil A soil with a pH higher than 7.0. *See also* pH.

allium vegetables Members of the genus *Allium*, with hundreds of species, including the cultivated onion, garlic, scallion, shallot, leek, and chives.

annual A plant that completes its entire life cycle in one year or less; must be re-planted each year. If allowed, many annuals will self-seed and come back as volunteers the following year. Most vegetable crops are annuals.

B

bareroot A plant that is sold in a dormant state with its roots exposed (typically wrapped in burlap) as opposed to in a pot with soil.

beneficial insects Insects that play a helpful role in the garden, such as acting as pollinators or eating pest insects. Common examples include bees, ladybugs, parasitic wasps, green lacewings, and praying mantids. Encouraging or releasing beneficial insects is a common practice in organic gardening or part of an integrated pest management strategy.

biennial A plant that lives for two years. Typically, biennials establish a strong root system and leafy growth in the first year of life, followed by fruiting/flowering, and going to seed the second year. Many biennial vegetables are treated as annuals.

biodegradable A material that will eventually break down or naturally decompose under the right conditions, such as with the help of bacteria, fungi, and oxygen.

bokashi A Japanese composting method, meaning "fermented organic matter." This method rapidly ferments food waste in an air-tight container with the aid of a specialized inoculant. *See also* compost.

bolt When vegetable plants quickly go to flower rather than producing the food crop. Environmental stress (such as extreme heat, inadequate sunlight) or late planting can cause plants to bolt early; negatively impacts eating quality, flavor, texture, and lifespan.

botanical tea A homemade natural liquid fertilizer that is made by "brewing" or steeping soil amendments, such as alfalfa meal, kelp meal, and/or neem meal in water to create a nutrient-rich solution used to water and feed plants.

brassica The cabbage plant family, Brassicaceae also known as "cole crops," which includes bok choy, broccoli, Brussels sprouts, cabbage, cauliflower, kohlrabi, mustard greens, radish, turnips, and others; generally grown as cool-season crops.

C

chill hours Also known as vernalization, it is the number of hours that a plant or seed needs to be exposed to temperatures between 32°F to 45°F (0°C to 7.2°C) in order to break dormancy and either sprout, flower, or bear fruit. *See also* vernalization.

chlorosis Yellowing plant leaves due to insufficient chlorophyll; caused by a number of issues, including disease, damaged or bound plant roots, highly alkaline soil, inadequate drainage, and/or nutrient deficiencies.

cold frame A small structure that covers plants, protecting them from very cold or freezing conditions. Like a greenhouse, a cold frame has a transparent roof in glass or plastic to allow sunlight in but is built low to ground, more closely shrouding the plants.

cole crops Several cool-season brassica vegetables that grow best at temperatures between 60°F and 68°F (15.6°C and 20°C); broccoli, cabbage, and cauliflower are the main cole crops, with several others, including Brussels sprouts, Chinese cabbage, and kohlrabi.

companion planting The practice of using specific combinations of plants growing near one another to provide various benefits, including attracting pollinators, deterring pests, encouraging healthy growth, or providing shade/support for one another.

complete fertilizer A plant food containing all three of the primary elements: nitrogen, phosphorus, and potassium. *See* fertilizer.

compost Decomposed organic matter that offers numerous benefits to soil and plant health. Home gardeners may either buy compost, or create homemade compost from things like collected leaves, straw, kitchen scraps, and garden waste.

compost tea A form of natural liquid fertilizer made by "brewing" or steeping finished compost or worm castings in water. The result is a mild, nutrient-rich solution used to water and feed plants.

cool-season crops Vegetable crops that prefer cooler soil and air temperatures to thrive, between 40°F and 75°F (4.4°C and 24°C). Most are very cold hardy and frost-tolerant; includes asparagus, beets, broccoli, Brussels sprouts, chives, cabbage, carrots, cauliflower, Swiss chard, kale, leek, lettuce, onion, parsnips, peas, radishes, spinach, and turnips. *See also* cole crops.

cover crops Fast-growing plants grown with the primary purpose to protect or rejuvenate the soil between seasons. They are planted to cover the soil rather than for the purpose of being harvested. They may feed the soil by fixing nitrogen, or act as a living mulch by reducing erosion, compaction, and runoff and may reduce weed growth. Ryegrass, oats, clover, barley, alfalfa, and other legumes or cereal grains are commonly used cover crops.

crop A plant that is cultivated for harvest, such as vegetables, fruits, and herbs.

crop rotation The practice of routinely rotating the types of crops grown in each plot; this practice can improve soil health and biodiversity, reduce the demand for fertilizer, and lessen disease and pest pressure.

cross-pollination When one plant pollinates a plant of another variety. The two plants' genetic material combines and the resulting seeds from that pollination will have characteristics of both varieties and is a new variety. *See also* hybrid.

cruciferous vegetables Members of the family Brassicaceae with many genera, species, and cultivars being raised for food production, such as cauliflower, cabbage, kale, garden cress, bok choy, broccoli, Brussels sprouts, mustard, and similar green leaf vegetables.

cultivar A specific variety of plant selected or bred by humans for particular characteristics. A cultivar name consists of a botanical name followed by a cultivar epithet. The cultivar epithet is enclosed by single quotes, e.g., the potato cultivar *Solanum tuberosum* 'Yukon Gold'.

cut-and-come-again To continually harvest from a single plant over an extended period of time, rather than harvesting the entire plant at one time (which kills the plant); most often used to harvest leafy greens, such as kale, romaine lettuce, or Swiss chard.

D

damping off When seedlings suddenly wilt and die; can be attributed to a number of different fungal diseases and is most common when seedlings are overwatered, have inadequate air flow, or when old, diseased garden soil is used to start new seeds.

days to maturity The length of time from when seeds are sown until the plant should be ready to harvest. A plant description or seed packet will usually outline a specific variety's expected growth timeline.

deadheading Removing spent or dying flowers from plants once the blooms are past their prime. The practice of regular deadheading channels the energy into the flowers, resulting in healthier plants and continual blooms.

deciduous Plants, including trees, shrubs, and herbaceous perennials, that lose their leaves during the autumn to winter months and regrow in spring.

determinate A growth habit in which a plant's main stem and branches will slow or halt growth once it begins to flower and bear fruit. Most often used to distinguish between types of tomatoes (determinate versus indeterminate), but also used to describe the growth habits of bean plants and others. *See also* indeterminate.

dioecious plant Plants that house the male and female flowers on different plants; in order to produce fruit and viable seeds, both a female and male plant must be present.

direct sow To plant seeds directly in the soil outdoors in their final growing location, as opposed to starting seeds indoors in small containers, and then later transplanting them as seedlings.

dirt As opposed to soil, dirt is devoid of the living organisms, nutrients, and well-balanced composition necessary for supporting health plant life.

dormancy The yearly cycle in a plant's life when growth slows and the plant goes into a resting phase. This period of rest is crucial to their survival in order to regrow each year and recover from stress.

double digging An intensive gardening method in which you prepare soil by systematically digging an area to the depth of two shovels, removing the topsoil layer and exposing the subsoil or hardpan beneath, to create a deep bed of loose soil.

dynamic accumulators A permaculture concept for certain plants that are reported to have an exceptional ability at drawing up nutrients from the soil and storing them in their tissues. Popularly used as green mulch, in compost, compost tea, homemade fertilizers, natural medicine or natural body care products.

E

erosion The wearing away, washing away, or removal of soil by wind, water, or humans.

espalier A plant pruning and training technique that creates a wide, flat structure; commonly used for fruit trees grown in small spaces.

evaporation Process by which water returns to the air; higher temperatures will speed the process of evaporation.

evergreen Plants, trees, and shrubs that do not lose their leaves or needles in autumn.

F

fertilizer Organic or inorganic plant foods, which may be either liquid or granular, used to amend the soil

in order to improve the quality or quantity of plant growth.

flat A shallow box or tray used to start cuttings or seedlings.

floating row cover A lightweight fabric spread or floated over a row of plants to trap heat during the day and release it at night; used to get a jump start in the spring, fend off pests, and extend the autumn growing season. *See also* row cover.

foliar feeding, or **foliar spray** Spraying plants, trees, or shrubs with a fine mist of liquid fertilizer (or other liquid amendment) from a sprayer. Pesticides can also be applied through a foliar spray.

frost The condensation and freezing of moisture in the air; tender plants will suffer extensive damage or die when exposed to frost. *See* frost date.

frost date Denotes either the average first date (autumn) or last date (spring) that an area receives frost. The days between are the most robust growing season for cultivating vegetables. *See* frost.

fruit A seed capsule that emerges from a flower, such as a tomato or melon; they are generally the sweet and fleshy product of a tree or other plant that contains seed and can be eaten as food.

full sun Typically refers to a minimum of 6 hours or more of direct sunlight

G

germination When a seed breaks dormancy and sprouts its first growth; the emergence of a new seedling from a seed.

GMO "Genetically modified organism"; refers to plants and

seeds genetically modified by humans in a lab setting for select qualities, such as pesticide resistance.

grafting The uniting of a short length of stem of one plant onto the root stock of a different plant; often done to produce a hardier or more disease-resistant plant.

green manure Certain crops grown exclusively to be turned into the soil or allowed to decompose on the soil surface as mulch to enrich the soil with nutrients.

H

hand pollination When humans aid in the pollination process by physically transferring pollen from one flower or plant to another.

hardening off Readying tender seedlings raised indoors to be planted outdoors; the process usually involves gradually exposing seedlings to conditions such as wind, cold and direct sun over the period of a week or more, so they can become increasingly strong and resilient.

hardiness The ability of a plant to withstand low temperatures or frost, without artificial protection. *See also* hardiness zone.

hardiness zone Refers to a geographic area defined as having a certain average annual minimum temperature, a factor relevant to the survival of many plants. The term is most often used in conjunction with USDA Hardiness Zone Map, a system created by the U.S. Department of Agriculture. Areas in the United States are grouped and designated into particular planting or hardiness zones (3a through 11b) based on similar climatic conditions; used to define what plans grow best in what areas, as well as provide guidance on when to plant what. Most of the larger countries and regions of the world have their own version of a hardiness map. Australia, New Zealand, Africa, Canada, China, Japan, Europe, Russia, South America, and many more have a similar system. *See also* hardiness.

hardpan The impervious layer of soil or clay lying beneath the topsoil that impairs drainage and prevents plant growth.

heat tolerance A plant's ability to resist heat-triggered issue, such as poor pollination, bitterness, premature flowering, and lack of fruit-set.

heirloom Refers to a plant or variety of vegetable that is at least 50 years old; the seeds must be either open-pollinated or self-pollinated to be considered heirloom, not a hybrid. *See also* hybrid.

herbaceous A plant with soft rather than woody tissues.

Hugelkultur A garden bed style that utilizes collected natural materials such as logs, branches, leaves, pinecones, or other organic matter to provide bulk below a layer of soil. As the bulky materials break down, they release nutrients and become a part of the soil.

humus Finished compost from natural organic materials, such as leaves, food scraps, or other garden waste; it is dark, nutrient-rich, and improves the moisture retention and overall condition of soil.

hybrid The offspring of two plants of different species or varieties of plants. The result of cross-pollination, when the pollen from one kind of plant is used to pollinate an entirely different variety, resulting in a new plant altogether. *See also* cross-pollination.

hydroponics The science of growing plants in a water-based nutrient solution, instead of in soil and can include an aggregate substrate, or growing media, such as vermiculite, coconut coir, or perlite.

I

indeterminate A plant that continues to grow in size and bears fruit over a longer period of time, as opposed to a determinate plant that is shorter lived with a more concentrated fruiting period. Most often used in reference to varieties of vining tomato plants. *See also* determinate.

integrated pest management A pest-control approach performed in an organic, sustainable manner that focuses on minimizing health, economic, and environmental risks.

K

Korean Natural Farming (KNF) An alternative natural farming practice that emerged in the 1960s in South Korea; focuses on building soil and plant vitality by promoting the growth of indigenous microorganisms (bacteria, fungi, nematodes, and protozoa) using fermented teas and other natural concoctions and avoiding chemical fertilizers or pesticides.

L

leaching The removal or loss of excess salts or nutrients from soil; soil around overfertilized plants can be leached clean by large quantities of fresh water used to "wash the soil." Areas of extremely high rainfall sometimes lose the nutrients from the soil by natural leaching.

leggy Overly tall, stretched-out seedlings that are usually weaker than other plants and prone to toppling. Often a sign a plant isn't getting enough light.

loam A rich soil composed of clay, sand, and organic matter that possesses good moisture retention and drainage properties; considered the ideal type of soil for growing food crops.

M

macronutrients The elements nitrogen, phosphorous, potassium, calcium, magnesium, and sulfur that are essential to plant health and growth; usually added to the soil through amendments and/or cover crops. *See also* N-P-K.

manure Organic matter excreted by animals that is used as a soil amendment and fertilizer.

medium In horticultural circles, a medium is the material plants grow in, such as outdoor soil or indoor potting mixes.

microclimate Variations of the climate within a given location, usually influenced by hills, hollows, building structures, or proximity to bodies of water.

microgreens Young, leafy vegetables or herbs that are harvested just above the soil line when the plants have their first pair of leaves, called cotyledons, and possibly the just-developing sets of true leaves.

micronutrients The elements boron, chlorine, copper, iron, manganese, molybdenum, and zinc, which are essential for healthy plant growth; can be added to the soil through compost, organic matter, and rock dust.

mild climate these are regions without extremes temperature variations—no freezing temperatures in winter and relatively temperate summers with low humidity.

monoculture The practice of growing one crop species in a field at a time. *See also* polyculture.

mulch Any material placed on the surface of otherwise bare soil that reduces erosion and runoff, suppresses weeds, increases moisture retention, and protects the soil and plant roots.

mycorrhizae Specialized fungi that colonize the root system of a plant to form a mutually beneficial or symbiotic relationship. They act as extensions of the plant's root system, increasing the surface area and exchange of nutrients and water between the soil and the plant's roots.

N

native plant Any plant that occurs and grows naturally in a specific region or locality.

nightshades The Solanaceae plant family that includes tomatoes, potatoes, peppers, and eggplant; their leaves are considered mildly toxic and are not safe to eat.

nitrogen-fixing When nitrogen is taken in from the atmosphere and turned into stored nitrogen in soil, where plants can then utilize it to support growth. The process is facilitated by specialized bacteria (rhizobia) that colonize plant roots; legumes are particularly effective at fixing nitrogen.

no-till gardening A gardening style in which the soil is disrupted as little as possible and is not intentionally tilled or turned over every season

as in traditional agriculture. Letting the soil go undisturbed preserves the living soil food web and can increase soil fertility, plant health, and productivity. Also known as 'no dig' gardening.

N-P-K Nitrogen, phosphorus, and potassium, three macronutrients essential for plant health and growth. The "NPK ratio" is listed on fertilizer containers, such as 8-2-1 (a high-nitrogen fertilizer) or 4-4-4 (a well-balanced fertilizer).

O

OMRI The Organic Materials Review Institute, a nonprofit organization that certifies whether certain agricultural inputs are safe to use in organic farming. *See also* organic gardening.

open pollinated Seed that will generally breed true (produce offspring roughly identical to the parent plant) when the plants are pollinated by another plant of the same variety. Good for seed-saving and consistency.

organic gardening The method of gardening utilizing only materials derived from living things, such as composts, manures, and natural soil amendments, and avoiding the use of toxic, chemical, or otherwise synthetic fertilizers and pesticides.

organic material Any material which originated as a living organism, such as peat moss, compost, manure).

P

partial sun/partial shade This refers to three to six hours of sunlight daily.

peat moss The partially decomposed remains of various

mosses; a good, water-retentive addition to the soil, but tends to add the acidity of the soil pH.

perennial Plants that can grow or live for more than two years.

perlite A mineral that when expanded by a heating process forms light granules; good addition to container potting mixes to promote moisture retention while allowing good drainage.

permaculture A principle of cultivation that focuses on the intentional, careful design and maintenance of agriculturally productive ecosystems (including garden spaces) so that they mimic the diversity, stability, and resilience of natural ecosystems.

pest Any insect or animal that is detrimental to the health and well-being of plants.

pH A measure of the amount of lime (calcium) contained in your soil; a soil with a pH lower than 7.0 is an acid soil, and a soil pH higher than 7.0 is alkaline soil.

photosynthesis The internal process by which a plant turns sunlight into growing energy.

pollination The transfer of pollen from the stamen (male part of the flower) to the pistil (female part of the flower) that results in the formation of a seed.

pollinator Anything that aids in the transfer of pollen between plants or flowers, including but not limited to bees, butterflies, birds, bats, insects, the wind, humans, or other animals. *See* pollination.

polyculture The horticultural practice of growing many types of plants in one garden bed, container, or space, including a mix of companion plants to create biodiversity in your garden, attract beneficial insects, and reduce the chances of widespread devastation by pests or disease that typically inflict the same types of crops. *See also* monoculture.

potting soil A soil mixture designed for use in container gardens and potted plants; it should be loose, light, and sterile.

potting up The act of moving a plant from a smaller container into a larger one. Typically done with seedlings as they grow bigger to prevent them from becoming rootbound and stunted.

propagation The process of growing new plants through any variety of methods, including from seed; root, stem, or leaf cuttings; grafts; or other plant parts.

R

relative humidity The measurement of the amount of moisture in the atmosphere.

rhizome An underground stem that grows horizontally from nodes rather than vertically like most other plants. An example of an edible rhizome is ginger; mint is a notoriously invasive plant because it spreads through vigorous underground rhizomes, also sometimes called "runners." *See also* runner.

rootbound A plant, shrub, or tree that is growing in too small of a container that in turn restricts roots and stunts plant growth. Some rootbound plants can recover by being potted up into a larger container or into the ground. Some severe cases, however, can leave the plant permanently stunted. *See also* potting up.

rooting hormone A powder or liquid growth hormone, used to stimulate root growth on fresh cuttings during the propagation process, while also protecting the new cuttings from disease; rooting hormone can be purchased in a powder or gel form.

root vegetable A term to describe underground plant parts eaten by humans as food; includes potatoes, sweet potatoes, carrots, celery, onions, radishes, and beets, among many other vegetables.

row cover Fabric used to either exclude pests or raise temperatures of the area beneath it. "Remay" is a type of polyspun row cover material commonly used in farm and garden settings and it comes in several different thicknesses. Row covers may or may not have hoops under it to create a low "tunnel." *See also* floating row cover.

runner A slender stem growing out from the base of some plants that terminates with a new offset plant; the new plant may be severed from the parent after it has developed sufficient roots. *See also* rhizome.

S

salad greens Vegetables that are grown for their leaves and commonly used in salads, such as lettuces, spinach, arugula, watercress, or escarole.

scarification The process of breaking through the hard outer covering of a seed to allow moisture to penetrate and enable the seed to germinate.

season extender Any structure or tool used to protect plants from harsh conditions to extend the growing season. Most commonly used in reference to a shelter

against frost, but the term can also be applied to things that deflect extreme heat and sun, such as shade cloth; examples include cold frames, cloches, greenhouses, and hoops that support various row cover material, such as plastic sheeting or frost blankets.

self-seed, or self-sow When a plant grows or spreads naturally from seed that was dispersed or dropped by a parent plant without human intervention. *See also* volunteer.

sheet mulch The process of mulching an area with wide and fairly solid sheets of material, such as cardboard, burlap, newspaper, rolls of painters paper, or synthetic materials like plastic or landscape fabric.

slow-release fertilizer Fertilizer that will slowly degrade in the soil to make fresh nutrients available to plants over time instead of a strong boost of nutrients at once, such as granular or dry meal–type fertilizers often applied as a top-dressing and then watered in. Generally pose less risk of "burning" or shocking plants compared to liquid fertilizer. *See* fertilizer.

soil amendments Materials, either organic or inorganic that are added to soil to increase the health, nutrient content, moisture retention, and/or soil structure, such as perlite or compost. *See also* fertilizer.

soil food web The symbiotic relationship between soil and the network of living things within it, including beneficial microorganisms, fungi, protozoa, nematodes, earthworms, mycorrhizae, and other arthropods and critters. These living organisms work together to break down organic matter, introduce nutrients, and improve soil aeration, drainage and moisture retention. Also known as "organic living soil."

south-facing Garden space located in an area that receives unobstructed sunlight from the south; in the Northern Hemisphere, a south-facing garden is an ideal site to maximize sun exposure in all seasons and throughout the day; the opposite is true in the Southern Hemisphere.

sprout Germinated seeds that are not grown in medium but instead rinsed in water and drained several times a day.

staking Driving a stake into the ground next to and as a support for a plant.

stratification A process used to break the dormancy of a seed; usually requires that the seeds be placed in a moistened rooting medium and kept in the refrigerator or freezer for a designated length of time.

succession planting, or s**uccession sowing** The practice of continually planting new seeds or seedlings in a staggered timeframe over a growing season to offset harvest dates to provide a slower, continual harvest over many months instead of all large amounts of crops maturing all at one time.

T

tap root The main, large, and thick root growing straight down from certain plants.

tender perennial A warm-climate perennial that is not cold hardy in all temperate zones.

tender plant A plant unable to endure frost or freezing temperatures.

tendril The twisting, clinging, slender growth on many vines, which allows the plant to attach themselves to a support or trellis.

terminal bud The portion of a plant where new growth originates from, most found often in the center or top "leader." If the terminal bud is cut, it often causes the plant to stop or slow upward growth and can encourage branching instead.

thinning Separating or reducing the number of plants in one space or container; promotes fast and healthy growth.

top dressing Applying fertilizer or amendments to just the top of the soil, as opposed to tilling it in.

topsoil The top layer of native soil; the term may also apply to good-quality soil sold at garden centers.

transpiration The release of moisture through a plant's leaves.

transplanting Relocating plants from one location to another; used to describe when young seedlings are taken out of their starter containers and planted outside.

tuber A flat underground stem that stores food and plant energy and from which a plant grows.

U

umbel A mostly flat-topped flower cluster in which individual flower stems radiate from a common point, like the ribs of an umbrella; seen in the members of the carrot family (Apiaceae or Umbelliferae).

untreated seed Seed that does not have a chemical treatment such as fungicide applied to it.

V

variegated Plants that display patches or streaks of varying colors, most often white and green.

vermicompost Composting with worms; typically accomplished in a dedicated closed system, such as a worm bin or tiered worm farm.

vermiculite A sterile soil amendment created when the mineral mica has been heated to the point of expansion, like popcorn; a good addition to container potting mixes, it retains moisture and air within the soil.

vernalization Exposing seeds or bulbs to a prolonged period of cold temperatures to satisfy the plant's natural requirement for chilling in order to break dormancy and successfully sprout, flower, and/or bear fruit. *See also* chill hours.

volunteer A plant that germinates and grows with little to no help from the gardener; typically grow from a plant that went to seed previously in the general vicinity. *See also* self-seed, or self-sow.

W

warm-season crops Vegetables that need consistently warm conditions to grow, will thrive when temperatures are 75°F (24°C) or above, and do not tolerate frost or cold conditions unless protected; include tomatoes, melons, summer squash, winter squash, beans, peppers, corn, sweet potato, cucumbers, and eggplant.

worm castings Another word for vermicastings, or worm poop. When food passes through a worm's body, it is broken down into concentrated, highly bioavailable nutrients and beneficial microbes for plants that result in better moisture retention abilities and improved drainage in soil. Though potent, worm castings are very mellow, slow-release, and can't "burn" plants as other animal manure or fertilizer can.

INDEX

PHOTO CREDITS

FOREWORD: 7t Gardening Know How; 7ml Gardening Know How; 7mr thka/SS; 7b Tom Gowanlock/SS

INTRODUCTION: 8 Viktor Sergeevich/SS; 9 sanddebeautheil/SS

PART ONE:
THE VEGETABLE GARDEN'S FOUNDATIONS
10-11 Andrea Obzerova/DT

Chapter One
Edible Garden Basics
10-11 Andrea Obzerova/DT; 12-13 Visivasnc/DT; 14 Alexx60/DT; 16 Joanne Dale/SS; 17 Rob Walls/AL; 18ml Vaivirga/DT; 18bl Rawpixel.com/SS; 18tr Donfink/DT; 18br Serge Mouraret/AL; 18mr epiximages/SS; 19tl AYAimages/DT; 19ml Helinloik/DT; 19bl Shadow Inspiration/SS; 19tr Skyler1519/DT; 19mr Studio2013/DT; 19br Bricolage/SS; 20m Varbenov/DT; 20tr Bertoldwerkmann/DT; 20br Chernetskaya/DT; 20box Syomayo11/DT; 21tl Vkph/DT; 21ml TatyanaL/SS; 21bl Fbxx71/DT; 21m Tibor13/DT; 22 Freshhouse/DT; 23tr Helinloik/DT; 23 box BIOSPHOTO/AL; 24 Nura M/SS; 25 filippo giuliani/SS; 26 Ronstik/DT; 27 Disobeyartphotography/DT; 28 Dragonimages/DT; 29bl Lucy M Ryan/SS; 29tr public domain sourced / access rights from Mark Robertson/AL; 30tl box christopher miles/AL; 30bl box F42pix/DT; 30tr box Hounen Kihan; 30br box Elenfantasia/SS; 30bl Stsvirkun/SS; 30br Kristi Blokhin/SS; 31l pryzmat/SS; 31m lp-studio/SS; 31box kryzhov/SS; 32l Yekatseryna Netuk/SS; 32r Vlarvix/DT; 33tr Yurich20/SS; 33mr Oleg Mayorov/SS; 33bl Alisonh29/DT; 34t Photosergii/DT; 34bl Halfpoint/SS; 34br faithie/SS; 35tl eurobanks/SS; 35bl mimagephotography/SS; 35tm Alena Brozova/SS; 35bm Angela Nott/AL; 35r PhotoSGH/SS; 35box garden-scoot; 36l Brinja Schmidt/SS; 36r Chrislofoto/DT; 37l Duramax; 37r Altitudevs/DT; 38l Rido/DT; 38r Upixa2/DT; 39l Wavebreakmediamicro/DT; 39r encierro/SS; 40-41b pundapanda/DT; 41 Andreypopov/DT; 42ml ABO PHOTOGRAPHY/SS; 42bl Matthew Taylor/AL; 42tr Lordn/SS; 42mr Svett/SS; 42br Arina P Habich/SS; 43tl kram-9/SS; 43ml La Huertina De Toni/SS; 43bl Deborah Vernon/AL; 43tr Malcolm Haines/AL; 43mr La Huertina De Toni/SS; 43br Leklek73/DT; 44 Alisonh29/DT; 45l Glebska/DT; 45r Feldarbeit/DT; 46 Rghenry/DT; 47 Rycream/DT; 47 box Mashiki/DT; 48 Dabisik/DT; 49tl Fotoevans/DT; 49bl Simonapavan/DT; 49tm Iredding01/DT; 49mc Mangkelin1/DT; 49bm Simonapavan/DT; 49 Simoncountry96/DT; 49 box Byon35/DT; 50 Zlikovec/DT; 51l Island Images/AL; 51r Janet Horton/AL; 52 box Daniel Borzynski/AL; 52l Msgrafixx/DT; 52m Richsouthwales/DT; 52r Luschikovvv/DT; 53tl Inavanhateren/DT; 53ml Idenviktor/DT; 53mr Barmalini/DT; 53bl Irina274/DT; 53bm Mkos83/DT; 53br Sergejsbelovs/DT; 54tl Noomhh/DT; 54tm Dleonis/DT; 54tr Jijikalinkova/DT; 54bl Dleonis/DT; 54bm Dleonis/DT; 54br Will1877/DT; 55tl Darkop/DT; 55tm Stevanovicigor/DT; 55tr Ishmeriev/DT; 55bl Faddy6/DT; 55bm Zvonko59/DT; 55br Lianem/DT; 56tl Kslight/DT; 56tm Lyudmylagromova/DT; 56tr Mila722/DT; 56bl Anettphoto/DT; 56bm Peternanista/DT; 57 Martin Kemp/SS; 58 Reefer/DT; 59bl Gartland/SS; 59t Dewcreations/DT; 59br vaivirga/SS, 60 Tomas Bazant/SS; 61t Caftor/DT, 61b Pauws99/DT; 62 Radovan1/SS; 63tl Sasiwit/DT; 63bl Art4Picture/SS; 63tm Tomasz Klejdysz/SS; 63bm Irina Liebscher/SS; 63tr Lertwit Sasipreyajun/SS; 63br Tomasz Klejdysz/SS; 64tl Lertwit Sasipreyajun/SS; 64bl Avalon.red/AL; 64tr Hatthakon/SS; 64br Ombee Ly/SS; 65tl perspective_lensreflex/AL; 65bm Nigel Cattlin /AL; 65tr Mwli670323/DT; 65br kale kkm/SS; 66tl Tomasz Klejdysz/SS; 66bl Fotoz by David G/SS; 66tm matunka/SS; 66bm Gina Schubbe/AL; 66tr Gardening Know How; 66br Thomas Barrat/SS; 67tl Rabbitti/SS; 67br m.bonotto/SS; 68l Stef22/DT; 68m Boarding1now/DT; 68r Zigzagmtart/DT; 69 Tim Gainey/AL; 70 Amenic181/DT; 72 Jacob Lund/SS; 73 Simone Hu/SS; 74 Raymond Keller/SS; 76 Goddard on the Go/AL; 77t Grundsteins/SS; 77b Guy Banville/SS; 78 COULANGES/SS; 79tl Olga Mazo/SS; 79br Julie Sotomura/SS; 80bl LaineN/SS; 80tr Wollertz/DT; 81tr H.Angelica Corneliussen/AL; 81 box Luimi/SS; 82 Floki/SS; 83bl Anniota/SS; 83tr Piyachok Thawornmat/SS; 84 Lithiumphoto/SS; 85 Igor Klyakhin/SS; 86 Ivana79/DT; 87bl 13Smile/SS; 87tr Jamie Farrant/SS

PART TWO:
PLANT PROFILES
88-89 Ivonnewierink/DT

Chapter Two
Fruits and Vegetables
90-91 Photomailbox/DT; 92 Iuliia29photo/DT; 93 Photographerlondon/DT; 94 Marti157900/DT; 95 Markskalny/DT; 96tm Dleonis/DT; 96ml Trong Nguyen/SS; 96bl Juanjomenta/DT; 96tr Jlueders/DT; 96mr Curtoicurto/DT; 96br Lvenks/DT; 96box flameWinwinartlab/DT; 97tl Chiyacat/DT; 97ml Gabes1976/DT; 97bl Johnpierpont/DT; 97tcl Mr.Somchai Sukkasem/SS; 97mcl Debbieannpowell/DT; 97bm Gasparij/DT; 97tcr Wpmcb1997/DT; 97mcr swa182/SS; 97br Luigi1984/DT; 97tr Carlosneto/DT; 97mr Kaarsten/DT; 98 Sirawitmarch/DT; 99 Boonmeekim/DT; 99 box Bhofack2/DT; 100 Viviansviews/DT; 101 Darkop/DT; 102tl Gvictoria/DT; 102ml Mkos83/DT; 102bl Nipolbe/DT; 102tr Rawlik/DT; 102mr Shariffc/DT; 102br Creativefire/DT; 103tl Natureexplorer2/DT; 103ml Yorozu520/DT; 103bl Peter Turner Photography/SS; 103tcl Thalabhula/DT; 103mcl Konfetko113/DT; 103bm yuratosno3/SS; 103tcr stockphotofan1/DT; 103mcr Papava/DT; 103br Worapong/DT; 103tr Motorolka/DT; 103mr Rumata7/DT; 104 Irinka7/DT; 105 Kyznehova/DT; 106 Johnsarkar/

DT; 107 Pstedrak/DT; 107 box Stevanovicigor/DT; 108 Irina88w/DT; 109 Grafzero/DT; 110 Ustunibisoglu/DT; 111 Jurga85/DT; 112 Dennisvdwater/DT; 113tl agefotostock/AL; 113tm Slovegrove/DT; 113tr Midosemsem/DT; 113ml Wellesenterprises/DT; 113mc Ulphoto/DT; 113mr Davidgn/DT; 113bl Grazza23/DT; 113bcl Olyas8/DT; 113bcr Artography/DT; 113br Atosan/DT; 114 Madajar/DT; 115 Kimopfinder/DT; 116 Alcyon/DT; 117 Simonapavan/DT; 118 box Bialasiewicz/DT; 118tr Wideonet/DT; 118mr Kenishirotie/DT; 118br Olhaafanasieva/DT; 119tr Insanet/DT; 119mr Rbiedermann/DT; 119br Eballard13/DT; 119tm Boonsom/DT; 11mc jenwolfphoto/DT; 119bm Booba123/DT; 119tr Rmorijn/DT; 119mr Brebca/DT; 119br Kwangmoo/DT; 120 Altinosmanaj/DT; 121 Mgrigorjevs/DT; 122bl Ustunibisoglu/DT; 122tr Tuayai/DT; 122mr Ahmet Cigsar/SS; 122br Yareta/DT; 123tl Claudio Saba/SS; 123ml Annieannie/DT; 123bl JBGerchicoff/SS; 123tr Dashkouski/SS; 123mr Agban99/DT; 123br Ste208/DT; 124 Alexcr1/DT; 125 Olenafoto2332/DT; 126 Rittis/DT; 126 box Captivatinglightphotos/DT; 127 Alison Thompson /AL; 128 Idenviktor/DT; 129 Milaquarter/DT; 130tl Kampwit/DT; 130ml Davidgn/DT; 130bl Jen Wolf/SS; 130tr Jfeinstein/DT; 130mr Wildkatphoto/DT; 130br Ffranny/DT; 131tl Jfeinstein/DT; 131ml Aleela/DT; 131bl Darkop/DT; 131tcl Melastmohican/DT; 131mcl Herreid/DT; 131bcl Sheila2002/DT; 131tcr Debchephotography/DT; 131mcr Zigzagmtart/DT; 131bcr Raymona/DT; 131tr Amzphoto/DT; 131tm Dinictis/DT; 131tb Mlhead/DT; 132 Unge255/DT; 133 Markit/DT; 134 Denny128/DT; 135 Jane McLoughlin/SS; 136 Jackf/DT; 137 Lizaazarova/DT; 138tl Saiko3p/DT; 138ml Pstedrak/DT; 138bl Darkop/DT; 138tr Rifberlin/DT; 138mr Zhukovsky/DT; 138br Tangsphoto/DT; 139tl Ramvseb1/DT; 139ml VittoriaChe/DT; 139bl adimpetrov/DT; 139tcl Brebca/DT; 139mcl Willamette Biology/Creative Commons Attribution-ShareAlike 2.0 Generic; 139bcl Simonapavan/DT; 139tcr Lianem/DT; 139mcr Zabavna/SS; 139bcr Sydeen/DT; 139tr Anantaradhika/DT; 139mr EMFA16/DT; 139br Wirestock/DT; 140 Chernetskaya/

DT; 141 Ahundov/DT; 141 box Jabodo/DT; 142 Russell102/DT; 143 Freshhouse/DT; 144 Anettbulano/DT; 145 Tchara/DT; 146t Lunamarina/DT; 146b Lipa23/DT; 146m Morgancapasso/DT; 147tl OlgaKorica/DT; 147tm Dreamer Company/SS; 147bm Lunamarina/DT; 147tr lzf/DT; 147tm Fotoeventstock/DT; 148 Atlantisprints/DT; 149 Fotofreak001/DT;

**Chapter Three
The Herb Garden**

150-151 Plateresca/DT; 152 Shaiith/DT; 153 Aamulya/DT; 154 Qwartm/DT; 155tl Ekaterina79/DT; 155br Albinayal/DT; 156 Andreyrut515/DT; 157 Mruckszio/DT; 157box Karayuschij/DT; 158 Sokor Space/SS; 159 Chernetskaya/DT; 160 box Kargona/DT; 160tr Robynmac/DT; 160br Dorling Kindersley ltd/AL; 161tl Pheby/DT; 161bl Bhofack2/DT; 161tr Funandrejs/DT; 161br Michelle3900/DT; 162 Dcmamiel62/DT; 162 box Rinofelino/DT; 163 Amradul/DT; 164 Ikeroesia/DT; 165 Manfred Ruckszio/SS; 166 Mruckszio/DT; 167 AndrisT/DT; 168 Zutosekale/DT; 169 Miragec/DT; 170 Sillu654/DT; 171 Barmalini/DT; 172 thala bhula/SS; 173 Sagegardenherbs/DT; 174 Erikapichoud/DT; 175 Tarfullhd/DT; 175 box Larrymetayer/DT; 176 Subcomandantemarcos/DT; 177 Marjattacajan/DT; 177 box Kalebkroetsch/DT; 178 Kathryn Roach/SS; 179 Snowboy234/DT; 180 Sevenday3/DT; 181 Zoonar GmbH/AL; 182 Goncharukv/DT; 183 Kewuwu/DT; 184l Paulmaguire/DT; 184tr 585036/DT; 184mr Tang90246/DT; 184br Kewuwu/DT; 185tl Michaela Pilch/SS; 185ml Silviacrisman/DT; 185bl Paulmaguire/DT; 185tr Tanusree Edbe/SS; 185mr Kazakovmaksim/DT; 185br Anneriekeschuurman/DT; 186 Albinayal/DT; 187 Jobrestful/DT; 188 NadyaSo/DT; 189 Fotokate/DT; 190 Soniabonet/DT; 191 Sheila2002/DT; 192 Vinicius Souza/AL; 193 Areeyatm/DT; 194 Jokue-photography/SS; 195 Chamille White/SS; 196 Fermate/DT; 196 box Raudonkepuraite26/DT; 197 Westhimal/DT; 198ml Nikolaydonetsk/DT; 198bl Kobeza/DT; 198tr Adri Smuts/SS; 198mr Ivana79/DT; 198br Matka_wariatka/DT; 199tl Geografika/DT; 199ml Liwei12/DT; 199bl Morellir/DT; 199tr

Wiktory/DT; 199mr Anatema/DT; 199br Elenathewise/DT; 200 Mila722/DT; 200 box Alpaksoy/DT; 201 Correodehierro/DT; 202 Orest lyzhechka/SS; 203 Martina889/DT; 204 Julitt/DT; 205 Zoonar GmbH/AL

APPENDICES
206-207 Akarawutl/DT; 208 ClassicStock/AL

ACKNOWLEDGMENTS

GARDENING KNOW HOW
Brand Director: Peggy Doyle
Senior Editor: Elizabeth Baessler
Creative Director: Sean Collins
Marketing Director: Kyle McCann
Head of Operations: Uwe Kerkhoff
Marketing Communications Manager: Caroline Bloomfield
Junior Editor: Laura Walters
Digital Community Manager: Amy Draiss
Manager of Analytics & Advertising: Allison Kerkhoff

**PRODUCED BY
MOSELEY ROAD INC.**
Irvington, New York
www.moseleyroad.com

President: Sean Moore
Art and Editorial Director: Lisa Purcell
Production Director: Adam Moore
International Rights Manager: Karen Prince
Editors and Contributing Writers: Nancy J. Hajeski, Finn D. Moore